People, Places and Dogs
Columns from the Casa Grande Dispatch

Bill Coates

Also by Bill Coates

Pug Ugly and Pretty Dead

Needles Arizona

Rancho Javelina

Table of Contents

PLACES

DOGS

Introduction

I started writing columns for the Casa Grande Dispatch in 2013. My first column was largely an extended correction.

Medical marijuana became legal that year in Arizona. Pinal County's first pot shop opened that April in Eloy. I went there for a story. I was the newspaper's Valley Life editor. I interviewed the very first customer, as he walked out with his prescription of weed. In the print version, I had the numbers right, but the units wrong. By my miscalculations, he'd bought three times the legal limit.

The shop's managers were upset.

So I wrote a column to correct the record. I played it for laughs. We're talking pot, after all, the giggle drug. That column is on page 83.

I organized the book around three themes. Hence, the title: *People, Places and Dogs*. I added a fourth section, one for the columns that didn't quite fit the first three. It's called "Loose Ends."

I noted the date each column appeared in the newspaper.

For "People," I had a wealth of material. People of all walks.

There are a number of war veterans, as well as a former governor you could look up in the phone book. A state senator doing the people's work, a retired police sergeant and a barber's revered grandmother.

Some of the people I wrote about have since died. The columns ran during their time on earth, with one exception. I looked back on the life of Dick Myers, who died in 2021.

I ended up leaving out a lot of noteworthy people. I had to make choices. It wasn't easy. I sifted through every column I had written since 2013. The cutting room floor was a mess. I went back and forth on a number of columns. Taking some out. Putting some in.

The second section leads you to "Places." Places where people live, work, play and sometimes catch the bus. Here you'll find my mea culpa for suggesting a medical marijuana shop sold pot by the pound. Other places include: A car-repair garage that, in an earlier life, was a draw for 1960s dance bands, including Alice Cooper. Site of a mystery cargo plane's fiery crash. A feisty radio station punching above its weight.

Three columns visit Casa Grande's Greyhound bus stops. They moved around. From mini-marts to a truck stop.

I wrote a number of columns about dogs over the years. They get their own section in "Dogs." You can read about the all-hands-on-deck search for a dog named Alice. About dog walkers named Linda. And about my own variously named dogs.

The final section, "Loose Ends," is largely a collection of personal musings – from bad drivers-license photos to colonoscopies.

The low-hanging fruit of humor.

I threw in a few columns about my domestic life. From the zen of washing dishes to my wife's knitting. She's a good sport about it all. I'm pretty sure.

Overall, "Loose Ends" columns are just that. Here, the city of Casa Grande prepares for the unthinkable. There's a story about a lost tortoise. And a COVID-19 column on social distancing. The section ends with a city councilmember's plan to water the desert by tapping into the Mississippi.

The columns, for the most part, appear as they ran in the Dispatch. I made a change or two here and there. In one column, the last line seemed a bit flippant for the subject. I took it out.

For the record, Casa Grande, Arizona, is home to more than 50,000 people. It's about midway between Phoenix and Tucson, though it leans slightly toward Phoenix. It has a good manufacturing base, plenty of winter visitors and a view of desert mountains. Farming in the area is still big, but threatened by drought.

Columns set in Grande don't have datelines. It's pretty much Casa Grande throughout the book, so I left them out. Other towns and cities, when it's called for, do. Most are nearby, in western Pinal County. From Florence to Maricopa and points in between. I wrote a few columns from Kearny. It lies in copper-mining country to the east, just the other side of the Gila River.

You might see a reference to a PinalCentral staff writer or editor. PinalCentral is an umbrella group. The Casa Grande Dispatch falls under it.

The book is not a cover-to-cover read. Or doesn't have to be. Thumb through it. You might find a nugget or two. Somebody interesting. A bit of humor. And, of course, dogs.

Putting it together was, at times, like make-work. More cut-and-paste than writing. But it gave me the chance to look back on all the people I've talked to. The places they lived and worked.

And to reflect on the privilege afforded me week after week.

For that, I have to thank Donovan Kramer Jr., managing editor and co-publisher of the Dispatch. He always made space for the column. It's real estate editors don't give up lightly. You can't take it for granted.

And when I send in a column, I always look forward to his answer back: "Great, Bill."

PEOPLE

She's Still 'Judge Judy'
To Her Fans

August 23, 2013

Judy Ferguson was once a high-flying city judge, if you include the time she went to Eloy to perform a wedding.

"I get there, they start slipping this parachute on me," Ferguson said.

She told me the story of the airborne wedding across from a booth at the CookEJar in downtown Casa Grande, the city she held a gavel to for 24 years — until her forced retirement in July.

I should disclose that Ferguson paid for my coffee and cookie, well below my usual asking price of two cookies and a free refill.

Talking of her years on the bench, Ferguson, 68, was outspoken and congenial. This is a recap of our conversation.

The wedding in the clouds, sometime in 2000, united a bride and groom who both liked to sky-dive. Ferguson went along, part way. She wasn't going to jump. The parachute she wore was just a precaution, in case she accidentally fell out of the airplane.

She performed part of the ceremony on terra firma, then boarded the plane to finish tying the knot at 10,000 feet.

"We get down to where I say, 'You're now man and wife' — they kiss and jump out of the plane."

She did not mention the ring. Maybe the groom slipped it on as they plummeted toward earth. Ferguson collected her usual fee.

"For that ride, I charged 30 bucks," she said.

The pilot took the plane down fast but made a safe landing.

The landing that marked the end of her career was not so smooth. Under the city charter, the City Council appoints the judge every two years. Her reappointment was all but automatic each time. But in July, the council voted to replace her with Christopher O'Neil, who was a staff attorney with Pinal County Superior Court.

"It hurt," she said. "Nobody said thank you and you did a good job."

She hinted her final job interview didn't go well. "I hate to interview," she said.

Perhaps, too, it was simply the case that city leaders wanted a professional upgrade, bringing in a Bar-certified lawyer.

Ferguson isn't a lawyer. And that, she said, was a plus when she first got the job in 1989.

"They didn't want an attorney, because they wanted people to be treated like people," she said.

And she knew just about everybody in Casa Grande. Ferguson was raised here and went to school here. She left, then returned in 1973 after living the peripatetic life of an Army wife.

She eventually found a job as an office manager for a mobile-home maker. The principals, she said, weren't always on the up-and-up.

She had a good view of the parking lot.

"I'd yell, 'The police are here!' They'd hit the block fence. They always had warrants and were in trouble for something."

After that business folded, she took a secretarial job with Justice of the Peace William Gastelum. She began working as a judge pro tem for him in 1986, often presiding over initial appearances at the jail, a small lockup in the county complex on Cottonwood Lane.

Her first case involved an attractive young woman. She had shot and killed her boyfriend. She had clearly been abused, Ferguson said.

But she killed her man, so no bail for her.

Soon Gastelum began to loan Ferguson out as a pro tem to then-City Judge Bill Moore. When Moore retired, Ferguson succeeded him

She took over a court that was housed in, well, a house. It was small and cramped with little security. Cash from fines was kept in an unlocked drawer. She got a safe. She worked to make a more efficient court. And she looked after the court's bottom line, going

4

after slackers who didn't pay their fines. She jailed people who had outstanding warrants.

Ferguson made her mark.

"I've been known as the biggest bitch in town," she said, with a smile.

But she liked being a judge because she likes people. And she wasn't averse to giving someone a break, as long as the person didn't try to spin the same excuse time and time again.

Now, she's a month into her new life as Citizen Judy. And has since started one long-neglected project — cleaning out her house. She never had time for that as judge, what with getting called out at all hours to sign search warrants and the like.

To many people, though, she's still queen of the bench. One random passerby proved the point with the greeting: "Hi, Judge Judy."

From Omaha Beach
To a Graveyard Shift

Arizona City, October 17, 2014

Albert Malin is on the road a lot for his job.

Driving is not the job itself. That's just to get to it. From his Arizona City home, he drives 50 miles one way to an insurance company in Chandler. His car is a 10-year-old Mercury Sable.

He's a security guard. He spoke about his job from his kitchen table. It was Malin's day off, but he wore his crisp uniform for the interview and photos. The hat didn't match. It read: World War II Veteran.

Malin's beat is a 150,000-square-foot complex. He walks his rounds. He monitors security-camera screens. He issues company

IDs.

Usually, the work's trouble-free.

"We've had a couple of homeless people stop people coming in and ask them for loose change," he said.

Malin works with one security guard who's 85. Malin is four years his senior, born in 1925.

He retired once, many years ago. But now he has expenses. His wife, Deborah, has medical issues, and the bills pile up.

"She's disabled completely, and that's the reason I'm working full time," Malin said.

She's 61, too young for Medicare. They looked into private insurance. Even with the government subsidy, it seemed out of reach.

"It's not what you make, it's what it costs you to live," Malin said.

He works the graveyard shift, 11 at night to 7 in the morning. But he's not a whiner. He seems almost upbeat. Perhaps it goes back to the hat. Perhaps it reminds him of the time he lived to see June 7, 1944.

Many didn't.

The day before, D-Day, Malin was part of the first assault on Omaha Beach. He was a 19-year-old draftee.

"I lost two buddies," he said. "They never made it to shore."

The war gave him his first job working security. He was a military policeman. As the Army pushed into France, Malin directed traffic as equipment flowed to the front. That's how he met Gen. George Patton, commander of the 3rd Army.

Malin had stopped the tanks to let artillery through. It was protocol. But that didn't matter to Patton, who happened by.

"He gave me hell because I pulled the tanks over," Malin said.

Patton ordered Malin aside and waved the tanks through.

At war's end, Malin, who's Jewish, visited the Belsen concentration camp. Twenty minutes was enough for him.

Once stateside, he returned to Baltimore, his hometown. He trained to repair radios and TV sets. He installed antennas, too. Malin worked at this for about 10 years.

He once fixed a TV for his hometown hero, Orioles third

baseman Brooks Robinson. In turn, Robinson invited Malin to join him in a round of golf.

Later, Malin moved to California and ran a silk screening company his brother had taken over. The company made a number of things. It was called Orange County Nameplate Co. It still is. I looked it up.

Under Malin, it went from being worth six figures to seven. He had a big house, cars and lots of money. A half-million in the bank.

He met Deborah there, too.

"She worked for me," Malin said.

Deborah stayed around. They've been together for 41 years. The money came and went. But mostly it went.

"I made some bad investments," Malin said.

One involved a lawyer. They pooled their money to buy up real estate. Instead, the lawyer took the money and made off for the Marshall Islands, never to be seen again.

In 1980, Malin was pushed out the door of his own company. It had something to do with shares of stock. With no job, he worked as a security guard for Orange County. He later moved to Oklahoma, where he found work with a Tucson publisher and author. Malin commuted when called on. He moved to Arizona City about 10 years ago. He was closer to his job and found a home that fit his budget. He paid cash.

The author specialized in legal advice, Malin said.

"One book he wrote," Malin said, "was 'Busted by the Feds.' And he was busted by the feds."

For drug dealing, Malin added. The Cleveland Plain Dealer had a 2008 online story about it. Federal prosecutors said Larry Fassler took part in a drug ring "that moved large shipments of marijuana from Arizona to Northeast Ohio." Wikipedia had a brief entry on Fassler, with a footnote linked to the Federal Bureau of Prisons. You learn Fassler died in prison three years ago.

So Malin probably won't see the money he loaned him anytime soon.

Fassler was a man of ideas. One was to develop a yard fountain that doubled as a memorial. It would have a nook for a funeral urn. All he needed was seed money. Malin offered to help and

7

mortgaged his house for $50,000.

Now he has mortgage payments.

And now five nights a week, 89-year-old Malin gets in his 10-year-old car and heads up Sunland Gin Road for an eight-hour graveyard shift. It's a tricky stretch of road. The speed limit is 25, right past a sheriff's substation. A deputy just has to park outside, a ham sandwich in one hand and radar gun in the other.

Malin's been pulled over a time or two. He always has his hat. He wears it on the drive up, if not on the job.

"This has saved me several times," Malin said.

Deputies spot it, thank him for his service and send him on his way.

They know hats like that are hard to come by.

Real Grandmother Lost
In Story about Clutter

May 2, 2014

Carmen Burrell came to Casa Grande in the early 1920s. She and her husband, Jose, made the trip in a horse-drawn wagon. They had six children who, in turn, gave her 32 grandchildren.

One of those grandchildren is Ralph Burrell Jr., who has cut many a head of hair over the years in Casa Grande.

His parents divorced when he was 6 and Carmen took him in. And raised him until he turned 18 and headed for barber college. He's now 77.

She raised four other grandchildren as well, all cousins from homes that didn't work out for them.

"She was a very lovely woman," Ralph said. "She was like my second mother."

Ralph has fond memories not only of her but the house they lived in, a small stuccoed adobe. It's still standing.

It sits on First Street across the alley from St. Anthony of Padua Catholic School. That same house recently drew complaints from the school's principal. The backyard had become an eyesore with piles of debris.

Anything could be under there, I wrote on April 18, even "Granny."

Before I finished the column, I learned there was a real grandmother, Carmen Burrell. Even so, I left in the granny reference and Ralph called.

He wasn't happy.

I offered to write about the Carmen Burrell he knew. So I met

Ralph on Monday at his barbershop on Florence Street. It was closed that day and he wore his street clothes. I sat in a barber chair and he stood, as he always does on the job.

He handed me a three-page biography about Carmen. He had written it in longhand. Carmen was born in 1883 in Oro Blanco, now an Arizona ghost town northwest of Nogales.

She became an orphan at 2 or 3 and was taken to Altar in Sonora, Mexico, by a relative. She was married at 14 to a man named Carlos Castro. They had three children, but the marriage was brief. Castro died of cancer.

Then Carmen met Jose Burruel. After they moved to Casa Grande, the family name became Anglicized. So Carmen Burruel became Carmen Burrell.

And all who came after her were Burrells.

Through the years, Carmen remained a devout Catholic. She attended Mass daily in the former St. Anthony sanctuary, now Murphy Hall. And she raised money for the church, baking and selling tamales through the Our Lady of Perpetual Help Society.

Jose Burrell worked as a stone mason. He helped build the Woman's Club and the old stone church that now houses the Casa Grande Valley Historical Society.

Carmen and Jose moved into the house on First Street in 1932.

"The building had at one time been a butcher shop. On one side was the living quarters. They had split it down the middle," Ralph said.

The Burrells made it into a home for their kids and, later, grandkids. Carmen kept a very neat house, Ralph said, even as space was tight. Some slept on couches. Some slept in sleeping bags. Ralph slept on an Army cot.

In the backyard, Carmen raised rabbits and chickens. The chickens often landed on the dinner table.

"She was an excellent cook," Ralph said. "And seamstress, too."

She made the clothes he wore to school. And she took in laundry to help make ends meet.

Later, Carmen learned how to make medicinal herbs from an older Yaqui woman. When Jose was sick and bedridden, Ralph said, she cured his bedsores with a salve made from creosote. She healed animals, too, once treating a chicken that had lost its feathers. They grew back.

Over the years, the cousins grew up and took different paths. Ralph, of course, became a barber. The oldest, Arthur, served during the Korean War, as a medic. After the war, he went to Tulane University Medical School and became a pathologist. He died in 2000. Larry became a plumber.

Larry got the house and let things go a bit. But now, with a bit of prodding from the city, he's working to clean it up.

Carmen outlived Jose. And late in life, in 1976, she got a visit from then-Gov. Raul Castro. He had been at a ribbon-cutting ceremony for a nearby radio station. After the formalities, he went down the block to shake Carmen's hand. She was 93. The radio station has since gone quiet.

Carmen Burrell died in 1978, three months shy of 95. For the record, she's buried at Mountain View Cemetery next to Jose.

Finding Himself in a Good Place
March 20, 2015

Charlie Shields headed down the sidewalk at rabbit speed. I was still in turtle mode and had to jog to catch up.

Apparently I don't have a rabbit setting. Shields, 72, has both on his motorized wheelchair. So when he wants to motor, he shifts from turtle to rabbit, actual icons on his control pad.

At the moment, Shields was cruising along Second Street toward the St. Vincent de Paul thrift shop.

"I have a lot of friends there," Shields said.

He deftly moved his chair around tree wells. And across side streets. I asked him about close calls.

"I'm very careful and I haven't had any problems. I've only been hit one time."

Somebody backed into him coming out of a driveway. He wasn't badly hurt.

And he didn't sound too put out by it. All in all, Shields is in a good place.

That wasn't always so. Years ago, Parkinson's disease ended his career as sous chef at Francisco Grande Hotel & Golf Resort. He developed tremors. People would stare. Neighborhood kids burglarized the small house he once lived in. They threw rocks at him.

I wrote about Shields and a life upended three years ago. He later moved to an assisted living facility in Mesa. Things did not get better.

"I had some bad experiences there," he said.

Sometimes residents would fall. And sometimes staff would ignore them, Shields said. He would hear them yell for help at night. And so he'd try to help, even if it meant getting out of his wheelchair.

But the worst part was — he had few friends.

"That's why I came back to Casa Grande," Shields said. "People here are very helpful. This is the best place for anybody."

I talked to Shields a few weeks back. He had dropped by the Dispatch. He rolled in on his new wheelchair, the one with turtle and rabbit settings.

I caught up on his new and improved life. He's since moved into The Garnet, a high-end assisted living center. The food is good. So he has no need to show off his own cooking skills. And he wouldn't, even if asked.

"You leave this chef alone," he joked.

As we spoke, he held out his hand. It looked steady as a rock. His neurologist has him on some new medication. The tremors have stopped, for now.

Shields says the doctor jokes: "The next time you come in here, I want to see you do the waltz."

He's not quite there. But he can walk a bit. And he writes poetry for other residents at The Garnet. Most are seniors. Some get depressed, he said. Poetry cheers them up.

Now he's learning to play the piano.

He used to paint, before he came down with Parkinson's. A friend thought he could take it up again. She brought him a set of brushes and paints.

"I told her I'd give her the first painting. I haven't done it yet."

And it might not get done, he added.

"I can't paint much anymore."

In Casa Grande, Shields has a social life. It's built into his daily routine. He heads out for St. Vincent de Paul most mornings.

"They've been very kind to me — with furniture, clothing and anything else."

Not to mention a dresser.

"I didn't have anything to put my clothes in."

Elli's Artisan Jewelers on Florence Street is another regular stop.

Elli Fritz runs the store. She welcomes Shields with chit-chat and hot chocolate.

"That's what we're here for," she said with a smile, later that morning.

En route to St. Vincent de Paul, Shields looked like a wheelchair cowboy. You couldn't miss him, going rabbit speed in a cowboy hat. He rolled up to the front door and downshifted to turtle. Inside, he greeted Betty Kohles, a 30-year volunteer at St. Vincent de Paul.

Around a corner, next to some lamps, Shields stopped at a display of paintings and reproductions. He was mildly critical. He wouldn't have painted them that way. One picture was set up on a metal-framed easel.

Yvette Tapia stood nearby. She's a St. Vincent de Paul receptionist.

Shields turned to her. "How much do you want for the easel?"

Uncertain, Tapia went to ask. She came back shortly. "Charles, it's 10 bucks."

He still can't waltz. But painting? Maybe it was time.

Leading His Flock to the River

April 24, 2015

Young Grady Whatley worked at a steel mill in Pueblo, Colorado.

It was June 1962. Whatley was 25 years old. He attended Bethlehem Baptist Church. It turned out that sitting in the pew, receiving the Word wasn't enough.

One day he heard a voice. The Lord had called him to preach. But Whatley doubted himself.

"I stutter," he said. "I said, 'Lord, how am I going to preach when I can't talk.'"

But the Lord insisted, Whatley said. And he wouldn't be denied. So Whatley told the pastor of his calling. And the pastor agreed. The Lord wouldn't be denied.

So on June 13, Whatley preached to the congregation at Bethlehem Baptist. He was nervous, but he overcame that. His sermon was about the Good Shepherd.

And his message came through loud and clear.

"I don't have a stammer preaching," Whatley said.

He told me about his first day as a preacher on Tuesday. Now his days of preaching are nearing the end.

Whatley, 78, is retiring as pastor of First Shiloh Baptist Church, a small whitewashed building on Pinal Avenue. He added up the years. Fifty-three preaching. Forty-six pastoring. Twenty-seven as pastor at Shiloh, a church he founded.

Whatley is a large and soft-spoken man. He delivers that old-time religion, an African-American Baptist whose preaching roots go back to his great-grandfather. And his grandfather.

The calling skipped a generation. Whatley's own father wasn't a preacher. He worked in Coolidge and Casa Grande as a farm foreman.

Whatley himself was born and raised in Coolidge. He attended Borree Corner Elementary School. It was segregated, all black. He was too young to be upset.

"At that time, we didn't know what it was .... we accepted it."

That changed in high school. Coolidge High was integrated. Students, black and white, got along, he said. He played sports. Not all of Arizona had gotten the word on integration. He learned that on a trip to Douglas. The high school track team went there for a meet. The coach booked them for an overnight stay at the Gadsden Hotel. But, he was told, no blacks.

Whatley remembers the coach standing up for them — for the team.

"The coach said you have to accept them all."

Money talked, Whatley said. The management relented. The track team, black and white, got a good night's sleep.

Jim Crow took a bit longer to die out in Hobbs, New Mexico. Whatley went there yearly for a church convention. He made his first trip in 1957. He and his traveling companions soon learned who would deny them a seat at the table.

"We'd take our own water and our own food," he said.

Eventually, the racial barriers fell. But Whatley still traveled in two worlds. On the secular side, he worked for a moving company in Phoenix. He got a degree through Central Arizona College. He substitute-taught at Coolidge and Casa Grande Union high schools until 2006.

On the religious side, he married Edna Marie. He led congregations in Mesa, Eloy, Coolidge and Randolph. Then, in the 1980s, he was encouraged to start a new church. He and church members set out to find a building in Casa Grande.

"We went all over the place to have our church, and we noticed the Rebekah Lodge."

The Sunshine Rebekah Lodge was part of a women's order. The First Shiloh congregation rented the hall on Pinal Avenue for Sunday services. The Rebekah members were aging and dying out.

In 2003, the few left were ready to sell. First Shiloh bought the building for $25,000. Whatley passed the hat.

"We paid for it in cash," he said.

For years, Whatley led Bible study every Wednesday and preached twice on Sunday. He drove a van to pick up kids for church. Kids that he baptized got a Bible, a baptismal certificate and a watch.

Kids would show off their watches. Soon everybody, it seemed, wanted one. Baptisms became popular.

Whatley joked. "I'd have to take out a loan from the bank to get all the watches and the Bibles."

Parents trusted him to discipline their kids, with a belt if need be. He didn't have to use it, too often. Whatley said he would run into some of the kids years later. They had grown up. And they would thank him for setting them on the straight and narrow.

Times have changed, though. Belts are largely out of favor.

And the things Whatley regarded as sins are now more widely accepted. Marijuana. Gay marriage. Tattoos.

"The younger people, they're not much into supporting the church," he said.

He's done all he can. Long ago, he heard the call. He preached for a half century and more. Now he's turning it over to a new generation. The Rev. Alex Day becomes pastor on May 3. He's associate minister at St. John Institutional Baptist Church in Phoenix.

Pastor Whatley delivers one more Sunday sermon. He gave me something of a preview.

He'll be leaving, he'll say. And a new pastor will be taking over. But God isn't going anywhere.

"Like when Moses told Joshua, the same God that was with me will be with you."

Whatley paused briefly. "I brought them to the river, and the next pastor has to carry them across."

Rough Landing in the Shower
Florence, July 24, 2015

Benjamin Fowler is an older man, 63. His whiskers are white. He gets around on a walker.

When I met him, he had to leave it outside the door. It wouldn't fit in the visitors booth.

By last Friday, Fowler had spent 33 days in the Pinal County jail, charged with two counts of DUI.

He's not a hardened criminal, as far as I know. But he won't get any accolades for his driving record. Fowler's DUI arrests came five months apart in 2014. It appears he later failed to answer a court summons. He was arrested last month on an outstanding warrant.

He ended up in jail, bail set at $2,000. He had no relatives or friends who could bail him out. Or were willing to. His wife died in 2007.

He had the $200 needed for a bail bond, he said. Social Security payments went onto a debit card. But he couldn't get to it. He offered to take out a title loan on his truck. He couldn't get to that either. He was inside. Everything else was out there. Apparently, it's a Catch-22 kind of thing.

He worried he'd lose that truck anyway, along with his motor home in Apache Junction.

Given his DUIs, I asked him about his drinking.

"I don't have a problem with drinking," he said. But he added: "I do like my beer."

That's OK. It's liking beer, then driving, that's at issue.

Anyway, he hadn't touched a drop in over a month. Jail sobered him up.

17

But it has also been hard on his health, he said. Fowler lost nine pounds behind bars. He blamed it on the food. Not enough meat.

Like his money, Fowler's doctor was on the outside, too. That's the doctor who did replacement surgery on both hips. One in December. The other a few months later.

Fowler was due. He had put some hard miles on those old hips.

"I rode rodeo a number of years," he said. "I was a bull rider, bronc rider."

He worked jobs that called for labor. Real labor. Not pushing buttons on a keypad. He rebuilt houses, did plumbing and electrical work.

"I worked for a pipeline company years ago down in Texas," he said.

The surgery went well. The slip-and-fall in the jailhouse shower on June 23 didn't. Fowler said he re-injured his right hip.

"It feels like it's loose," he said. "I'm in a lot of pain."

He brought it up with medical staff. He asked for an X-ray. He told a nurse it felt loose. He was told, he said: "That can't happen."

He was given an ice pack.

Fowler had a wheelchair for the first couple of weeks, then he got a walker. He wanted the wheelchair back.

"I don't feel the bone in the shaft moving when I'm in a wheelchair," he said.

Pain meds would help, he added — something with a bit more juice than the Tylenol he got.

He complained but nobody listened. That was his side.

There's another.

Tom Schryer spoke to that. Schryer is the director of Pinal County Health Services. The agency oversees health care for jail inmates.

Schryer was familiar with Fowler's case, though he couldn't talk about specifics over the phone on Tuesday. Privacy rules. But he could talk about the process. And there's a process for getting care. Fowler didn't follow it, Schryer said.

Health officials met with Fowler perhaps a half-dozen times, he said.

"He wants to prescribe the kind of treatment that he gets,"

Schryer added. "He doesn't get the answer he wants, he gets really irritated."

There's a process on pain management, too. Generally speaking, inmates don't get narcotics. Half of them would be seeking relief for pain they don't have. But you can't always tell. Fowler's pain seemed genuine. I'm giving him the benefit of the doubt. He's kind of old. I know how that feels.

As for grab bars in the shower, Schryer didn't have an answer. It was more a facilities issue, he said. A jail spokesman said he'd look into it. I didn't hear back.

Lastly, Fowler said he was unable to sleep.

He didn't stay awake worrying, he said. He stayed awake suffering.

It was the bed. He described it as a sheet of steel covered with a thin foam pad. "It's killing me."

Bodies in the morgue have it better, he added.

His message: It was no jail for old men.

Interview over, Fowler rose slowly and signaled to the officer waiting outside. He was ready for his walker.

Here's an update. Fowler had a hearing on Tuesday. He cut a deal and took his medicine. He received a four-month prison sentence and four years supervised probation.

It's the state prison. Not the county jail. Maybe he'll sleep better.

Iwo Vet Gets Souvenir Flag
The Hard Way

February 20, 2015

The flag in the picture belonged to a Japanese regiment on Iwo Jima. Bob Brutinel found it in a cave.

19

By then, he had survived this speck of an island for 25 days, with nine more to go. He arrived on Feb. 19, 1945, 70 years and a day ago.

Brutinel was with the first wave of Marines to set foot on Iwo Jima. They reached shore by landing craft.

"The sea wasn't too choppy," he said.

For Brutinel, this was a small blessing. He likes to say he invented sea sickness. Joining him in the first wave was William Perry, a high school friend from Clifton, where Brutinel grew up.

Perry joined the Marines about a year after Brutinel. They met up again at Camp Pendleton, California, where they trained for an island invasion. They made a pact. If each took a war souvenir, they'd trade.

"Souvenirs were a big deal in the Marines," Brutinel said. "You could sell them to sailors or other Marines."

Brutinel spoke to me Wednesday morning. We sat in the break room of the plumbing company he founded. It's now Brutinel Plumbing & Electrical. Brutinel sold it some years back, but he still works there.

At 90, he's part of a shrinking demographic. Few World War II veterans are still around. Fewer still show up for work every day.

Two Marine regiments were in that first wave. His was the 27th, Company H.

His platoon had 13 men.

Going ashore, he was apprehensive. When you're facing a hailstorm of bullets, artillery and mortar rounds, that's understandable.

"You always think, 'Is it my time?'"

His time nearly came on Day 28. A sniper's bullet clipped his nose, eyebrow and ear. He dodged a direct hit, tripping and falling as the sniper pulled the trigger. War involves random acts of survival.

Brutinel could have taken the next medical boat off the island. The wound was serious enough. But after he got his head bandaged, he kept fighting.

Perry got shot five days into combat. Brutinel says he took it in the rear. Perry was shipped out.

Brutinel spotted the Japanese flag three weeks after Marines raised the American flag on Mount Suribachi, and three days before he was shot. He was part of a demolition crew that sealed up caves. They blew up the entrances with C2, a plastic explosive. It had to be set off with blasting caps. Otherwise, it was stable. Marines even used C2 to cook their rations.

Brutinel tossed in a qualifier.

"Some of the meals I wish we could have blown up."

But they had to save the explosions for caves. The Japanese hid out in them. They came out at night to stage raids. Collapsing the entrances shut them out — or in.

One thing Brutinel didn't do was enter the caves.

"That's a way to get killed," he said.

But on Day 25, something caught his eye. It was some 15 feet inside a cave. Ignoring his own advice, he went in and spotted two flags, folded up. They lay atop a small mound. He grabbed them, got out fast, then sealed the cave.

He gave one flag to the doctor who would patch him up.

By March 26, the Marines had done their job. Iwo Jima had been secured. Brutinel left for Hawaii, where his regiment would regroup to invade Japan. They'd need fresh recruits, given the 80 percent casualty rate. That included 5,000 dead. And one William Perry, recovering in a Honolulu military hospital.

"I went to see him, and I gave him the flag," Brutinel said. "He was tickled. He said, 'You're a good buddy.'"

The invasion was called off. Atomic bombs had been dropped, and Japan surrendered. Brutinel went in as part of an occupation force.

After the war, Perry made his way back to Clifton, where he settled with his wife, Louise. They were married in 1948. Brutinel knew Louise from high school. She was a younger classmate.

The Perrys later moved to Morenci. William Perry worked as a bookkeeper for the Morenci hospital. He died in 1974.

"He was walking down the corridor and keeled over dead," Brutinel said.

Perry was 50. He'd had a heart attack.

The flag went to Louise. She remarried and outlived her second husband. Louise died two years ago. Brutinel attended her funeral in Safford.

"They had three boys," he said. "And they asked me if I wanted the flag."

Brutinel hadn't seen it since 1945, since he handed it to Perry, who kept it in storage.

"That's where his son went to get it."

On Sept. 4, Brutinel celebrated his 90th birthday at the Paramount Theatre. A party was thrown for him. The flag he captured was unfolded and put on display.

The rising sun of a fallen empire.

Two Women Who Take
Life Step-by-Step

August 21, 2015

Corrine Antone spends her days walking. I spoke to her last Friday outside Calvary Southern Baptist Church.

She walked there for lunch. It's a free hot lunch, compliments of Seeds of Hope, a nondenominational faith-based charity.

Antone, 49, is a part of an informal club. Its members spend their days walking. Just walking. They often meet here for lunch.

Many are homeless. Reasons vary, Antone said.

"Some get thrown out," she said. "Some are diabetic. I take walks and talk to them."

I'm not sure diabetes causes homelessness. But there's probably a correlation.

Antone is diabetic herself. She receives treatment through the Indian Health Service. She's a member of the Tohono O'odham tribe.

She's not homeless, she said. She stays with her daughter in a three-bedroom home on the south side. Her son lives there as well, along with her daughter's kids and boyfriend. It's a household of seven or eight. She couldn't pin down the number.

It sounded a bit tenuous. She had a roof over her head at night. During the day, she walked.

"Just to get out and exercise," she said.

Having finished lunch, she stood under a noon sun. Her face shined with a thin layer of sweat. It would get hotter, up to 113. It was already humid.

Antone didn't seem to mind the heat. She had water in a backpack. She didn't wilt. And neither did her hair. It was fixed in something of a wave that crested high atop her forehead.

Perhaps she once walked to work. She used to work at a laundromat.

"I could go back to my old job," she said.

But not today.

Her son, Ruben, listened as we spoke. Ruben was quiet. Like his mother, polite. He's 22 but looked much younger.

I thanked them for their time, and they continued their walk. They circled around to the west side of the church and cut across an adjoining lot. I followed, lagging behind.

Warm air is supposed to rise, but this heat broke the rules. It was thick and heavy.

I headed back to the office. Antone and her son walked to the Main Library.

It's a public space that welcomes all who are quiet. It's air conditioned and offers a place to sit, reflect and play games on the computer. Antone's not selfish. She leaves the books for others to read.

Before I spoke to her, I met Clancy Wayne Butler. I interrupted his hot lunch at Calvary.

Butler is outgoing. "Pull up a chair!" he said.

The system lets down people like him, he said. For one, hot lunches fall short of a roof over your head. And you have to work for them at that.

"We clean up the tables but we still got to sleep in the rain," he said.

The rain was a tree-toppling monsoon storm. It came and went early last week.

Lunch was almost over. Lola Martinez made her way from the table. She walked with difficulty — more than a simple limp.

By chance, I met her again on Tuesday. She was crossing Picacho Street, slowly headed for the shade of a tree in Reed-Mashore Park. It's a postage stamp of grass at Picacho and Fourth streets.

The Pinal Hispanic Council faces the park, across Picacho. It's a nonprofit that helps people with serious mental illness. Many of them are homeless.

Martinez, 40, lay on the grass in a sweat.

She gets by on disability.

"I broke both my ankles ... 2005," she said.

Some kind of accident. She didn't remember the details. Or wouldn't.

All the same, her legs didn't bother her as much as the heat.

She had this in common with Antone: "I don't drive. I just walk."

And like Antone, Martinez is Native American, a Ute from Fort Duchesne, Utah.

Things could have turned out differently for her.

"I had the option of going to college," Martinez said.

Instead, she got a job right out of high school. She did yard work and painted buildings. Then she had her accident.

Like Antone, she's not homeless. Not by her definition.

Sometimes she sleeps at a friend's house. More often, she stays with her grandmother.

"We have issues," she said. She didn't care to talk about them.

Her grandmother lives on the north side. How far north was left unsaid, but it seemed a ways away.

Martinez wouldn't go there now, in any case.

"I can walk at night," she said. "Right now it's too hot to walk."

At least she had cold water. She got a bottle from the Pinal Hispanic Council, the place across the street.

"They give it out to the homeless," she said. "I was just

24

pretending so I can take it home."

She smiled. She had them fooled.

Sense of Humor, a Badge
And a Pool Skimmer

November 13, 2015

At age 5, Junior Hernandez saw his future.

His family lived in Laredo, Texas. It would have been around 1952. He followed his mother into a store. There he spotted a man in a 10-gallon cowboy hat. He had a badge. And a holster with a gun, a big gun.

"I couldn't take my eyes off that gun," Hernandez said.

He asked his mother about the man. "He's a policeman," she told him. "He helps people. And the bad people, he takes them to jail."

By 1971, Hernandez had the badge and the gun, if not the hat. He was a Casa Grande police officer, helping the people in need of help. And taking the bad people to jail. He put in his time, then became a Pinal County sheriff's deputy. All told, his law enforcement career spanned nearly four decades. Thanks to the man with the big gun.

Hernandez is 68 now and retired for good. His real first name is Serapio, as was his father's. I sat down with him at the CookEJar last week. His speech is rapid fire. Laced with humor. He brought homemade tamales for me. I held up my hand and said I can't accept gifts.

Actually, I did no such thing. I took the tamales. Who doesn't like homemade tamales?

Like many families, Hernandez's came to Coolidge for the work.

And the work was farm labor. During the '60s, Hernandez worked a number of jobs himself. He was a cowboy on a ranch in Roll, about 40 miles east of Yuma. He didn't ride a horse. He was one cowboy who stood his ground.

He did his share of stoop labor. He picked cotton. He picked watermelon. He picked whatever was in season. Later, he worked at a cotton gin in Eleven Mile Corner.

In 1966, he moved to Casa Grande with his first wife, Lucy. And their baby. He got a job at South Elementary School. It later became Ocotillo. But he argued for a better job description. He didn't like being called a janitor. The principal suggested custodian. No, Hernandez said.

How about sanitary engineer? That sounded good to him. He'd go home and tell his family, "I'm an engineer."

But he wanted to be a cop. He hadn't finished high school, though. Without a diploma, he couldn't join the force. So Hernandez completed his GED and hired on with Casa Grande PD.

He was 24. His mentor was Sgt. Bill Gastelum, who later became a justice of the peace. Gastelum died in 2010. Here's the first thing Gastelum told him: "There's a shootout every night."

It was meant to scare the rookie cop.

"He didn't scare me," Hernandez said. Joking, he added. "I wanted a shootout."

As it happened, Hernandez never fired his gun. Not outside the practice range. He found other ways to deal with the bad people. In the early days, many of them could be found stumbling in and out of the bars on Main Street. Troublemakers fueled by alcohol.

But Hernandez kept tabs on them. He had, in his words, a CI. Confidential informant. He'd pretend to arrest him. Put him in the patrol car, get the low-down.

"As soon as we got out of town, I'd let him out," Hernandez said.

In just three years, Officer Hernandez became Sgt. Hernandez. He supervised a four-person squad. He was always first on backup. He reviewed the reports. He corrected spelling.

"I'm a good speller," he said.

26

He put in his 20 years and retired. It was a short retirement. Within six months, then-Sheriff Frank Reyes took him on as a deputy. Hernandez covered western Pinal County, from Stanfield to Florence. But he once answered a call in Kearny, a mining town along Arizona 177. It was a domestic dispute. The kind of call that always required backup. People are angry, ready to lash out.

Hernandez got there by way of Superior. A mother and her teenage son had been arguing. The mother came to the door. She took a look at Hernandez, by then in his 50s.

"She said, 'We need younger deputies.'"

The insults he could handle. But he never got used to crashes involving children.

"They were innocent," he said.

One innocent child fell into a swimming pool. She was 2. Hernandez was still with Casa Grande police. He made his way to the backyard. He couldn't swim. He grabbed a skimmer on a long pole and lifted her out. Another officer performed CPR.

Years later, Hernandez heard from the girl's cousin. The girl he rescued?

"She grew up and she became Miss Michigan."

Hernandez retired in 2009, a second and final time. He's now something of an amateur historian. He's visited the ruins of a long-ago Butterfield stage stop. A Mormon Battalion site. The ghost town of an abandoned mine. And he's read about all of them.

Otherwise, he spends his days with his wife, Eva. She'd like him to dig more weeds in their Casa Grande yard. He can't, he tells her. He jokes about the man across the way. The man's a spy. So Hernandez has to stay indoors. Away from the man's prying eyes.

Maybe she just needs a better job description. He might go for gardening engineer.

First and Last Mission

June 19, 2016

Max Swearengin was 18 when he last saw his brother, Billy. Max is 94 now and lives in Casa Grande. Everybody knows him as Gene.

Both Gene and Billy were born in Mount Vernon, Missouri. Their parents were Robert and Flora. Billy was the youngest of four. He was born in March 1924, two years after Gene. Evelyn was the oldest, followed by John.

In 1926, Robert packed up the family and drove to Arizona in a Model T Ford.

They lived in Glendale, briefly. Robert worked on a dairy farm. They soon moved to another dairy farm between Tempe and Mesa.

There were no neighbors. No other kids to play with. So Gene, John and Billy played amongst themselves.

"We played out on a dirt road, hockey with a can and a stick," Gene said. "We played together all the time."

And when they weren't playing, they drove dairy cows to and from the pasture. Gene got it in his mind one day to ride one. The boss caught him and barred him from the dairy works for three months.

It wasn't the kind of thing Billy would do.

"Billy was a good kid," Gene said. He was quiet. Kept out of trouble.

Just as Gene started high school, the family moved to Florence. Robert went to work for the state prison, making garments. Play became a luxury for Billy as well as Gene.

"He worked like most of us," Gene said. "We were a poor family. We had to make do ourselves."

Perhaps Billy played sports. Gene doesn't recall.

"He tried to get me to play basketball, but I was too busy working," Gene said.

Gene had morning and afternoon paper routes. When he finished high school in 1940, he signed up for the Army Air Forces, commonly known as the Army Air Corps. He followed in John's footsteps. It was the last time Gene saw Billy, then only 15.

Gene and John ended up in Puerto Rico, at separate bases.

Gene was the radio operator for his base commander. He was the first one there to hear about the attack on Pearl Harbor, Dec. 7, 1941.

Once out of high school, Billy briefly worked for a lumber yard. He soon signed up with the Army Air Corps himself. He wanted to be a pilot, Gene said. But he failed flight training.

"So he went back again to be a navigator," Gene said.

He trained for two years. Then he shipped out to England, joining the 480th Bomb Group. By then, the war was nearing an end. Victory in Europe would be declared on May 8, 1945.

Gene was in liberated Germany himself. His Air Corps ground unit followed Patton's final push. He was still a radio operator. If escort fighters lost their way, he'd help guide them back.

On April 19, 2nd Lt. Billy Swearengin's B-17 Flying Fortress took off from England. It was his first mission and one of the last bombing raids over Germany. He was the navigator on a crew led by Lt. William Edward McCallister.

Gene believes Billy's B-17 was over Hanover. Its target was Dresden, says Nancy Fassbender. She's a historian for the Pinal County Veterans Memorial Foundation, which is raising money for a memorial in Casa Grande. It will include a wall with the names of the fallen.

Billy Swearengin will be on it. His first mission was his last. His plane was shot down by a German fighter over Marienberg, Germany, near Dresden, according to the American Air Museum in Britain.

"One man who bailed out with him said that he knew that his chute opened," Gene said. "That's the last we knew."

That man was Paul Webb Jr., the tail gunner. He was captured

29

by Germans and became a prisoner of war, if just for a few weeks. He later lived in Tucson, where he attended the University of Arizona. He got in touch with Billy's mother, Flora. He told her he never saw Billy after that day.

Nobody did. He was listed as missing in action.

A dog tag was found four years later, along with Billy's remains. He was buried in Ardennes American Cemetery in Belgium. A memorial marker was placed in Florence Cemetery.

Billy was 21. Of the nine crew members, seven were killed. Two survived. Webb went on to become a wildlife biologist for Arizona Game and Fish. He died in January at age 90.

Glen Howard of Muncie, Indiana, was the co-pilot. He was captured, too. He would probably be in his 90s, if still alive. I think he might be. I could not reach him in any case.

After the war, Gene took over an established dairy farm. He put in 17 years, then went to work as a federal corrections officer in California. One of the inmates under his guard was H.R. Haldeman, President Richard Nixon's chief of staff. Haldeman went to prison for his role in the Watergate scandal.

He didn't get special treatment.

"I used to send him down to sewer work every day," Gene said.

Gene has since retired to Casa Grande. He lives with his wife, Philene. He's the last surviving Swearengin sibling.

And the last to know Billy, a good kid.

Note Brings Toll of War to Army Father
May 31, 2016

John Michael Turner was 22 when he went to Vietnam. It was December 1968.

Many went because they had little choice. They were drafted, handed a gun and told to stop the spread of communism. Turner went voluntarily.

He grew up in a military family. His father, John Thomas Turner, fought in World War II with the Army Air Corps. He was a gunner on a B-17.

The elder Turner left the Air Force and later joined the Army. He served for 32 years and retired as a full colonel.

To avoid confusion, everybody called his son Mike.

The elder Turner lives with his wife, Barbara, in Sisters, Oregon, outside Bend. I spoke to him by phone last Monday. He's 91 and Barbara's 87. They keep active. That includes daily trips to the gym. In Bend's last Veterans Day Parade, Turner was the grand marshal.

He lived in Casa Grande in the 1940s, after the war, working construction with his father, A.L. Turner. Mike was born at Lincoln Hospital in October 1946. The hospital is no longer in business, but the building still stands. It's on Brown Avenue and First Street.

As a military family, the Turners moved around. Mike was 3 when the family left Casa Grande. In the mid-1950s, Turner was stationed in Japan. Mike attended a parochial school.

The family then transferred to Fort Leavenworth, Kansas. Mike went to Leavenworth High School, where he excelled as an athlete.

In summers, Mike would visit his grandparents in Casa Grande. He worked as a flagman for his father-in-law's crop-dusting company. With the money he saved, he took flying lessons back in Kansas.

In the late 1960s, as the Vietnam War plodded on, Mike told his father he had signed up for the infantry. It was a delayed-entry program. Mike would be in uniform after his third year of college.

The colonel did not give his son a pat on the back.

"I told him he's crazy," Turner said.

Infantry, in Turner's mind, was a sure way to die. And Vietnam was a different war than the one he fought in. People wondered if it was a war worth dying for.

"People of the country didn't support it," Turner said. "They thought it was a bad idea. I thought it was a bad idea."

But soldiers, being soldiers, fought as ordered. And returned

31

home to treatment they didn't deserve, Turner said.

Mike did not return, despite Turner's best efforts. He pulled some strings so his son could be transferred to aviation. Mike's own flying experience helped.

"My reason for getting him out of the infantry — I thought I was saving his life," Turner said.

Mike ended up a warrant officer and flew a helicopter.

I watched the Vietnam War on television, throughout high school and into college. A number of images stuck. The body bags. Soldiers tramping through jungle. Soldiers clearing out caves. And the bulbous-nosed Huey helicopters. They became an enduring icon of the war.

Mike's final mission was near Pleiku, in the central highlands of Vietnam. Turner was stationed in Germany at the time.

He was in a meeting with a general when a junior officer entered. The officer handed him a note.

It read: "Warrant Officer John Michael Turner was last seen in a burning aircraft."

"My heart came up in my throat," Turner said. "I went home and I didn't tell the family."

Turner didn't learn the full details for another two years. Mike went down with a lieutenant. Both were killed. A search team went back to retrieve the bodies.

Maybe enemy fire brought the helicopter down. Maybe it was mechanical failure. The cause remains unknown.

The general in the meeting understood Turner's loss.

"His son had died three days before in Vietnam," Turner said.

Mike's time in Vietnam was short. He died March 26, 1969, 72 days into his tour.

Turner still doesn't know why his son signed up in the first place. He does know Mike was a good son, despite — or perhaps because of — being raised in a strict military family.

"He was a good kid. I thought an ideal kid. … Everybody liked Mike."

Turner added: "That's a father talking."

It's a father's right.

Mike was buried in Leavenworth National Cemetery. The fallen there will be honored on Monday, Memorial Day. Fallen veterans will be honored at Mountain View Cemetery as well.

Mike will not be forgotten here either. His name will join 240 others on a wall planned for the Pinal County Veterans Memorial. All were veterans killed in action. All from Pinal County.

Fundraising for the memorial is ongoing, said Nancy Fassbender, a memorial foundation board member. So far $89,000 has been raised. When organizers reach $100,000, they'll break ground at Ed Hooper Rodeo Park. That could be next year, Fassbender said.

The memorial will include an interactive kiosk with bios of the fallen.

When the memorial is completed, you can visit anytime. You won't have to wait for Memorial Day.

Korean War Vet Learned To Lead with His Left

October 3, 2016

Korean War veteran Billie Bell wasn't born left-handed. His right arm was shattered in combat and amputated shortly after.

In the mid-1950s, he enrolled at Arizona State University, then known as Arizona State College. He majored in accounting, but he still needed English.

One of his first assignments was to write a 500-word essay. The English professor who assigned it called Bell into the office.

He told Bell: "I have a 5-year-old daughter at home that can write better than this."

Bell replied: "Oh, I thought I was doing pretty good learning how to write left-handed."

The professor looked up and saw what Bell meant. He had no right arm.

For his part, Bell was just stating a fact — likely in his usual good-natured way. Good-natured is how Bell struck me in an hour-long conversation inside his Casa Grande garage.

He's made it into something of an indoor patio — with a couch and armchairs. There's still room for two cars. A filing cabinet stands in the corner. That's where Bell keeps his prosthetic arm.

On balance, Bell's a cheerful guy. He can't help himself. He's made that way. Perhaps, after the war, he had his moments of inner turmoil. And maybe he has his tough-guy side. He was a Marine, after all.

But I couldn't help but like him. He says of himself: "I'm a pretty likeable guy."

His thoughts meander at times. Bell suffered a head injury about 10 years ago. Visiting a friend at the Casa Grande hospital, he slipped and fell in the hall. He was airlifted to a hospital in Phoenix.

His wife, Melva, helps to keep him on track. She sat alongside him during the interview. He's 86. She's 82. They've been married nearly 50 years. They met in the Los Angeles area, where Bell worked as an auditor for the Internal Revenue Service.

The IRS hired him out of college. He was tapped to work in Phoenix, following training in Los Angeles. He went there in summer. Los Angeles was 80 degrees. Phoenix 117. He stayed in LA.

He retired to Casa Grande after 27 years, returning to his roots. Bell spent his school years here, from grades one through 12. His family had moved to Casa Grande from Moreland, Arkansas. He was 6 at the time, one of seven kids.

Bell's mother drove, leaving his father behind. She had her reasons. Now a single mother, she had a family to support.

"She worked at the school cafeteria," Bell said. "She did ironing and house cleaning for people."

During World War II, Bell and other students picked cotton for the war effort. He wasn't very good at it, he said.

He did better as a stock clerk at Prettyman's Market, since shuttered. He worked there after finishing high school. Later he landed a job in a warehouse at the Ray Mine, near the present site of Kearny, then owned by Kennecott Mining Company.

In the summer of 1950, the Korean War broke out. Bell wondered about his draft status and dropped by the draft board in Coolidge. He learned he'd soon be called up. He didn't wait. He joined the Marine Corps. In April 1952, he landed in Korea.

"On May 29th is when I got hit," Bell said. "Something that blew me up. I thought I was dead, but when I woke up I was on a tree stump."

One Marine was killed. His name was Donald. Bell named his younger son after him. Donald Bell would later serve in the Marines himself.

I asked Bell how he first reacted to the loss of his arm.

"First thing I thought: 'I'm going home.' Then I thought: 'Well, I'm going to be getting a check every month the rest of my life — so I want to make it a long one.'"

He returned to Casa Grande and his old job at Prettyman's Market. The boss was glad to have him back. Bell was a good worker. But the GI Bill and math skills led him to Arizona State.

In college, he wasn't all study and no play.

Bell and a handful of other veterans started the Sigma Nu fraternity chapter. They rented a house. And bought a keg of beer for a pledge initiation. An officer on patrol nearly caught them. Bell enlisted a frat brother to toss the keg in his car trunk.

The cop didn't find the beer, just a lot of drunk college kids.

In time, Bell's handwriting got better. And he learned to type one-handed. Hunt and peck, he said. He even figured out a way to tie shoelaces, only now he doesn't need them. He secures his shoes with Velcro straps.

After he retired, he and Melva took to the road. They've been to all 50 states and the District of Columbia, where they visited the Korean Veterans War Memorial.

"Sure a lot of people on it," Bell said.

"Is that when you stood there and tears came to your eyes?" Melva added.

He nodded. But he didn't dwell on it. Or the war's toll on him. Bell's not one for self-pity. Or holding a grudge — even against the

English professor who mocked his handwriting.

"After that," Bell said, "we became pretty good drinking buddies."

A Governor Who Was Just Plain Folk
December 24, 2016

You probably won't find too many ex-governors in the phone book. But Rose Mofford was there.

She died earlier this year. She was 94.

I spoke to her a number of times — twice while at the Dispatch.

I was editor of the Valley Life section. I picked up an Associated Press story about the beehive hairdo. It would have been four or so years ago. That's just a guess. And I don't remember the story's details.

It wasn't about the death of the woman who invented the beehive, Margaret Vinci Heldt. She died this past summer, just months before Mofford.

Heldt was 98.

When I saw the wire story, I thought of Mofford — Arizona's most famous beehive role model. I didn't have her listed on what passed for my Rolodex, a few dozen smudged cards on a plastic tray. I'd have to make calls. Find people who knew her. Cajole her number out of them.

But first I looked her up in the book. Wouldn't hurt to try, I thought. This was the electronic version of the phone book. And there was the name: Rose Mofford and a phone number.

I called and Arizona's first woman governor answered. And she was glad to talk. She let me in on a secret.

Her do was not a beehive. It was, she insisted, a French roll.

I wasn't clear on the difference. But I had to defer to the governor on that point.

I rang her up again in 2014. I got a tip a silver concho belt she had owned was in a display case at Western Trading Post on Florence Street in Casa Grande. Owner Jim Olson showed me the belt.

Mofford collected all kinds of Native American belts, jewelry and kachina dolls.

Most ended up in a collection now on permanent exhibit in Miami, Arizona. Mofford was born in Globe, just up the highway.

In 1997, the concho belt went for a good cause. Mofford donated it to a fundraiser for a Highway Patrol memorial. Whatever she didn't keep, she gave away, she said.

"I've only sold one thing, and that was the apartment next door."

The belt later ended up at a western antique auction. That's where Olson bought it.

Mofford said the donation was made in memory of her brother, John Perica. He was a Highway Patrol officer himself. He died at age 44. He didn't die in the line of duty. But he had the distinction of being the first to serve.

He had badge No. 1.

She was a No. 1 herself, of course. She became governor after her predecessor, Evan Mecham, was impeached and ousted in 1988. Mofford was secretary of state and next in line.

At the time, I wrote for a now long-gone afternoon newspaper. That's when I first met Mofford. I remember her as a governor wholly without pretense.

I've talked to other governors. I can't say that about all of them.

She was a person of good cheer and, well, just plain folk. I sat in her office on the ninth floor of the Executive Tower. This was where the bigwigs made big decisions — or in her case, the big French roll. But the atmosphere didn't feel rarified. I could have just as easily been chatting with my neighbor over the fence.

I talked to her predecessor in 1986. Evan Mecham was running for governor then. Everybody gave him as much chance of winning as they gave Donald Trump. Mecham showed them. He was elected governor, then made a mess of everything.

It was a complicated three-way race. I was assigned to interview Mecham for a feature story. Other reporters at the Phoenix Gazette — the long-gone paper — were assigned other candidates.

We had a list of questions. One was "What do you have in your pocket?"

I don't remember Mecham's answer. I do remember his somewhat rubbery face. It looked like a mask in a Hollywood movie. The bad guy would peel it off and reveal his true identity.

Of course, this was Mecham's real face. Still, he wasn't one to open up, ala Mofford. He wasn't unfriendly. It just seemed he kept a touch of mistrust in reserve.

As governor, his mistrust grew to open hostility against the press. And paranoia. He believed then-Attorney General Bob Corbin had focused a laser beam on him from across the Capitol mall.

That led to my favorite political cartoon by the Arizona Republic's Steve Benson. Mofford, in her newly appointed office, has a large hole burned into the middle of her beehive — or as we now know, French roll. She says: "Tell the attorney general he can turn off his laser."

Mofford was something of a caretaker governor. But she was just what the state needed, following the implosion of Evan Mecham.

And she was always in the phone book.

Homeless Man Had a Name
August 14, 2017

Dale Wallace was born in 1952, No. 4 of five brothers.
Don Wallace was No. 2. He's 76, some 11 years older than Dale.

Their parents, DeWitt and Kathleen, owned Casa Grande's City Cleaners on Sacaton Street, just north of Main Street.

Don remembered Dale as somebody who took his own counsel. He could come across as aloof, Don said.

"He was a very intense thinker," Don added.

Still, Dale wasn't a recluse. He made the honor roll in junior high school. He was a starting pitcher for the boys minor league team. Don recalls he pitched complete games as a lefty. The coach kept him in, despite rules limiting young arms to two innings or less.

He carried the team.

At Casa Grande Union High School, Dale was a varsity wrestler. He was wiry and competed at 102 pounds. But he wasn't all about athletics. He played Flamenco guitar, took lessons.

His mother encouraged his talent. She bought him a D-28 Martin.

These were pastimes, not lifelong pursuits. And maybe he became more the thinker after his father died in 1967.

DeWitt Wallace was killed in a one-car crash on the Papago Indian Reservation, now the Tohono O'odham Nation. He rolled his Volkswagen minivan heading back from a fishing trip in Rocky Point. He lost control on the narrow blacktop that becomes Chuichu Road.

But life went on for Dale. He graduated from Casa Grande Union in 1970. That fall he started his freshman year at Arizona State University.

Don visited him a time or two. Dale had moved out of the nice dorm his mother had arranged. His new dorm was somewhat shabbier. His new roommate shared his fascination for ASU's underground network of tunnels.

They spent their days mapping it out.

Maybe it was a network of storm drains. Or sewer lines. Don wasn't sure. I do know ASU's Tempe campus is connected by tunnels that can accommodate maintenance carts. I rode around in one for a summer job.

Dale's reading included works by poet-philosopher Kahlil Gibran, popular with the counter-culture set. His reading apparently didn't include textbooks.

And he didn't bother attending some classes. He flunked out. From there, he drifted.

He moved to Kearny and spent a year working for Kennecott Copper's Ray Mines Division. His job involved water purification.

"He was in a little building off by himself," Don said. "He was the perfect guy to do that kind of job."

But Dale moved on. He set out for Tucson and got a job with Truly Nolan. He sprayed for bugs in restaurants along Tucson's Miracle Mile.

He was married by then. And Don was living in Tucson at the time. He was a branch manager for a company that made industrial machine parts.

Dale seemed to settle in.

But it didn't last. In a year, maybe two, Dale and his wife, Susan, headed to Northern California. There was no planning. They just packed up the Pontiac and left.

Don ended up cleaning out Dale's apartment, boxing up what he could. Dale's sudden departure left him shaking his head. For Dale, it was a clean break.

"I lost track of them when they got to California," Don said.

Some news got through. News that was all but unavoidable. Dale lost Susan to illness and started drinking. In time, he sobered up.

Don heard little from Dale otherwise, until two years ago. By then, Don had retired to Mesa with his wife, Joyce.

He got a call from an in-law in Casa Grande. She said Dale had shown up. He wanted a place to stay, but she couldn't take him in. A police officer gave Dale a ride to a homeless shelter in town.

Don called the shelter. Dale got on the line.

"I talked to him maybe a minute and a half," Don said.

Whatever had come between them was still there.

The shelter closed last year, and Dale dropped off Don's radar. He took to camping out. Making the rounds. And making a few friends.

Daniel Tortorice was one of them. Dale was not given to self-pity, Tortorice said.

"He knew that he was homeless. Nobody had to remind him."

I came across Tortorice in Peart Park. Tortorice is 68 and retired. He's not homeless himself, but he likes to get out. And, in getting out, he got to know Dale Wallace.

"He was such a nice guy," Tortorice said. "He'd joke with you. He wouldn't tell you he was in pain or anything."

Peart Park had shade. It was a good place to dodge the heat. East of the park, Whataburger had cold drinks. And Dale was ready for his free refill. He carried bags of plastic cups, each from a different fast-food joint. He'd take out the cup with the matching logo and help himself at the soda fountain.

Whataburger was a favorite.

"Everybody at Whataburger knew him," Tortorice said. "They used to come out and give him biscuits and stuff."

I made my way to Whataburger, where I spoke to a young woman refilling napkins. She remembered Dale Wallace. She once brought him a meal somebody had bought for him. He talked about his days in high school. How he used to wrestle with her uncles on the varsity team.

Dale stopped coming after June 27. That afternoon he was found dead behind a behavioral health clinic on East Florence Boulevard. He'd had a heart condition. The heat likely triggered an attack. It had reached 107. Wallace was 65.

He had no ID. To the police, he was simply a "known transient."

The Pinal County medical examiner later identified him through a fingerprint match. He did have one arrest. He failed to appear in court to answer a trespassing citation. He had worn out his welcome at a Casa Grande McDonald's.

But for his arrest, Dale Wallace might have remained John Doe.

I learned his name from Casa Grande police. With a search of newspaper archives, I also learned he had a brother in Mesa.

I called Don Wallace Tuesday morning. I asked if he had a brother named Dale.

"Is he OK?" Don asked.

I told him Dale had died. That the county had paid for an indigent cremation. And that Legacy Funeral Home in Mesa had his remains.

The news came as a shock, Don said. But it wasn't entirely

unexpected.

It was the life Dale chose. But now he was in his brother's care. Don picked up Dale's remains soon after my call.

I visited Don the next day.

"I carried him as a baby," Don said. "But I carried him yesterday as an adult, and I never felt closer to him."

He'll lay his brother to rest at Mountain View Cemetery, alongside their mother and father.

Long Journey to a Final Resting Place
October 26, 2017

Dale Wallace was laid to rest in Casa Grande on Aug. 16. His brother, Don, wanted to place his remains next to their parents.

Those sites were taken.

But Mom and Dad aren't far. A short walk across a road and few rows down.

Dale's grave is marked with a small polished stone pillar. Earlier this month, a plaque was fitted on it. The plaque reads: "Dale Dwight Wallace – Son-Brother."

Don Wallace provided for the plaque. And he arranged to have Dale's ashes laid to rest here – in Mountain View Cemetery's Serenity Gardens. It's a pleasant place. Stone markers like Dale's are connected by ambling walkways. A fountain is nearby.

Dale Wallace did not have it so pleasant in life. At least not in his later years. He died nameless on June 27 behind a building on East Florence Boulevard. He was 65 and homeless. He'd had a heart attack, likely triggered by the heat.

I wrote about Dale last August, after learning his name from Casa Grande police. They learned it from the Pinal County medical examiner, who identified Dale Wallace through fingerprints. He had been arrested once for trespassing. It's an occupational hazard for the homeless.

Dale had four brothers. I was only able locate Don. The day I called, Don wasted no time. He picked up Dale's remains that afternoon. They had been in storage at a Mesa funeral home. The county had paid for an indigent cremation.

Don called me last week, just after the memorial had been placed atop Dale's marker. He said he'd never felt closer to his brother than he did now.

In life, Dale was a hard person to pin down. He seemed a free spirit. He often drifted from job to job, before giving up work all together.

He flunked out of college. In his case, it was for lack of trying.

After the column ran, I heard from Craig Scott, Dale's college roommate at Arizona State University. In an email, Scott confirmed what Don told me.

"Dale NEVER went to class, played his guitar and listened to music all day."

James Taylor was a favorite.

At night, Scott said, he and Dale and other roommates would wander the underground maintenance tunnels that crisscrossed the campus. Dale did broaden Scott's horizons a bit. He introduced Scott to the music of B.B. King, talking him into concert at Grady Gammage auditorium.

A niece of Dale Wallace also wrote to me. Her father, Randy, was the youngest of the five brothers. Randy learned from the column that Don was his last living brother.

She wondered why I hadn't contacted her father. I told her I had tried look up each of Dale's brothers. Don was my last hope. I found a phone number.

I first learned their names in a Dispatch newspaper article. They were listed as survivors in a story about their father's death. DeWitt Wallace died in a rollover accident in 1967. He was 50.

His wife, Kathleen Wallace, died in 1997. They're both interred in a grassy area, not far from Dale. The grave markers give dates of birth and death, brackets for time spent on earth. They also read:

43

"Mom." "Dad."

The Serenity Gardens, where Dale is, can be found right off the parking lot. I parked and got some maps from the office. I visited Dale's marker first. I took a few pictures, then headed over to his parents' graves. It was early afternoon. It was hot. The wind was gusting.

I held onto my hat. I didn't want to chase it across a cemetery.

To the south, beyond the grass, was a large flat expanse. It was dirt and had a few stakes here and there. It looked like a future development. Certainly, it had room for many who would follow Dale, DeWitt and Kathleen. Someday.

Across the expanse, I saw another collection of graves. It was maybe a quarter mile away, in the southwest corner. Curious, I crossed the dusty expanse.

The burials here seemed a bit more casual. On closer inspection, there was an order to it all. The graves formed rows. They all faced east. The dirt atop them was well packed. The wind tried, but couldn't kick up much dust.

A number of gravesites were little more than mounds, like something out of the Old West.

Others had nice polished stone markers. Some were decorated with an array of flowers – plastic – and little statues.

Somebody still cared.

Pinal County paid for most of the burials. This was the section for the indigent and the unclaimed. The John Does and the Jane Does. But the burials have largely stopped. The county no longer pays for them. Now indigents are cremated. And their remains sit in storage at a Mesa funeral home.

Until somebody comes to claim them. Somebody like a brother.

Finding Love in Kearny

Kearny, June 18, 2018

The photograph dates to the 1930s. It was taken shortly after the grand opening of Gabe's gas station and auto repair.

It's mounted high up near the entrance of Norm's Hometown Grocery. The market is on the main plaza in Kearny. Norm Warren co-owns the store with his wife, Myra Fontes-Warren.

There's a bakery. There are shelves stocked with groceries. Then there are the historic photographs, all enlarged. Norm gave me a brief tour of the collection.

I paused at the gas station. It was owned and operated by Gabe Avenetti and his wife, Antonia. The picture shows a vintage car parked behind vintage glass-cylinder gas pumps. Vintage now. They were new then. Gabe is on the far left, in a cap and holding up an inner tube. Antonia is the pretty woman off to the right.

She got her hands dirty, just like the guys. She fixed tires for buses. She could listen to an engine and tell you what was wrong with it.

Five of Gabe's young sons are in the picture.

A little girl sits next to one of the pumps. She's Molly, the Avenettis' daughter. She later married Luis Fontes and now goes by Molly Fontes.

The gas station was part of the commercial hub in Sonora, Arizona, once located near what's now State Route 177, south of Superior. The town of Ray was next door. Another smaller community, Barcelona, was nearby.

Molly, now 83, remembers some of the older houses. They lacked insulation. They lacked plumbing.

"There were some outhouses. There were a few indoor toilets," she said. "We were one of the few that had indoor toilets."

She and Luis settled in Sonora. They had six children. Myra was born in 1960.

In Sonora, Myra recalled, the houses weren't all that great. But the soil was rich with minerals. Trees thrived.

"Apricots, peaches, grapefruit, lemon, citrus, lime — everything grew down there," Myra said.

She remembered her favorite treat.

"The lady had a little store where everyone would go to get their snow cones."

Sonora had things to do, and not just for kids, Molly said. The town had a swimming pool, theater, and tennis and basketball courts.

Norm's family lived in Ray. He was born in 1957.

The two families likely didn't mingle much. Ray and Sonora were segregated.

Not so much by race but by nationality, and along ethnic lines, Molly said.

Anglos, including ethnic English and Scots, lived in Ray. Sonora had people of Mexican heritage, but others as well.

"We had Syrians," she said. Her own family, the Avenettis, were Italian.

The Spanish settled in Barcelona.

Segregation was the rule, Molly said.

"The mine separated us."

Kennecott Copper Co. owned the Ray Mine, at the time. Ray and Sonora sat on land owned by Kennecott. People worked for the mine or for businesses dependent on Kennecott paychecks. Luis worked in a shop that serviced mining trucks. Norm's father worked for the mine. He was a painter.

Sometimes labor disputes led to strikes. And strikes led to hard times. With no checks coming in, people relied on government assistance. Families helped each other out. Things could get rough.

In an earlier time, Myra said, mine bosses would take to concrete pillboxes, seeking refuge from angry strikers.

In Luis's time, it didn't come to that.

One way or another, the strikes were resolved. Miners returned to work. Life went on as usual, until the 1950s.

By then, Kennecott had gone from underground to open-pit mining. Crews began digging their way toward a large ore deposit under Ray and Sonora. To get to it, the towns would have to go.

Families were uprooted. Many scattered to nearby and not-so-nearby towns, Molly said. Breadwinners stayed on the job. Only now they had to commute, she said.

"They would drive," she said. "We had people driving from Globe. We had people driving from Superior. We had people driving from Phoenix."

But many, if not most, resettled in a new town, one created by Kennecott. Kearny was officially founded in 1958. Kennecott named it after Gen. Stephen Watts Kearny, who followed the Gila River with a contingent of troops in 1846, during the Mexican-American War. He was just passing through, on his way to California.

The town of Kearny sits just above the eastern banks of the Gila.

The migration from Ray and Sonora to Kearny took place over several years. People left ahead of the growing pit.

It was a short drive to Kearny. Ten miles. Maybe more.

But families packed more than suitcases. They loaded up furniture and other belongings. Some moved entire houses. The Catholic church and parts of the Baptist and Methodist churches were relocated. The dead were reinterred in a new cemetery, now along State Route 177.

The Fontes family and the Warrens pulled up stakes in the mid-1960s, among the last to leave. They moved into new houses built for a new town.

"The move was hard, expensive," Molly said.

Her six kids took it well, though. They found the move exciting. Something new and different.

Myra was 5. She was in kindergarten. Many people, she recalled, were heartbroken, sad.

Norm was 8. He was in second grade. In Sonora and Ray, Myra and Ray would have attended separate grade schools.

In Kearny, things were different. Segregation ended. Norm and

Myra went to the same schools. People of different walks were all thrown together. Norm summed up the fallout.

"We just all lived in harmony," he said.

Well, there was some tension, at first. But it faded. People intermarried, Molly said. And the youths in Kearny discovered an attraction all could appreciate. The Gila River. It was down the slope, beyond the town's swimming pool.

"We were called river rats," Norm said.

The river was something of a warmup for the pool, Myra added.

"We'd go to the river and swim and go to the pool … and do our swim team."

She took synchronized swimming. Her mother, Molly, taught it.

Families picnicked by the river. They still do. And Molly and Luis Fontes still live in the house they bought in 1965. Luis, 85, retired from the mine after 41 years.

In 1974, Norm got a job at the grocery store. It was Gordon's IGA. He became manager in 1987.

Two years later, Norm married Myra. He was the boy from Ray. She was the girl from Sonora. Kearny made it possible.

In 2015, they bought Gordon's and renamed it Norm's Hometown Grocery. It also goes by Norm's IGA. Myra had the historic photos enlarged and placed on the wall. She plans to do more. She'd like to create a museum dedicated to Ray, Sonora and Barcelona. And Kearny.

Hayden and Winkelman won't be overlooked, Myra said. They're just the down the road and part of the Ray Mine story.

Norm walked me past the bakery. He stopped beneath a picture of a girl in a flowing white dress. She's a teenager. Perhaps 17. Very pretty. She's Norm's mother, Les.

She came with her family from Oklahoma. It was the time of the Dust Bowl.

"They packed everything in a beat-up old truck," Norm said.

Whole families up and left. It was the mass migration captured in "The Grapes of Wrath."

His mother's family got as far as Glendale. Sometime later, she was in Ray raising a family and facing another migration.

The one that put Kearny on the map.

The Girl from Riverside Refused to Quit

Kearny, June 2, 2018

Stephani Yesenski made a racket whenever she drove to Kearny.

The gears on her blue Yugo moaned with every shift. It was a very proletarian stick shift. The car rattled like a bucket of bolts, or so one longtime resident said.

Yesenski lived in Riverside, a village of modest homes and house trailers. She'd cross the Gila River on a one-lane bridge, built in 1916. Locals flash their lights to let the other guy cross first.

The bridge leads to Kelvin, near the eastern terminus of the 30-mile Florence-Kelvin Highway. Half-paved. Half dirt.

Kelvin isn't a real town anymore. Boom to bust. Yesenski would pass through it on the way to Kearny, 7 miles down the road on State Route 177. She shopped in Kearny. She had friends in Kearny. She took classes at Central Arizona College, down the road in Aravaipa.

Yesenski's aunt and uncle bought her the Yugo. It was a high school graduation present. Maybe it groaned. Maybe it rattled. But I have no doubt Yesenski appreciated the gift.

I just can't ask her about it. Yesenski died of cancer in the waning hours of 1999. She had just turned 20.

Yesenski received a much better gift, in any case. A Yugo couldn't stack up against the generosity shown by family, friends, neighbors and all kinds of people from Oracle to Superior. People who came together to help Yesenski fight her illness. Republicans, Democrats, Mormons, Baptists, Catholics. White collar. Blue collar.

She was a unifying force.

I'm sure she didn't plan it that way. Few things in Yesenski's

49

early life went her way. Her mother died at the age of 37. Yesenski lived briefly with her father and stepmother, then her older brother.

Neither placement worked out. So Jackie and Roy Mann of Riverside, the aunt and uncle, took her in. She was 15 and already had cancer.

Yesenski, it turned out, wasn't a moper. And she wasn't a quitter.

Jackie Mann offers this story. Yesenski went out for volleyball at Kearny's Ray High School. The coach said she was too ill to play. So she decided on track.

The track coach took her on. He decided she deserved a shot.

Mann recalls the track meet in Apache Junction. Yesenski ran hurdles. But she failed to clear the first one and fell. She got up. She moved to an outside lane, running alongside the hurdles.

She leaped as she passed each one, as though jumping over it. She finished the race, Mann said. The crowd loved it. They laughed. They cheered. They gave Yesenski a standing ovation.

"She just wouldn't quit," Mann said. "She wouldn't give up."

She didn't give up fighting her cancer either. I admit, everybody seems to battle cancer. It sounds a bit cliché. But that's just what Yesenski did, though she had an army to back her up. People in and around Kearny, led by L.S. Jacobson. Just call him Jake.

He's the president and CEO of the Copper Basin Railway. Its main job is to haul ore from ASARCO's Ray Mine to the smelter in Hayden. Jacobson knows railroads, going back some 60 years.

Railway Age magazine named him Railroader of the Year in 1994.

Soon after, he became the engine behind efforts to get Yesenski into alternative treatment.

She had been undergoing chemotherapy in Arizona. But the chemo was taking its toll and the cancer wasn't backing off. She was 18, and 19 looked doubtful.

More needed to be done.

Yesenski and her aunt decided to pay Jacobson a visit. Yesenski had seen a painting by Winkelman artist W. Mitchell-Tucker in the local bank. It showed Jacobson, shovel in hand. Behind him, railroad tracks descended into a torrent of water. He'd do whatever it took to save them. And he pretty much did.

The painting was made from a photograph taken during the flood of 1993.

The same flood had nearly topped the bridge Yesenski would later rattle across in her Yugo. The bridge held, for the most part. Houses that smashed into it didn't.

In the painting, Yesenski saw somebody she could relate to. Somebody who wouldn't quit.

Jacobson was soon leading the charge with old-fashioned fundraisers. Bake sales and the like. He played groups off one another. Look how much the Mormons raised. Surely the Catholics can do better.

Donations rolled in and Yesenski made the flight to New York City. She stayed at a Ronald McDonald House. She was one of the older residents, helping smaller children with their studies, Mann said.

"She loved children so much, she wanted to be a schoolteacher," Mann said.

ASARCO paid for cabs to and from the hospital.

The plan was to get Yesenski started on stem cell therapy at St. Vincent's Hospital Manhattan, since torn down. The plan fell through. The lead doctor was booted out of the insurance network. A second doctor at Sloan Kettering Cancer Center in New York said stem cell therapy would kill her.

The doctor recommended an experimental treatment, one the Food and Drug Administration had not signed off on.

Jacobson went on a letter-writing campaign. He wrote the FDA. He called on a fellow Vietnam veteran, John McCain, who in turn wrote the FDA himself. The senator didn't ask the agency to rule in Yesenski's favor. He simply asked it to reply to Jacobson's earlier letter.

"This way they can't throw it in the damn waste basket," Jacobson said.

Others pitched in as well. Then-Sen. Jon Kyl and U.S. Rep. J.D. Hayworth made calls.

The FDA responded, months later. It gave Sloan Kettering the go-ahead with a treatment known as TNP-470. Here's what the National Cancer Institute says about it: "It may prevent the growth of new blood vessels that tumors need to grow."

The FDA opened the program to nine other patients. For Yesenski, it was something of a bonus.

"Even if it doesn't help me," she told her aunt, "it might help someone else."

Yesenski had one more hurdle. Her insurance provider balked. Pete Rios, then a state senator, got on the phone. The state insurance director got in on the conversation, Mann said. Things were said. Coverage was restored.

Yesenski received the treatment.

She returned home in the summer of 1999. She was greeted by yellow ribbons along 177. Jacobson's railway was sponsor of a cleanup mile. He and his crew tied the ribbons to signs and posts along the way.

In New York, Yesenski did well at first, Mann said. The cancer was in remission, briefly. Back home, she continued to receive treatment. But the cancer came back. It spread quickly. She died two days after her 20th birthday.

Jacobson spoke at her funeral. People filled the high school auditorium.

He recalled the girl who wouldn't give up. The girl you could hear a mile away, rattling across the old bridge in a rickety Yugo. To honor her, he said, he'd push for a new bridge. It would be a bridge of unity, named in her memory.

The bridge did, in fact, get built. It's all but ready for showtime. Ribbon cutting is 9:30 Friday morning. It's a promise kept, Jacobson said.

"If I hadn't been stirring the pot, it wouldn't have happened."

There's a parallel story behind the new bridge, one told by Pinal County. Planners saw the need to replace the old bridge nearly 20 years ago. But planning was complicated. Federal buy-in a must.

It took some time, but things fell into place. Construction started in February 2017. The bridge was completed at a cost $6.5 million. Feds paid a million. The county footed the rest.

The new bridge will have two lanes and span the Copper Basin railroad tracks. It will be named the Kelvin Bridge Replacement Project. Not much sentiment in that.

The old bridge will remain. It will become a foot bridge and part of the Arizona Trail. It doesn't span the railroad tracks, just the river.

Crossing the old bridge, you see the sign Jacobson put out, right next to the tracks. It says: "The 'Jake' Jacobson Bridge of Unity: In memory of Stephani Yesenski."

There's a toll for crossing the new bridge, the sign says. It's not a monetary toll. You pay by reaching into your heart and finding compassion and mutual respect for all people.

It's a good sentiment. I won't quibble about the bridge's name, in any case. I'll just picture the girl who crossed it in her blue Yugo. The girl who wouldn't quit.

Senator Offers Glimpse Of People's Business

Arizona State Capitol, March 31, 2019

I went to see sausage being made last Monday. Instead I witnessed a vote for lemonade.

I had a nice visit with Sen. Frank Pratt along the way. Pratt is part of the sausage-making industrial complex known as the Arizona Legislature. He's a Republican and represents Legislative District 8. He lives in Casa Grande.

I dropped by the Senate about 10:30 last Monday morning. It was a cold call.

"John Q. Public, reporting for duty."

Pratt's assistant told me the senator had visitors throughout the morning. But he would make time for me. Squeeze me in.

I waited in the third-floor lobby outside Senate offices. I was easy to spot. I was the only guy not wearing a dark suit, though I did have on my professional reporter's uniform. Khaki pants and a polo shirt.

The suits and well-dressed women were lobbyists. All sitting around, waiting to get their two cents in with a sausage maker.

Jojo Taylor was standing nearby with her mother, Lori. Jojo was wearing a sash. It read: Miss Pinal County Outstanding Teen.

That's about all I learned. They were quickly led into the inner sanctum of Senate offices. I was left to wait. Maybe it was the sash. Maybe if I had one. It might say: Mr. Can't Find His Car Keys Runner-up.

It probably wouldn't work. So I waited instead. Lobbyists came and lobbyists went. About an hour later, Pratt made time for me — as promised.

Here's an observation. Pratt's diffident, easygoing and as about as far from political bombast as you can get. Talking with him was like a chat with a neighbor.

He's a businessman. So the GOP suits him. He owns Pratt Pools in Casa Grande. His son Bryan runs it day-to-day.

I first met Frank Pratt in January 2009. He was part of a new crop of representatives in the Arizona House. I worked at the Arizona Capitol Times. I had the job of taking mug shots of the new arrivals.

He's 76 and conservative, but not rigidly so. He was among nine House Republicans to back then-Gov. Jan Brewer's 2013 push to expand Medicaid in Arizona.

He won his Senate seat in 2016. He was re-elected in 2018. In 2020, he'll be part of a term-limit shuffle. District 8 Rep. T.J. Shope can't run again for the House. Pratt agreed to leave the Senate, opening the seat for Shope.

Pratt might, in turn, run for Shope's House seat. He hasn't decided.

I think returning to the House would cramp his style. You have to cram twice the number of lawmakers into pretty much the same square footage.

Pratt looked around his Senate office. There was room for an executive-size desk and a comfy couch.

"It's pretty nice in here," he said with a laugh. "Pretty

comfortable, you know."

I settled into a chair. I asked Pratt what he's done for Pinal County. He cited a bill he sponsored to free up money for firefighter and police pensions. He sponsored SB1186 with Florence in mind.

Here's the nutshell version. It's a bit wonky. Better grab some coffee.

In years past, Florence set up a pension plan for part-time and volunteer firefighters. Now the town has a full-time fire department. Today's firefighters are covered by the Public Safety Personnel Retirement System, separate from the volunteer plan.

Florence settled its volunteer pension obligations. And had a quarter million dollars left over, said Benjamin Bitter, assistant to the town manager.

It was money the town couldn't touch.

Pratt's bill allows Florence to put the money toward the full-time public safety pension, for firefighters and police. It would certainly help. The town's public safety retirement plan is currently $1.5 million in arrears. The $250,000 would knock it down to $1.25 million.

"Quite a big percentage," Bitter said.

It's not a partisan issue. Pratt's bill passed the Senate 29-0. It's now with the House.

Another Pratt bill, SB1257, would let Globe, Miami and Gila County set up a district to build and maintain a community swimming pool. It would be supported by a property tax, if approved by voters.

It's like a fire district, but for a swimming pool, Pratt said.

I have a swimming pool. They're welcome to mine. But I suppose they'll want to start off new.

Well, on to the important stuff. The Senate has before it a bill to deem lemonade the official state drink. I asked Pratt about it. He demurred. He had bigger fish to fry. And I immediately thought of the Apache trout, the official state fish.

But that was not up for discussion.

Pratt, it happened, sat on the committee for the lemonade bill, the Senate Government Committee. It would meet at 2 o'clock, for a final time this session.

So it was now or never for lemonade. I showed up at the hearing room. The seven committee members, it seems, all got swag from the lemonade lobby. Bottled lemonade next to every nameplate.

The first order of business dealt with amendments. One would specify pink lemonade. Another would make sun tea the official state drink. Another went with jamaica, a Mexican hibiscus-flavored tea. Margarita was also in the running.

In the end, the committee approved the lemonade bill, unamended. It was on to the full Senate. It could still be amended on the floor. I'd go for making water the official state drink. That is, until we run out.

Pratt didn't vote on lemonade. He had stepped out. He had other matters to deal with. Some might say more important.

He did sit in for other bills. He voted in favor of naming an Estrella mountain peak after a war hero. Charles Keating IV was killed in a Kurdish-led firefight with ISIS, in Iraq. But the naming honor would have to wait until 2021. The U.S. Board on Geographic Names, the committee learned, will only accept proposals for a person "deceased at least five years."

Keating was killed in May 2016.

After the hearing, I made small talk with Pratt in the hall. We talked about scuba diving. Some years back, I went diving with my daughter. And Pratt used to be a diving instructor. He hasn't dived lately, though. No time, he said. He spends 12-hour days on the people's business. And that doesn't count the drive time between Casa Grande and the Capitol.

Maybe he'll take some time this summer. Don his flippers and air tanks. Go diving off the coast of Cozumel with his son.

And maybe relax on the beach with a lemonade.

Writer's Sheriff Shaped
By War and Wyoming

October 21, 2019

Bob Schrader follows the old rule. Write what you know.

And what he knows led him to write about a larger-than-life deputy sheriff in the fictional county of Banner, Wyoming. It's rural. It's rugged. And it's got bank robbers.

Schrader introduces the man in his first novel, "Jerry's Story." He writes under the name Robert W. Schrader.

Jerry is Jerry Burkley.

More about Jerry in a bit. First, I want to touch on Schrader's street cred in crafting the character. The setting. The supporting cast.

I spoke to Schrader, who's 75, at his Casa Grande home last week. He winters here and summers in Wyoming, his home state. Betty, his wife, sat nearby. Dusty was at the ready. He's Schrader's 4-year-old black Labrador. He's a service dog, trained to guide Schrader about the house and in public.

Schrader has Parkinson's disease, fallout from his exposure to Agent Orange in Vietnam. He went there in 1968 as a newly minted second lieutenant. The symptoms first appeared in 2010.

Schrader was born and raised in Cheyenne, Wyoming. His grandfather, Wesley, started a funeral business there in 1924. In 1928, he bought the Idelman House, just across the street from the state Capitol.

"I was a poor deprived little kid," Schrader said, with a hint of irony. "I grew up in a mansion."

He showed me a picture. The mansion looks like a towering

Gothic house from a Hardy Boys mystery.

Wesley repurposed the house as a funeral parlor. He took care of business on the first floor. The third floor was open and sometimes served as a ballroom. Three generations of Schraders lived on the second floor.

Young Robert Schrader remembers escaping from his crib as a tot. He'd wander about the house. One morning his parents found him next to an open casket. He had pulled up a chair to stand on. He had a glass of water.

"I was flicking water in this body's face, trying to wake him up to come play with me."

You won't find this bit in "Jerry's Story."

The funeral home and the old house, however, have a starring role in Schrader's next book, "Tunnel Secrets." It's due out in a few weeks.

"Jerry's Story" starts in Vietnam. Jerry Burkley flies helicopters, picking up the wounded.

Schrader's own Vietnam job was that of a battalion surgeon assistant, a forerunner to today's physician assistant. He led a surgical unit on a ship that patched up wounded soldiers and Marines.

They were first brought to smaller boats by helicopter.

"We floated up the Mekong River," Schrader said.

He kept busy. One particular night comes to mind. He treated up to 200 South Vietnamese marines. Most took mortar rounds in an ambush.

After Vietnam, Schrader spent a year in the family funeral business. He left to sell insurance. Four years later, he began law school.

The insurance company was not on board.

"They fired me." The company told Schrader: "We don't want any part-time agents."

It worked out for the best. Schrader got a job as a deputy sheriff in Laramie County. During the semester, he worked as a dispatcher. In summer, he patrolled the county. His experience informed Jerry's character.

Schrader finished law school, passed the bar exam and worked at small firm in Buffalo, Wyoming. Population: 4,000. In the years to follow, he became a justice of the peace, Wyoming state insurance commissioner, a state district court commissioner and, following a brief retirement, a substitute teacher.

He also put in 28 years with the Wyoming Air National Guard, retiring as a lieutenant colonel.

He flew a lot as well. He had a commercial pilot's license.

Betty was, and is, his constant companion. They had known each other since grade school. In high school, he needed a date. He called her up. They hit it off. They've been married 55 years.

Schrader began writing "Jerry's Story" between jobs.

"I went to up the forest area next to Cheyenne, and sat in a camper there and started working on the story," he said.

Jerry, it happens, is not Schrader under a different name. He couldn't be. Schrader makes an appearance in the book as himself. Jerry is a composite. And he's got a past that differs from Schrader's. Jerry Burkley was divorced and something of a drifter with a chip on his shoulder.

That was before Sheriff Tom Flanigan took him under his wing.

Jerry wasn't new to law enforcement. He was a Denver cop. He graduated first in his class at the police academy. He became Sheriff Flanigan's best deputy.

"He just seems to get most of it done pretty well," Schrader said. He's modest on Jerry's behalf.

The writing reflects Schrader's own droll sense of humor. Characters aren't cardboard. They draw parallels to real people. Sometimes Schrader uses their real names, with permission. Jerry has a love interest, of course. Cheryl is a laboratory technician at the local hospital in Caribou, Wyoming.

Like Banner County, it's fictional.

I won't give away too much. I'll just say Cheryl becomes essential to the plot. And that picks up when robbers hold up the bank. They make their getaway on horseback, taking their loot through the rugged Wyoming wilderness.

Jerry follows.

Schrader has these scenes locked down. He knows about horses. He learned to ride before he could walk. And he knows the

Wyoming wilderness by heart. He's worked as an elk-hunting guide.

No salary. Just all-expenses-paid camping trips.

Jerry's story isn't finished yet. He'll be back in "Tunnel Secrets." It involves a super computer the size of a laptop. Its whereabouts had been a mystery, until 10-year-old Brynna discovers it in a tunnel leading from the old Grubb mansion.

Grubb stands in for the old Idelman house, the mansion of Schrader's childhood. Brynna is fashioned after Schrader's own granddaughter, also named Brynna.

Betty is Bob's editor. She just finished scouring the final proof of "Tunnel Secrets."

All writers need an editor, however much it bothers them.

For Some, Lockdown Means Locked Out

July 20, 2020

Christina Marn and her friends help each other out on hot summer days. They head for a convenience store. Whoever has food stamps will buy a big bottle of water. And maybe some ice.

They share.

"We pass water to each other," Marn said. "Pour water on ourselves, and when the sprinklers turn on, sit under a shade tree."

What they don't share is a roof. Marn and her friends are homeless.

I spoke to her last week in a dining room run by Seeds of Hope, a faith-based charity. Free hot lunches are served daily. The dining room has a new floor. The walls have new paint.

It's housed in the Fountains of Living Water Church on Second Street. Diners are expected to help with cleanup and other chores.

Like Marn, who's 50, many of them are homeless.

I have to state the obvious here. Now is not a good time to be homeless. Not July in Casa Grande. The day I spoke to Marn the high was 109. The day before it was 114.

A bit of shade under a tree is much appreciated.

Peart Park offers that, plenty of shade and grass. It's a 10-minute walk from the church. People there look out for each other, Marn said. If someone falls asleep in the sun, they'll get a wake-up call and be led to a spot under a tree. Shade.

I asked her about other places she could go to cool off.

"The only place I can think of is the skate park," she said. "They have like a water thing for kids."

The water thing is at Carr McNatt Park, also home to the skate park. Kids can splash around in cool geysers of water.

"I'm pretty sure adults get wet, too," Marn said.

Parents with their kids most likely.

Marn can only watch and perhaps dream of resetting the clock. Become a kid again and run freely through the cool spray.

"That's a good idea right there," she said.

Childhood, of course, is no longer an option.

Before the pandemic, Marn had other places she could go. Public spaces where people of all walks were welcome. A favorite was the Casa Grande Main Library, adjacent to Peart Park. It offered a cool place to sit. It offered water.

It was listed as a cooling and hydration station in what was known as the street sheet. The one-page foldout was a resource guide for the homeless. It was in wide circulation last summer.

This summer, not so much. Cooling stations like the library have largely shut down anyway. The coronavirus can't spread if people aren't around to spread it. The library closed its doors in mid-March, part of a statewide lockdown. It opened the lobby in May.

Then, as COVID cases spiked in Arizona, it closed again.

Before the lockdown, everybody was welcome, Library Manager Amber Kent said.

"People could come in as long as they needed."

Now books are checked out curbside. And the doors aren't completely shut. People can go in to use the computers. Six have been set up, 6 feet apart. Barriers separate the stations. They're cleaned after each use.

"A lot of people need those computers. They're looking for jobs or filing for unemployment benefits," Kent said.

For now, library cards aren't required. People can just cool down while surfing the web.

I spoke to Princelee as he finished lunch. He sat one table over from Marn. He didn't want his last name used. He planned to head to the library later, use the computer.

"They'll let you in there for an hour," Princelee said. "But you have to be very, very quiet."

It is, after all, a library.

I asked Princelee how long he'd been homeless.

"To be honest, this is my 15th time, since 19. I'm 25. My dad's in prison for life. My mom, she hasn't really been there."

He doesn't handle it alone, he said.

"If I didn't have a relationship with Jesus Christ, I would not be able to get through it," he said.

He spoke philosophically about Jesus as the way.

Seated next to him, Carl Benner said: "That's pretty deep, man."

Benner, 50, gets by with a higher power himself.

"When I want to be cooled off, I ask God for a nice cool breeze. Usually, he'll give it."

He didn't get it Sunday before last. He was walking in the 114-degree heat.

"I felt like I was going to pass out, until I made it to the park, and then I sat down for a while."

Pre-COVID, he could have grabbed a cold bottle of water at the library. Not at the moment. The library stopped taking donations, Kent said. There's simply no place to store the water.

The nearby CGHelps Resource Center was another cooling and hydration station. It sits on the northeast corner of Peart Park. It's a one-stop shop for the homeless and people needing help with housing. It's mostly shuttered now. Pandemic fallout.

The doors are open for a few hours Monday and Wednesday. The homeless can pick up their mail then, in care of CGHelps. One person staffs the mailroom. She hands out water as well.

The Community Action Human Resources Agency manages CGHelps. Mary Lou Rosales is CAHRA's executive director.

CAHRA is looking into places that can offer cooling and hydration. They won't be left high and dry, Rosales said.

"We have water that we'll share with anybody who has a hydration station," she said.

Some faith-based centers already offer food and water.

The library and CGHelps want to resume business as usual. That includes offering cool respite to people who could use a bit of comfort. How soon depends on getting the virus under control. No one has the answer.

Benner rose from the dining table. He shouldered his backpack and braced for another scorching afternoon. I asked if he planned to visit the library.

"I don't know how to use a computer," he said.

Dick Myers, Eloy's Homespun Historian

May 17, 2021

Once a year, I'd head east on Jimmie Kerr Boulevard, turn off at Toltec Road. A block or two more and I'd end up at the Old Toltec Elementary School in Eloy. Dick Myers would be there. He was there most days. Or so it seemed.

The school was built in 1930. I first met Myers there in 2010. He showed me around.

What I saw was an old building — abandoned, cluttered and dusty. Myers saw a school restored as a museum, one that spoke to the history of the area. From Hohokam to early settlers and cotton farming.

Every year, on my return, I saw less of my first impression and more of Myers' vision. He first restored a smaller wood structure nearby. It was built in 1928 and known as the "colored school," a relic of Arizona's segregated past.

The main building, the 1930s school, now houses a museum. Displays of the region's history line the walls, as do restored blackboards. The Sunland Visitor Center occupies a part of the building.

The work wasn't a one-person job. Early visitor center members saw a need to restore the school. The Santa Cruz Valley Historic Museum was created to raise tax-exempt funding. Myers was the board president.

Volunteers pitched in.

But nobody pitched in more than Myers. He was always right there, hands-on-getting-it-done. He put in at least 20,000 hours of sweat equity. He stopped counting after that. I went through some of the stories I wrote about him and the school. One had "labor of love" in the headline.

I'm sure that's true. But "love of history" might be more on point.

I recall standing outside the school. We faced north. Myers spoke about the families who showed up to pick cotton. They had children. And the children would fill the old school to bursting. Once the cotton was picked, the families would leave. And classrooms emptied out.

Myers was tall and, well, homespun. Truly homespun, raised in Eloy and full of stories about it. He spoke plainly, like someone who just happens to know these things. Not a musty academic. But Myers was a true historian. He dug through old newspapers. And historical records. He'd tie all that into his own experiences.

Then he'd tell you a story.

He had a personal attachment to the old school. He didn't attend it. But his wife, aunt and kids did. He was born in Phoenix. His parents moved to Eloy when he was 4. They ran Eloy's Greyhound bus station. He recalled a job he had bagging potatoes, stuffing them into burlap bags. Pay was by the pound. I nodded. I had no idea Eloy farmers once grew potatoes.

64

Myers later worked for El Paso Natural Gas Co. It led to a 30-year career, 15 as a welder in Topock, in northwest Arizona. On retirement, he moved back to Pinal County and became a historian of all things Eloy. He had a regular radio show. He gave talks about Eloy's history.

I went to one at Dorothy Powell Senior Center in Casa Grande. He spoke of the migrant camps, populated by seasonal farmworkers. The bars lining Frontier Street, then part of the old Tucson Highway. He had a story about a wild sheriff's deputy, long-since departed. Word had it he shot up his own car.

Then Myers turned to the naming of Eloy. The generally accepted version didn't hold water, he said. It went something like this: A man stepped off the train, took in the bare desertscape and shouted, "Eloi, Eloi lama sabachthani." A biblical phrase roughly translated as: "My God, my God, why has thou forsaken me!"

Didn't happen like that, Myers said. The name arises from an acronym used by Southern Pacific, which built the railroad — going from Yuma to Tucson. Eloy stands for East Line of Yuma, Myers said. He had pored through documents. He interviewed a dozen retired Southern Pacific railroaders, among others. They all backed him up.

Myers the historian was also Myers the tour guide. Once a year, he gave a Tag-A-Long Cotton Tour. Tourgoers would jump in their cars and trucks and follow Myers to B&J Farms. I went along once as well. While a big cotton harvester went up and down the rows, Myers spoke about the life of a cotton farmer. Not an easy one.

He gave tours of Central Arizona Project works as well. I missed that one. Too bad. Probably a good story there.

I didn't pass up a chance to see his artwork. He specialized in wind chimes. He worked out of his garage. Or wherever it was convenient. He kept something of a scrapyard for the parts. His wind chimes were not all light and pingy. For one set, he welded a beam atop a post and suspended discarded oxygen and CO_2 tanks. When the wind blew, they clanged like Big Ben.

He used to take his sculptures and wind chimes to Casa Grande's Art in the Alley. He sold them to raise money for the Old Toltec School. He also donated his art to an annual dinner-and-dance auction. Proceeds went for the school's restoration.

Myers' own yard is something of a sculpture gallery. There are the chimes, of course. Then there's the mailbox. Art as humor. It's actually several mailboxes fixed to a 12-foot pole, in ascending order. There's snail mail. Junk Mail. Email. At the top, airmail.

On my visit, Rosalind, his wife, had made cookies. She was kind and offered me a few. I thought: Dick has it pretty good.

The house is tucked up against the desert. Myers loved to see javelina parade through, especially the babies. He appreciated nature.

He lived just a few blocks from the Arica Road Trailhead at Casa Grande Mountain Park. The mountain had a history, and Myers had stories. He gave me a personal tour, flanking the park in his SUV. He pointed to a rise, known as Chimney Hill.

That's where Old Bill on the Hill built a fireplace with a chimney, Myers said. Old Bill would drive up there with his Jeep. He'd switch on his portable radio.

"He'd come up there, listen to Paul Harvey, because he couldn't get a signal because the mountain would block it," Myers said.

Old Bill's gone now. And Jeeps aren't allowed on the mountain trails. But development is planned for desert flats hugging the mountain. Areas now used by hikers. Myers looked into the proposal. Not a good fit, he decided. Not for a place of quiet, solitude and desert beauty.

He was all for free enterprise, he said. Developers were within their rights. Still, he said, not a good fit.

I recall another ride-along. Myers showed me the remnants of old farms. Foundations for houses. Housing for abandoned wells. Mesquite reclaiming a land once plowed for cotton.

He knew who had lived in the houses. Who had raised the crops. He knew just about everything about anything you could see, if you looked around.

He had stories about it all. And he shared them. Now he's gone. He died April 1. I'll miss him.

Film Looks at War's Toll on Wives
March 15, 2021

Terri Topmiller was married to a Vietnam War veteran. The war was something he never got over. It was something she never got over.

Both lived with it every day.

"He never found peace," Terri said.

Robert couldn't stop thinking about the war's lasting toll, especially on Vietnam. He and Terri visited Vietnamese orphanages. And children scarred by the defoliant Agent Orange. They supported an orphanage for a year, sending $600 a month.

It wasn't enough. The nightmares continued.

"He had so much guilt from Vietnam," she said.

Terri shares her story in the documentary "I Married the War."

His burden became hers. Maybe burden's not the right word. It's a sharing of all the injuries men bring home from war. From the physical to the emotional. From brain injuries to post-traumatic stress disorder.

Terri is one of 11 women interviewed for "I Married the War." All wives of combat veterans. Their stories are personal. Each is different. But all tie into the idea that war isn't left on the battlefield. It's brought home.

And depicted in the moving film produced and directed by Betty and Ken Rodgers.

"I Married the War" isn't quite a sequel to their first documentary, "Bravo! Common Men, Uncommon Valor." It's more of a natural progression.

The first film focused on the Battle of Khe Sanh. Marines in

1968 held off a 77-day siege by North Vietnamese troops. The movie put the battle front and center, with archival photos and footage, as well as ear-ringing explosions. Khe Sanh veterans spoke about the battle and its lasting effects.

Ken had a personal interest. He grew up in Casa Grande before joining the Marines. He was at Khe Sanh. He still carries shrapnel from a mortar explosion.

"Bravo!" won best documentary at the 2015 GI Film Festival in San Diego. Ken and Betty screened the film around the country, often at Marine Corps reunions. They kept in touch with Khe Sanh veterans.

And their wives.

The film's editor, John Nutt, had a suggestion. Do a movie about the wives of the men in "Bravo!"

Nutt, a professional film editor, had come out of retirement to edit "Bravo!" He's also a Vietnam veteran. He returned to edit "I Married the War."

Betty would hear from other women: "You know the wives are Vietnam veterans, too."

Betty and Ken took to the idea. But they went beyond Khe Sanh. And Vietnam. They interviewed wives of veterans from War World II, up through the wars in Iraq and Afghanistan.

The film deals with conflict beyond the battlefield. Conflict borne by returning soldiers. Conflict that tests marriages. And families.

"Anytime there's conflict, some kind of relationship between humans," Ken says, "there's a story there."

Terri Topmiller was their first interview, in late 2015. She lived near Betty and Ken in the Boise area of Idaho. Betty met her at a screening of "Bravo!"

"It was an instant friendship," Betty said.

Terri agreed to sit for an interview. It wasn't an easy decision. Once you see the film, you understand why.

She was one of four Boise-area women featured in the movie.

The Idaho public television station showed an interest in the project. And suggested a more diverse group might appeal to a wider audience. So Betty and Ken expanded their search.

They took their film crew to shoots in Texas, Indiana, Wisconsin, California and Atlanta. The movie became one of diversity in color and ethnicity, as well as geography. And in wars fought.

Gloria Jabaut lived in California. Her husband, Ron, served in the Navy. He returned from the Korean War a different man. He couldn't stop washing his hands. He scrubbed until his fingernails came off.

She told him: "You have to talk to me about it. He just wouldn't."

Ron was a sonar operator on a destroyer. At Hungnam, Korea, he volunteered to help evacuate Marines who had fought their way out of a major Chinese assault. With heavy losses. He helped the injured board the ship. He carried the dead. His hand washing obsession followed.

"The name they put on it was PTSD," Gloria said.

Precious Goodson's husband, Leonard, came back from Afghanistan a broken man. He had PTSD, along with mild traumatic brain injury. TBI is the shorthand. He was easily angered and easily upset.

"If I closed the refrigerator door too hard, it would set him off," Goodson said.

Precious never left his side. She completed her doctorate online, all the while helping Leonard out in any way she could. In one scene, she counts out pill after pill and blends them in a medical milkshake. All for Leonard.

Later we see Precious and Leonard walking their two dogs. A form of therapy, perhaps. I'd give the dogs credit. Betty and Ken do, at the end of the film.

Stacie Vaughan of Indiana recounted her husband's flashbacks. At one point, Drew pinned her to the floor. He didn't recognize her. She spoke his name calmly and firmly, over and over. "Drew, Drew ..." He came out of it.

"I don't know what he did in Iraq," Stacie says.

She knows what it did to him. Still, she stayed with him and, as best she could, kept him grounded. You see them both later, strolling around Nashville, Indiana, enjoying the sights.

He's a presence in the film. But he's not interviewed. None of the husbands are. Nor does the film feature men married to women who fought in combat.

The filmmakers didn't want to lose focus.

"I have a philosophy about these films," Ken said. "Keep it simple. Keep the story simple."

Having veterans tell their side would add all new storylines. New wrinkles. And complicate a film that had already generated 25 hours of unedited footage.

It was, of course, edited. Nutt did most of the work. Betty and Ken collaborated. Now each wife's story runs about five or 10 minutes. Betty had thought about going on camera to tell hers. But it would have meant cutting into the time afforded the others. She decided against it.

Here's what she told me.

She met Ken in 1984, 16 years after Khe Sanh. They both lived in Cloudcroft, New Mexico, high in the Sacramento Mountains. Betty helped to manage a resort. Ken was a regular.

They met in the bar, Ken said.

Not quite, according to Betty. Ken sought to make reservations for his parents. He didn't have a credit card, though. Betty was called in to deal with it.

"I thought, well, we'll give him one chance."

Ken's parents showed up, credit card in hand. Ken and Betty married the following year.

Betty cited a quote from the film: "We just started talking and we've been talking ever since."

In 2008, though, they both came to realize: Ken carried with him the baggage of war. PTSD. It explained mood swings and emotional flareups.

It was something they both had to acknowledge and work through.

I viewed the film at home, something of a private screening.

I wondered afterward, where would these veterans be without the wives? The women not only absorbed the pain. They kept them grounded. Kept them from spinning out of control. In some cases, kept them alive.

Ken recalled the interview with Sally Zepeda. She lives with her husband, Luis, on their mini-ranch in Hondo, Texas. A Vietnam veteran, he developed cancer attributed to Agent Orange. He began radiation and chemo-therapy.

At some point, he decided it wasn't worth it. He told Sally he was ending his treatment.

Sally said she would not let that happen. She was telling us that. We could see her telling her husband, "I won't let you die." He completed his treatment. The next scene shows the two on a walk through the ranch. Luis is very much alive.

Not all stories end well.

Terri Topmiller's husband took his own life, 40 years after Khe Sanh. He couldn't shake the guilt. He carried with him what psychologists now recognize as moral injury.

I asked Betty what she would say, if she sat for the camera.

She answered as a filmmaker, not a subject.

"This is what happens when we ask people to go to war, and it's something that hasn't been talked about. It's something that is not known about the true impact of the ripple effect, that they do bring the war home with them."

Ken adds: "I think this really is a story to tell women who are going through this, that you're not alone. That millions of people are going through this."

Seeds of Nursery Ownership
Planted Years Ago
Signal Peak, October 4, 2021

Adel Diego remembers her early childhood in rural Mexico. She lived on an hacienda. She remembers playing in the river. She remembers the fruit trees.

She doesn't remember getting polio. She doesn't remember a day without polio. She was too young for that, only a year and a half old.

It hasn't slowed her down. She greets customers at the Avocado Nursery with a smile, a knowledge of all things plants and a willingness to show them where to find what they want. Sometimes customers note her limp. They tell Diego not to go out of her way.

In Diego's words: "They say, 'Don't worry, just point where it's at. You stay here.'"

She tells them: "There's no problem. I walk this nursery every day."

She's walked it for 20 years. She rose to become the manager, working for Phil Bond. He founded the Avocado Nursery, along with his wife, Julie. She died in 2013. Phil carried on until his death, just last August.

In his will, he turned the nursery over to his most loyal workers. Diego, of course, as well as Marisol Rodriguez and Guadalupe Rodriguez, Marisol's mother. Marisol handles the landscaping end of the business, Distinctive Earthscapes. Lupe, as she's known, helps with landscaping.

The Avocado is a distinctive nursery. Its brick-lined paths meander through greenery labeled with hand-crafted signs.

Diego's own life path took a few detours. But she had help along the way. And a few timely encounters.

She's 45. That's young for a person who's had polio. Vaccines were widely available by 1975, when Diego was born. Except in parts of rural Mexico, she added. For her parents, who had no car, it was a four-hour walk to the clinic.

She did get a first polio vaccine, she said.

"When I needed to get the second vaccination," she said, "I didn't get there in time."

It could have been worse. She at least had some protection. The doctor told her: "You were lucky. You didn't get completely disabled."

She could walk, with difficulty.

When Diego was 7, her family moved to the Picacho area. Her

mother and father worked on a citrus farm. Workers used tractors to pick ripe oranges. One drove the tractor and — as it passed by — another picked the fruit.

Diego attended Picacho Elementary School. The students, she said, did not tease her for her disability. Only for the tube socks she wore with a dress.

She walked with a foot turned inward. Only surgery would fix that. Robert Noe, the district's superintendent at the time, helped her get insurance.

"He made everything to where it was possible for me to get the treatment, surgery, the checkups and everything," Diego said.

Without surgery, Diego might have needed a wheelchair or a cane. Now she walks with a leg brace. That's walk, as in good luck keeping up with her.

In 1998, Diego moved to Casa Grande with her mother, Reyna. Adel dreamed of becoming a pediatric nurse. She wanted to be like the nurses who treated her. One of her doctors shot the dream down.

He said: "You can't do it because you can't walk."

He was wrong. Just the same, Diego switched dreams.

She liked working with numbers, so she took accounting courses at Central Arizona College, Signal Peak. She eventually got degrees in business administration and communications, as well as accounting.

Her business communications professor was Julie Bond.

"She would get to know her students and talk to them," Diego said.

Diego told Julie that she and her mother were building their own house. They did the framing, tiling and landscaping.

She told Diego: "If you've done landscaping, if you've done irrigation, you might be interested in coming and helping us."

And so began Diego's two-decade career at the Avocado.

Julie brought Diego in to help with the paperwork. Julie Bond was like an aunt to her.

"Like a family member," Diego said. "That's how she treated us."

She was a compassionate aunt in matters of illness and personal

73

issues. A stern aunt in matters of business.

If Diego did something wrong, Julie had her do it over. Under Julie, she learned to handle bookkeeping, accounting and sales. The paperwork end of running the business.

Phil Bond showed her how to run a nursery.

"He was like a father to me," Diego said.

Here, she teared up. She paused. Then she gathered herself and went on.

"He didn't see that I was weak, because of my disability."

He told Diego she could do anything anybody else could. And with his guidance, she did it.

"I had to run around an eight-acre nursery," she said. "I started watering, and working with cactus."

From there, Phil Bond taught her about the different plants. How to deal with pests. How to propagate new plants from seed and cuttings. She took courses and became a certified Master Gardener.

Most of all, she said, "he taught me the value of work. For anything to get done, you need to get up front and do it yourself."

Around 2010, during the recession, the three future owners got the chance to prove themselves.

"We weren't getting the clientele," Diego said.

In part, suppliers dried up. Landscapers and other customers couldn't get the plants they needed. So Diego, Marisol and Lupe went to work. They increased the plant stock. They worked to keep the Avocado on its feet.

"The three of us were the ones that stayed and we kept pushing each other."

They'd set their own goals. "OK, by this week, we want to have so many plants upgraded — 500 plants, 1,000 plants, upgraded by this week."

Upgrade is shop talk for propagating new plants.

Phil Bond took notice. Four or five years ago, he called the three into his office.

He told them: "I talked to Julie before she passed ... this is what our thoughts were."

They wanted Diego, Marisol and Lupe to carry on the business.

It includes the 10 acres the nursery sits on. Bond left the underground house he lived in to his daughter, Susan. It fronts the nursery and faces Overfield Road, about a mile off CAC at Signal Peak.

He gave Diego his 3-year-old rat terrier, Chad-O. Chad-O roams the nursery with his best friend, an 8-year-old German shepherd named Cujo. Unlike the dog of fiction, this Cujo is very friendly. He was abandoned at the nursery as a puppy. Diego took him in. He and Chad-O compete to greet customers.

With ownership comes a few new tasks. Mainly payroll and taxes. But otherwise, the job's the same.

Work hard. Take care of customers. Just like "when Phil was here."

PLACES

Much Ado about a Gram of Pot
Eloy, April 12, 2013

People still read newspapers. That's the good news.

Five people showed up at Pinal County's first medical marijuana dispensary on Wednesday. They had all read about it in the Dispatch. Not the online Dispatch, but the ink and pulp Dispatch.

They showed up because of an article I wrote about the dispensary. The not-so-good news is that the article had an error. I had unwittingly exaggerated how much marijuana you get at the dispensary for $125 or so. Apparently by a big factor. People showed up, newspaper in hand, looking for a smoking deal — so to speak.

The error was corrected in the online edition. That deal never existed.

The transaction was in grams. I converted it to ounces. It went something like this: 8 grams equals 8 ounces. I guess there was some math involved that I missed. Anyway, you'd never be able to buy 8 ounces of marijuana at a legitimate medical marijuana dispensary. And I knew that amount wasn't allowed by statute. I noted that in the article, way below the offending error. I didn't put two-and-two together. Again, more math.

All the same, I didn't think 8 ounces was such a big deal. That's nothing but half a loaf of bread. But it apparently takes a lot of bread to buy that much marijuana. One informed editor of a sister weekly told me: "That's enough to supply half a college dorm."

I'm a baby boomer. I never lived in a dorm, but there was marijuana in college — back in the day. Maybe wholesale dealers talked about grams and ounces. I never saw that end of the business.

From what I remember, all marijuana came in sandwich bags, also known as baggies. These were low-tech. Ziplock bags hadn't yet been invented. There was no weighing them. They were just $10 baggies and out of my price range. I had rent to pay and gas to buy on a car that didn't run half the time anyway.

So all this business about marijuana and grams and ounces is new to me. Especially the grams part.

The marijuana dispensary sells to patients by the gram. But it reports sales to the Arizona Department of Health Services by the ounce. All that metric-to-English conversion can lead to trouble. Well, first off, anything metric is trouble to a person like me — educated in a system where everything was feet and pounds and ounces. Grams and kilograms and liters were never taught, except perhaps in high school chemistry. Maybe I was exposed to them there. But I was exposed to French, too, and I can't remember three words.

So the metric system remains foreign to me and conversion is not to be taken lightly. Just ask the rocket scientist who forgot to convert to metric on the 1999 Mars Climate Orbiter.

The thrusters were on the English system. The guidance on metric, or something like that. Anyway, the $125 million spacecraft was off course by 60 miles. Of course, when the ground is 60 miles closer than you thought, you can hit it pretty hard. It became the Mars High Impact Debris Field.

The guy who blew that one likely drowned his misery in beer, by the liter.

Historic House Has Seen Better Days

August 16, 2013

Tom Hickman went house hunting in the early 1980s. He liked the old adobe house he saw on West First Street. It's known as the Meehan-Gaar Home.

He ended up buying it. Hickman, 57, later learned about its history.

In turn, he became an early advocate for historic preservation, securing an appointment on the Casa Grande Historic Preservation Commission in August 1991. The commission had just been created. Hickman was a charter member.

He saw other historic buildings around town being torn down or neglected. The commission would seek to protect them.

"I thought it would benefit everybody," Hickman said.

Life, however, is full of ironies. And Hickman is living in one. Just a few years back, the Meehan-Gaar Home was listed as one of the state's most endangered historic places by the Arizona Preservation Foundation — one of two in Casa Grande. The other is the Fisher Memorial Home a block north of Florence Boulevard. Windows are boarded up at the Fisher house. Maybe the owner still lives there, and maybe not. It's something of an open question.

Hickman, for his part, has no plans to move, though his house is showing its age. It is, after all, a hundred years old, or close to it. One account says Tom Meehan built it in 1903. Another says he built it in 1909, six years after he moved to Casa Grande. Hickman places the date at 1907.

All agree it's made of adobe and an example of Colonial Revival architecture.

Along with the house, Meehan owned the Gilt Edge Saloon on Main Street, which he bought in 1905, according to the Casa Grande Valley Historical Society. He ran the saloon for the next nine years before going into surgery for stomach problems. He died on an operating table in Florence. He was 43.

His widow, Frances Meehan, sold the house to Fanne Gaar in 1920. She became mayor of Casa Grande in 1927, a first for a woman in Arizona.

Gaar lived in the house until her death in 1971. It was listed on the National Register of Historic Places in 1985.

Now it's one of Casa Grande's most prominent fixer-uppers.

The most outward sign of its ailing condition lies in the roof's shake shingles. They're in disarray, many scattered about like cards in a game of 52 pickup. In some places, they don't cover the roof at all. Where they do, Hickman said, there are two layers. A second layer likely was put on top of the original, which was painted green.

What the years didn't take care of, nature did, Hickman added.

"A wind storm in the '80s pulled up a lot shingles."

The house once had a wraparound porch, he said. What's left has not fared well. The low adobe wall in front sags badly, sitting on the edge of a 12-foot hole. A well once supplied water for the house, Hickman said. He dug the hole to explore it. Now he plans to fill it in.

The plaster is peeling off some of the porch posts, exposing the adobe. The adobe, in turn, is deteriorating. The porch roof — made of wood planks — has large holes.

It's not all bad, Hickman said.

"The adobe in the house is in good shape," he said.

My own take on the house's condition, it turns out, might have been understated. In 2008, the city hired Phoenix architect Jeffry Swan to do an assessment, with Hickman's permission.

The conclusion: The house needed more than a fresh coat of paint.

"Overall, the Meehan-Gaar House is in poor condition," the report said, spelling Gaar as Garr. "Unsympathetic building alterations and additions, poor craftsmanship, weathering and neglect have not been kind to certain exterior and interior elements

...."

In other words, it was in bad shape inside and out. In 2008 dollars, the report estimated it would take $132,000 just to restore the exterior. The interior would run another $39,000.

A morning drizzle, entering a gap in the porch roof, dampened my notebook as I spoke to Hickman earlier this month. He's an easygoing man with a trim moustache. He was born in Buckeye.

In all his years in Casa Grande, he never met Marge Jantz. She now sits on the same Historic Preservation Commission that he helped to launch. Jantz is perhaps the commission's most outspoken member. Her recommendation helped to land Hickman's house on the endangered places list.

Jantz is a passionate defender of Casa Grande's landmarks, from historic buildings to old signs.

"It's almost in my DNA," she said.

She sees the Meehan-Gaar Home, however, as a lost cause. Or nearly so.

"It's a disgrace. It's just a disgrace," she said on the phone. "It was just such a cool place. There's so much history in that house."

"I agree, it's a disgrace," Hickman replied.

But help initially promised by the city did not materialize, he said. The architect's assessment was to be a first step, followed by $100,000 in loans and grants, Hickman said. It fell short of the architect's estimated cost, but Hickman would make up the difference with sweat equity. He works in construction as a heavy equipment operator, specializing in concrete.

The recession, however, hit the public pocketbook hard. Schools let go of teachers. State parks were closed. Hickman didn't get his loan.

"The funds dried up all of a sudden," he said.

Since then, he has heard little from the city. Certainly no offers of help.

"I pretty well have given up."

But he has a plan B. He'll go ahead and do the work himself. He's slowly gathering all the building material he needs. He has some on hand already, much of it by way of donation from his employer. It's stacked on his driveway and the porch.

If he picks up a hammer now, Hickman might get a head start. He'll probably need one. He's got a hundred years of restoration to catch up on.

Catching Next Bus
In Search of a Better Life
August 1, 2014

The bus depot is little more than a strip of shade fronting a mini-mart. The view is one of concrete, gas pumps and traffic converging on downtown's Five Points.

A big sign says Chevron. Two smaller signs on the front and side say Greyhound.

Sam Cetwinski stood in front, a backpack at his feet. It was a little after 8:30 Friday morning last. He was nicely dressed. A nicely pressed casual short-sleeve shirt and jeans. Hair neatly combed. People don't think of him as homeless, he said.

But his last address was the MASH Mission, a homeless shelter south of the railroad tracks.

He had worked for a drilling company at one time. He ended up in Casa Grande about a year and a half ago. He lost his apartment — or perhaps just gave it up.

"I kind of got lost along the way," he said.

Now he had a sense of direction. Now Cetwinski, 39, waited for the Greyhound bus, the 9:10 headed for Phoenix. He would stay there just long enough to pick up his surfboard. His father had it.

From there, it was the California coast, his true home.

"I'm going to go out there and start surfing and start living my life all over again," Cetwinski said.

He had an easygoing California manner about him.

He kept to the shade offered by an overhanging roof. The morning was still bearable. Another half dozen or so people stood nearby, around the side. They weren't taking the bus. They were just hanging out.

They were hoping to strike it lucky, Cetwinski said.

"A lot of them are waiting for the hundred-dollar man."

The story goes that a man just pulls up — without warning — and hands out 100-dollar bills.

"I thought that was a myth," Cetwinski said.

Maybe it is. Maybe it isn't. But California is real. The surf is real. And the Greyhound would take him there.

A few minutes later, an SUV pulled up. A woman got out and struggled to work a cardboard box out of the back. She asked for help but didn't wait for it. She lifted the box out herself. She set it down in front of the store. The car left.

Her name was Michelle Hartman. She had just spent three days in a domestic violence shelter. She had fled an abusive boyfriend in Dallas-Fort Worth.

When I look over my notes from Hartman, I see a lot of unfinished sentences. She spoke faster than I could write. Hartman, 45, was something of a live wire. She could hardly contain herself.

"I'm ADHD and I'm flipping out," she said. She smiled a wild kind of smile.

I'm pretty sure she wasn't on drugs. I just think it was her hyperactive yin to Cetwinski's mellow yang.

Inside the box was a large trash bag. It held her clothes. She also had a purse, a smaller box of packaged candy and a rock shaped like Texas, if you held it up a certain way. Like Texas, it was big. The candy, she said, came from a trash container behind a drugstore.

The box for her clothes was falling apart. The store manager let her use his tape dispenser to patch it up. Ronnie Muñoz lent her duct tape to fix her flip-flops. He lives next door.

Like Cetwinski. Hartman was headed home. She had been on the move two years, following her father's death. A free spirit on overdrive. Now she was returning to her daughters and granddaughter in Colorado Springs, Colorado.

She had a brightly colored tattoo on her ankle — a zodiac sign for each daughter.

Her thoughts raced from one topic to the next. Out of nowhere, she had to have a Whataburger. She asked if I could give her a ride, though the bus was due any minute. Before I had time to say no, she was onto something else.

Later, she said, "Pot's legal in Colorado."

Pot might do her some good, I thought.

The bus, it happened, was running late. As 9 headed toward 10, it was getting warmer. The island of concrete offered little relief.

Cetwinski and Hartman retreated to the only seating available — a block window ledge.

At one time, Casa Grande had a real bus depot.

Frank and Dorothy Wiles owned it. It was at 117 E. Second St., where The Living Center is today. Linda Wiles, their daughter, grew up at the depot. It was in her family from 1957 to 1995. If they were shorthanded, her father would pull her out of school to fill in.

Linda, 62, now owns the Secondhand Treasures consignment store on Jimmie Kerr Boulevard.

In its heyday, the Wiles Greyhound depot had all the amenities.

"We had a lobby and games and pinball machines," Linda said. "We had a restaurant and a barbershop."

A bus would come and go every hour. In the late 1960s, Interstate 10 from Tucson to Phoenix was completed. Downtown was no longer on the main route. Business fell off. Fewer buses pulled in. Wiles' father died in 1982 from a heart attack. He was 49. Stress from working three jobs, Linda said.

When Dorothy retired, she sold the business. The Greyhound depot moved to North Sacaton Street. Sometime around 2013, judging by phone book entries, it moved to the Five Points mini-mart.

It's short on amenities. No restaurant here. Hartman settled for a bag of chips and a kiwi strawberry juice.

The bus pulled in about 9:50. The driver stepped out and opened up the cargo hold.

Hartman showed the bus driver her Texas-shaped chunk of geology.

"It's my rock," she said.

"You can't have that on the bus," he said.

The bus driver cautioned her. She had to calm down. She said she would. She did.

Cetwinski lifted the big box with her clothes and the small box with her candy into the cargo hold. Then he placed the rock next to them. He did it with care. He knew it meant something to her.

Five minutes later, the bus swung out onto Pinal Avenue, heading north. Two souls leaving town, going home to something better. So they hoped.

Not a Road Less Traveled

July 18, 2014

I drive Interstate 10 daily. Like me, a number of co-workers commute to Casa Grande from the great heat island to the north. I joke I like the weather down here.

I often see the same cars on the freeway heading in the same direction. Their drivers have the same commute. I sometimes see a pickup with a bumper sticker on the rear window. It says, "I give three feet." I think it refers to going around bicyclists instead of over them.

I remember taking I-10 once or twice a month from 1977 through 1978. I was going to journalism school at the University of Arizona and my parents lived in Ahwatukee. They were Ahwatukee pioneers.

Whenever I wanted a decent meal, I would make the drive. Picacho Peak, halfway there. McCartney Road, getting warmer. The Gila River. I can almost smell dinner.

Admittedly, some stretches weren't all that scenic. If I wanted scenic, I'd take the Tom Mix Highway up through Florence.

Just the same, I-10 was like a drive through the country. I could travel for miles without having to pass a car. Or a big truck. Or without having anyone overtake me — more often the case.

That was then. Now I-10 is like a river of steel and plastic from Phoenix to Tucson. Big trucks, little cars and everything in between. I'm something of a Type B driver, though a colleague at a different newspaper once pegged me for a Type D. I guess I flunked.

Anyway, I'm the guy in the right lane. I hesitate to pass. But some big trucks are too slow, even for me. So I pull into the left lane, the tailgate lane. Then I see it's not just one truck. But truck after truck after truck. It's like passing a freight train.

That can be nerve wracking.

It could be worse. I could be driving I-10 in a dust storm.

I've done that, too. But then, who hasn't?

Last summer, I recall driving through an ocean of dirt. I tailed a big rig, making sure I stayed close. I didn't want to lose sight of it. I put on my blinkers, hoping the truck driver behind me didn't mistake them for landing lights.

No little particles of dirt were going to stop me. I had a beer in the fridge. If I had a jingle, it would be: "I can't see, but that's OK."

All right, my jingle doesn't rhyme. Even if it did, officials at the Arizona Department of Transportation wouldn't be impressed. They don't think much of people who drive blind.

ADOT has its own catchy jingle: "Pull aside, stay alive."

Well, if you put it like that.

I spoke to Dustin Krugel on Tuesday. He's an ADOT spokesman, and he practices what he preaches.

He got caught in a dust storm driving from Phoenix to Tucson last November. He was just outside Casa Grande. He followed the company line. He pulled over, turned his lights off.

He found out he wasn't alone.

"There were more than 10 cars pulled over off the side of the road," he said.

Everybody lived. So good advice.

Krugel happened to be en route to a TV interview in Tucson. He was going to talk about some then-recent dust storms. One in late October led to a pileup on I-10 that killed three people. Twelve were hurt.

Here are some other numbers, courtesy of The Associated Press. Among the 25 vehicles involved, six were 18-wheelers. News photos showed cars crushed by big rigs.

When dust is a factor, long-haul trucks are often part of the wreckage.

It's simple math. Dust storms are part of the desert. Disturbed landscape, like abandoned fields, can make them worse.

Here's the other part of the equation.

"I-10 has the most commercial truck traffic of any highway in the state," Krugel said.

No surprise there. What's more, not all truckers — crossing into Arizona for the first time — are dust-storm savvy. They probably think "haboob" is something you don't say in polite company.

ADOT is working to educate them. Truck drivers get a pamphlet on dust storms at the state border crossings.

But ADOT wants all the state's drivers to know about dust storms. The agency has started a year-round awareness campaign. It co-sponsors a website, www.pullasidestayalive.org.

A survey asks how people learn that a dust storm's on the way.

I, for one, pop my head out the door.

My wife's cellphone beeps with dust-storm alerts. It's a sensitive warning system. If there's a dust storm in Lukeville, I'm pretty sure it beeps. And I think it beeps when I sweep the patio. Weather forecasters, however, refer to that as a rare event.

My phone doesn't beep warnings, though I can calculate tips on it.

I took the survey and learned about the ADOT haiku contest. The agency invited people to write haikus about driving in dust storms.

Here's one from the ADOT website: "Oh snap, crackle, pop / Dust has you blind / Pull over or you'll want to cry."

I don't think his problem is dust. He shouldn't be eating Rice Krispies on the interstate.

Monk with Money Draws a Big Crowd
February 13, 2015

Tim Cary sat on a curb. He faced Third Street. At his back was the Woman's Club, a sturdy stone relic from the early 1900s. It's fixed up inside. The city owns it. Parks and Recreation has yoga classes there.

Cary's wife, Sarah, stood a few feet away. This was last Friday. A modest crowd had gathered, maybe a dozen or so.

People waited for the monk bearing cash. And food boxes and bananas. Here's what I'm told. The monk rides in an SUV from St. Anthony's Greek Monastery near Florence. He has a cap and a white beard. He hands out $100 in 20s.

I don't know if it's always the same monk. He has a driver, possibly a monk. Possibly not.

He usually arrives in the morning, before 10, but there's no appointed day. It's a random act of giving alms.

Cary, 36, could use some alms about now.

"We're pretty much homeless," he said.

He and Sarah, also 36, have three kids, ages 4, 11 and 13. They used to live in his grandparents' house. But it was foreclosed on. Now they live in the Se-Tay Motel on Pinal Avenue.

It's not exactly upscale. And, Cary said, it's not a good place for a family.

He's a Navy veteran, a Seabee from 1997 to 2003.

In 1998-99, he was in war-torn Kosovo.

"Most of us were tasked to find mass gravesites."

They found a few.

He doesn't work now. He was injured on the job. He takes odd jobs. He continues looking for full-time work. Later, he'll head to a job center on Florence Boulevard. He'll be on foot. He had a motorcycle, but thieves backed over it with the pickup they were stealing.

Sarah can't work herself. She has seizures from a brain tumor.

They started waiting for the monk about a month ago, Cary said. They thought it was rumor at first. They heard any number of rumors about the monks. They heard the monks had been robbed in Eloy and Coolidge. The monks don't go there anymore, he said.

But word was they still made their way to Casa Grande. The Carys decided to find out. The Se-Tay is little more than a stone's throw from the Woman's Club.

They learned the monk was for real.

Cary spotted him once. But the crowd apparently became unruly, and the monk's driver kept on going. No money. No bananas.

Sarah got a payout, though. It was a Wednesday. Their son Nathan, 11, was with her. He was skeptical.

"He didn't believe it," she said. "He was like, 'Nobody's going to be dumb enough to hand out a hundred dollars.'"

The monk proved him wrong. On a cool January morning, Sarah was handed $100. She showed her son the money. He started crying.

When you have nothing, $100 is like a gold mine.

Step back a bit, though, and you get a different picture. You don't see the personal struggle of a single family. On some days, you see as many as 30 or 40 people. They crowd around the sidewalk and a small parking lot, waiting for the monk.

They're starting to draw attention. A week or so back, I saw a Casa Grande police officer parked nearby. A casual observer, it seems.

Ralph Burrell knows about the monk. His barbershop is next to another gathering place.

I spoke to Burrell Wednesday morning. Outside his shop, at Florence and Second streets, more than a dozen people stood and waited. Two sat in lawn chairs. Others took to city benches.

There was some spillover onto a small parking lot. Customers park there for Burrell's shop, as well as a bookstore and a Cuban restaurant.

Not everybody's comfortable with the arrangement. Customers are scared off, Burrell said.

"A woman told me she wouldn't come here anymore," he said. "She's intimidated."

Burrell complained to City Hall.

"One council member told me there's no law against giving away money," Burrell said.

And he was told people had a right to assemble. He couldn't remember the council member's name.

I called St. Anthony's Greek Orthodox Monastery in Florence. I've called before. Rarely does anybody answer. This time somebody did.

I didn't get the man's name. He sounded young. Monks did give out cash and food boxes for the needy, he said.

"We had to stop both the financial help and the food boxes," he said. "We stopped for now."

He was polite but kept the conversation brief. I didn't get in all my questions. He said: "OK, thanks."

Then he politely hung up.

Last Friday, at the Woman's Club, I hung around a while longer. People began to disperse. No monk today. And perhaps no monk tomorrow, if I heard the man on the phone correctly.

Two or three women pulled up in late-model cars. They were seniors, perhaps on their way to yoga. The new arrivals didn't make eye contact. Not with this crowd. But nobody gives anybody any trouble, Cary said.

Then he and Sarah kissed each other goodbye. She would head home. He would head to the American Legion.

Everybody would go their own way, empty-handed.

Tuneup for School Band Rentals
July 4, 2016

Michael Francois might not have 76 trombones. But he's ready to fill the need. He's got everything demanded of the well-equipped school band — from fifth grade on.

Francois, 39, works at De-No Music Center on Florence Boulevard. He's Casa Grande's go-to guy for band-instrument rentals.

And students — with parents and pocketbooks in tow — will soon be at the door. High school starts Aug. 5. Elementary and middle schools follow on Aug. 8.

I spoke to Francois on Tuesday. Cases with French horns, trombones, tubas and other big brass music makers lined the showroom floor — ready for halftime. They'll join Casa Grande Union High School marching band's rousing cacophony of sound. First practice was set for that night.

All that brass will carry a tune, in the right hands. Francois saw to that. Now he turns his attention to band-class rentals. Here's something of a price list. Clarinets and flutes run $20 to $25 a month. On the high end, a saxophone rents out for $30 to $35 a month.

It's a rent-to-own setup. Students who stay with band all through school often end up with a trombone and clear title. Francois will buy replacements as needed.

In the back, band cases stacked on shelves tell a different story. They're rentals returned. The young musicians graduated to other interests. Here saxes, clarinets and trumpets await a whole new set of lips and fingers.

And here's where Francois's true skills come into play. As it happens, not all instruments come back in the shape they left. Francois is there to repair them. He puts the shine back in. He tunes them up. And makes sure every note is as it should be. The A sharps are sharp.

He'll probably repair a couple hundred for schools. All told, he repairs some 2,000 instruments a year.

Sometimes it's like body shop for auto collisions.

"I hammer out dents," he said.

He has a rod called a mandrel. He can slip a trumpet on it and tackle dents with a few deft swings of a hammer. He solders and replaces broken pieces.

"Especially the marching horns, like the bigger saxophones," he said. "The heavier the instrument, the more they get banged around."

Saxophones often need pads replaced. They cover what are known as tone holes. Francois will shine a light from inside the sax. If any light shows through the pad, he'll replace the pad.

"We got tons of pads. We try to keep a little bit of everything," Francois said.

The instruments often need a cleanup as well.

"We clean quite a few, like trumpets, where we pull them apart and we'll clean them and sterilize them."

His job would be a lot easier if students used the spit valve once in a while. It drains moisture that builds up. If let untapped, a green scum forms. And cleaning it — after a year of neglect — is something of a nightmare.

There are good band teachers, Francois adds. And the good ones usually include care of the instrument as part of the curriculum.

Still, kids manage to leave all manner of things in trumpets and saxes.

Here's a partial list compiled with the help of Store Manager Noel Kirkland: soda pop, mouthpieces, tennis balls and old sheet music.

For Francois, few repair jobs are beyond his reach. He's been at it for 21 years.

He recalled his first day on the job. He was hired by Dennis

Kirkland, De-No music founder and Noel's father. Dennis is now retired.

Dennis, Francois said, "pulled me aside and said, 'Listen, if I ever have to tell you what to do, you won't be working here. You need to find something to do — and do it good.'"

And he did.

Francois played trumpet in school bands himself, as well as guitar. Today, his original rent-to-own trumpet stands on a shelf like a trophy. His daughter, who's 11, is in band now.

She plays a trumpet he bought in high school. It replaced the original.

He keeps his daughter's trumpet in good shape, as he does all the instruments destined for band class.

And, as he said, few are beyond repair. Of course, there's always the exception.

"One kid, he didn't want to play anymore and they made him stay in the band —— his parents did," Francois said.

Every time he asked to quit, his parents said no. So he placed the saxophone, case and all, behind the car. His father, or perhaps his mother, backed over it.

Francois keeps the sax in the back. He pulled it out of the case and showed me the dent. It looked like a size 15 Michelin.

Well, band isn't for everybody.

Making Plans for the Big One
January 18, 2016

Casa Grande Mayor Bob Jackson dispelled the rumor I tried to start. I asked him about the secret bunker, buried deep inside Casa Grande Mountain.

The mayor and City Council would ride out the big one there. The unthinkable. Nuclear Armageddon. They'd have a bowling ally. A movie theater. And "Seinfeld" on DVD, seasons one through five.

"Sorry," Jackson said. He meant sorry, no such place exists.

Just the same, the city does have plans for the unthinkable. And every other disaster you'd care not to think of. Floods. Fires. Flu pandemics.

Nowadays people don't dwell on the one true unthinkable.

I'm a baby boomer. In my childhood, during the Cold War, everybody thought about it. School kids were told to duck and cover. Hide under their desks, until it all blows over. Desks back then were solidly built. Real wood. Lots of metal.

Duck and cover is now out of fashion. But then they don't make desks like they used to.

Mayor Jackson is a boomer himself. Growing up, he remembered the Cold War. And a real fear of nuclear attack.

"We had people that actually went out and bought bomb shelters and put them in their backyard," Jackson said.

His own family stuck with duck and cover.

Fear of nuclear war continued into the 1980s. "The Day After" played into that. It was a TV movie about the big one. I think some town in Kansas got nuked. Maybe the idea was nobody's safe, not even in Kansas — which has more wheat than people.

As I recall, the movie made no mention of the 1980s federal evacuation plans. People in big cities would be told to hit the road. Get out of town. Go somewhere safe. Your ZIP code determined your destination. My Phoenix ZIP code had me shelter in Show Low, or someplace nearby.

I drove there to write a story. I worked for an afternoon paper, one that has since gone the way of the carrier pigeon. The shelter, as I recall, was a basement in a nondescript building. It's nondescript partly because I can't remember what it looked like. It was stocked with water and soda crackers. I gave it a thumbs up. I like soda crackers.

Bomb-shelter drinking water came in olive-green tin cans. I learned this from Julie Syrmopoulos, operations manager for

Maricopa County Emergency Management.

"I'm looking at one at my desk right now," she said. I spoke to her by phone. "Mine is dated 1952 ... property of the U.S. government."

That's definitely Cold War-era drinking water. The Cold War ended a quarter-century ago. But the world is still full of nukes. North Korea has the bomb, if not the hydrogen kind as claimed. Russia has 5,000 of them. Enough to go around. And things are tense these days. The Doomsday Clock is now at 3 minutes to midnight. It's set by the Bulletin of the Atomic Scientists. It tells us how close we are to, well, doomsday — metaphorically speaking.

In 2012, it was 5 minutes to midnight. It hasn't been at 3 minutes since 1984, when flee-by-ZIP-code was the plan.

I asked Syrmopoulos about today's evacuation plans. Getting everybody out of greater Phoenix to somewhere safe. Well clear of the Arizona Legislature.

"The answer is, it depends. It depends on a number of things," she said.

ZIP codes are out. Cellphones could play a role. Mine already beeps for things like dust storms.

"There's all kinds of new ways of warning people," Syrmopoulos added.

Just where they'd be told to go, well that depends, too. Casa Grande should be ready for them, in any case. This is according to the big book of emergencies, the city's 3-inch-thick ring binder titled "Emergency Response and Recovery Plan."

City Manager Jim Thompson let me flip through a copy. I stopped at Page 176. It read: "War-related: Pinal County has been designated as a host area."

It added there might be fallout. It's nuclear war. That's to be expected.

Anyway, the refugees from Phoenix would be welcome with glowing arms. In Casa Grande, school gymnasiums and churches would open their doors. Agencies at all levels would coordinate things. Nonprofits like Salvation Army would assist.

Jackson, the council and top officials like Thompson would settle into the emergency command center, housed inside the Public

Safety Facility on Val Vista Boulevard. Fire and police officials already are housed there. The media would have a spot, though they'd probably complain the crackers are stale.

All would be thankful they were not stuck on Interstate 10 with a million other people.

But Casa Grande, Syrmopoulos said, might still be too close for comfort.

"I don't know if Casa Grande would be far enough out of what we consider a hot zone or a danger zone."

That's easily solved. We'll meet in Arizona City.

Tragic Story on a Reservation Road
Chuichu, Tohono O'odham Nation, April 10, 2016

Travel south from Casa Grande on Chuichu Road. You'll end up on Indian Route 15. It runs north-south through the Tohono O'odham Nation. It's a scenic drive. The desert is filled with mountains and saguaros.

And crosses. Nine of them appear 15 miles or more south of Casa Grande. They're lined up, side-by-side. Another, larger one, looks over them.

Each smaller cross stands for a life taken, all in one horrific accident.

Johnny Crawford's sister-in-law, Rosemary, was in it. She does not count as one of the crosses. She lived to tell Crawford what happened.

I met Crawford, 64, to hear the story. We sat near the back of Denny's on Florence Boulevard. His wife, Maltilda, sat next to him. They met in high school. She's Navajo. He's Tohono O'odham. They live in North Komelik Village off Indian Route 15, near the

102

Pima County line.

Rosemary died about a year ago, Crawford said. He couldn't remember her maiden name. And he hadn't kept in touch, he said. She and his brother had parted ways some years back. She lived into her 80s, he added. She would have been 15, maybe a little older, when the two trucks approached each other on a narrow bridge over a wash.

It was Oct. 20, 1951 — a Saturday evening, about 7:20.

Rosemary was riding in the open back of a large stake truck, one that has railings. She was with a group from the Tohono O'odham tribe. They were coming from Eleven Mile Corner, where they spent their days picking cotton. It was done by hand and bent backs in those days.

They lived in row houses, Crawford said. But most called Pisinemo Village their home. It's south of State Route 86 and west of Sells. By Google Maps, it's an 82-mile drive from Casa Grande.

All were en route to Pisinemo for a religious festival, according to an Oct. 25, 1951, article in the Casa Grande Dispatch.

Indian Route 15 can be treacherous. It's a narrow two-lane blacktop. Crawford was once forced off the road by a drunk driver. Police caught the man. He wasn't a tribal member.

Crawford had driven that same road for years. And for years, it was unpaved. And much less forgiving.

The stake truck would have driven over that same dirt. It would have been a rough ride. People would have had benches to sit on, Crawford said. Most of them were related in some way, the article added. They were family members, young parents and children. Ages ranged from as young as 4 to as old as 40.

I'm guessing the mood was light, though that wasn't mentioned in the news clip. The riders, I imagine, would have just wrapped up six days in the fields. Now they were joining family and friends for a day of celebration. They would have chatted. Laughed. And looked forward to catching up on all the news.

That's speculation, but it sounds right.

A semi-tractor-trailer was headed the other way, going north. It had a flatbed. On it, a large bulldozer blade was tied down, extending out over the side. Lawrence Ruff of Eloy drove the GMC rig, the article said.

As the two trucks passed, Ruff failed to account for the blade's reach. It swept across the oncoming stake truck and people seated on the left side. It left in its wake nine mangled bodies, the article said.

A coroner's jury faulted Ruff for the accident. An inquest drew everybody from the FBI to a Pulitzer Prize-winning writer by the name of Oliver La Farge.

Rosemary might have been among the dead, had she not switched seats.

She told Crawford: "I traded with somebody."

She didn't say why. Nor could she remember what happened to the person she traded with. People and bodies were everywhere.

"Ambulances were kept busy for over two hours bringing the injured and dead bodies to Casa Grande," the Dispatch reported.

Amid the chaos, Rosemary helped out where she could, Crawford said.

She may have comforted 4-year-old Edward Manuel, listed among the injured. He was in his mother's arms when the blade cut her life short. He would be about 68 now, the same age as Tohono O'odham Chairman Edward Manuel.

Like the boy, he's from Pisinemo.

I spoke to Matt Smith, the tribe's information officer. He said the chairman probably was that boy. I asked to speak to Manuel. I made three calls. He didn't call back.

Perhaps he was too young to remember. Perhaps he didn't want to remember.

Search for Ears in a Tough Market

January 14, 2017

Maybe July isn't the best time to start a new gig in the Arizona desert. Not if you're from Wyoming. February or March would be better.

But for Phil Riske, July it was.

It was 1979. He became general manger of the newly minted KSAA-FM — CASA 105.5 on the dial in Casa Grande.

He remembered one day in particular.

"It was 113 degrees," Riske said. "I'd never been to Arizona."

Like many people who'd never been to Arizona, Riske, 75, ended up staying.

That's a lot of Julys.

KSAA spun Top 40 pop out of a reconverted house on First Street, just across Hermosillo Street from St. Anthony of Padua Catholic School.

The building now houses Brutinel Plumbing & Electrical, founded in 1949 by Bob Brutinel. He fought on Iwo Jima in World War II. He later sold the business but stayed on as an employee. As far as I know, he still shows up for work every day.

Riske, the Wyoming native, now lives in Chandler. He's married with three adult daughters and plenty of grandchildren. He reports news on behalf of the Rose Law Group in Phoenix. I worked with him at the Arizona Capitol Times in the ought-2000s. He had worked at other newspapers before that.

But his voice lent itself to a career in broadcasting. It's a calming tenor that carries authority, a voice that draws your attention.

He worked on-air for radio and TV. He preferred radio. In 1969,

Riske worked for a Cheyenne radio station owned by the late sportscaster Curt Gowdy. Riske reported on a controversy known as the Black 14. In brief, the University of Wyoming football coach in Cheyenne booted 14 black players from the team. They had spoken out against the Mormon Church for barring African-Americans from the priesthood, a policy since changed.

Tensions grew. The National Guard was called out. Rumors floated that blacks with clubs were en route from Denver.

Riske insisted on reporting both sides, irritating some advertisers. They called for his firing.

He weathered the storm and stayed on the job.

In 1973, Riske went to work for Wycom, which owned radio stations in Wyoming and New Mexico.

Riske's partner at Wycom, it happened, had friends in Casa Grande.

"He wanted to have a station where he could come and visit them, and we thought it was a good market," Riske said. "It didn't turn out that way."

KSAA lasted three years.

Of course, nobody plans for failure.

So expecting a brighter future, Wycom bought KBFE and the house on First Street from Brett Eisele and changed the call letters. Eisele is now a real estate broker in Casa Grande.

Riske hired people he had worked with in Wyoming and New Mexico. Fitting in didn't come easily, Riske said.

"We found Casa Grande to be very parochial." He added: "They weren't very welcoming."

But he and staffers worked hard to make a go of it. One key was local news.

"We had news on the hour," Riske said.

Community involvement played a part as well. Riske sat on the board for Hoemako Hospital, which predated what is now Banner Casa Grande Medical Center. He ran for City Council. He campaigned on bringing a more progressive outlook to a small town. He lost by 40 votes in a runoff to Dewey Powell, father of current Councilman Dick Powell.

Riske also fought to bring the pronunciation of Casa Grande in line with proper Spanish. Casa Grande is, after all, Spanish for Big House. He wrote a letter to the editor, published in The Arizona Republic.

"Why don't these people pronounce Casa Grande correctly?" he asked.

Seated across from him, I didn't have an answer. I'm one of those people.

In its brief life, KSAA had as many as 10 people on staff. Sales staff cooled their heels in the living room. Reporters and other staff retired to the bedrooms, set up as offices.

One room had the studio. It was equipped with a state-of-the art computer setup dubbed "Hal." Except for the live newscast, hours of banter, music and ads would run on a continuous tape. It freed up staff for other jobs.

"You could put your program on for a couple of hours, go out … and mow the lawn," Riske said.

All the staffers had their turn with a mower. They took a radio to monitor the broadcast, just in case something went wrong.

They'd mow around trees and the broadcast tower. I checked Google maps. It still identifies the building as KSAA, but the tower's not there anymore.

KSAA spun popular songs like "Betty Davis Eyes" by Mistaken Identity and "Sultans of Swing" by Dire Straits.

The year 1980 started with "Please Don't Go" by KC and the Sunshine band at No. 1, according to Billboard. It ended with "(Just Like) Starting Over" by John Lennon, murdered that December.

KSAA went with NBC's coverage of Lennon's death. It followed up with a playlist of Lennon's music. Three months later, it covered the assassination attempt on President Ronald Reagan.

In 1979, Jimmy Carter still had the job. Riske had heard Carter was inviting community reporters to the White House. They could get a one-on-one interview with the president.

"So I wrote a letter to the White House and requested that my news director be invited some day," Riske said. "And, son of a gun, she was."

JoAnne Ross met with Carter for more than a half-hour.

Riske likened KSAA's cast of characters to the crew on the TV sitcom "WKRP in Cincinnati."

Scott Young was KSAA's own Dr. Johnny Fever, WKRP's envelope-pushing DJ. Young was 6-foot-10, Riske noted in an email.

"When people asked him if he played basketball, he said, no, he was a jockey."

Interviews with politicians were a staple. Riske once sat down with Morris Udall at a local restaurant. While Udall was fitted for a headset, Riske stepped away for a moment. He returned to find Udall barely able to lift his head. It was almost flat on the table. Riske figured his Parkinson's disease was getting worse. Just the same, he went ahead with the interview.

When they finally broke for a commercial, Udall asked, "Do you think you could get the cord on these headphones a little longer?"

The cord had caught on a chair.

"Oh, God, it was embarrassing," Riske said with a laugh.

But KSAA wasn't brought down by equipment failure. And it wasn't brought down by KPIN, the Casa Grande rival with a country-western format.

It was competition out of Phoenix. The well-funded stations from the big city had no problem reaching Casa Grande radios.

"We just couldn't compete with that," Riske said.

By 1983, KSAA was off the air. Riske left radio for good. But he never lost his voice.

Good Place for Garage Bands
October 14, 2017

Late last week, I met Roy Mejia at Ed Whitehead's Tire Pros on Maricopa Street downtown.

It wasn't always a place to buy new tires or get a tune-up. In decades past, it was home to a Chevy dealer.

But in 1966, it was Ma's Place, a dance club for teens. Mejia was one of them. He goes by Rabbit, by the way. He got the name as a boy. He used to chase rabbits.

Things changed at Ma's Place. It was his entry to the music and culture of the 1960s.

You entered where the counter now stands, he said. You paid admission and got your hand stamped. The ink showed up under a black light.

I followed Mejia to the garage in the back. Cars were on lifts, getting fitted up for the road. Of course, in '66, it was a whole different scene. The place was rockin'. Teens took to the dance floor and boogied to chart toppers.

Mejia pointed to a nook where a sink now stands.

"This is where the band played," he said.

The house band included Lewis Storey. He would later make his name as a singer-songwriter in Nashville. He maintained his base in Casa Grande, where he and his wife raised a family, and he was a teacher. He still records.

But you have to start somewhere. In 1966, he and his young bandmates were right here, in Ma's Place, covering the Beatles, Stones and whatever made feet move. It was all about the beat.

By the latter 1960s, the dance club was under new ownership. It had a new name, the Village Theater. Everybody just called it the Village.

The music evolved. Trippier. Edgier. But danceable, just the same. Different bands made the rounds. Perhaps the best known was the Spiders, Alice Cooper's early band.

Bands on the road often stopped and played at the Village, Mejia said.

It made sense. The main highway from Tucson to Phoenix, and beyond, went right through Casa Grande. Bands heading for California would stop off and perform a set.

"Of course, we didn't know it at the time," Mejia said, "but things were happening from the East Coast to the West Coast, especially during the Summer of Love in '67."

Then Mejia showed me a sign of the times. He led me up a flight of stairs, behind a door usually kept locked. We stepped into a loft, largely empty. A file cabinet stood in one corner. It was pushed up against a brick wall. On the wall was a mural, drawn in colored chalk.

The file cabinet dates to an era before computers. The mural dates to 1967, that Summer of Love. It's something of an indoor marquee. The name, "The Village," flows across the brick in the distorted lettering of hippies and flower children.

The artist, unknown, drew other flourishes. Swirls define a large face, with eyes staring out. And some kind of bug has its own big eyes. I think that's what I was looking at. The work's a bit faded, though it's held up well, considering its age and the medium. Chalk. And because the Whiteheads left it untouched.

Band members wrote their names on the wall, Mejia said. But those were lost to time, Alice Cooper's included.

The loft overlooked the dance floor. Up here, people could sit, relax or just hang out. You'd find Mejia here, living out the '60s.

But, like the Summer of Love, the Village's time came and went. It lasted another year or so. Then the building went from the beat of the bands to the hum of industry.

It became a textile mill. The loft no longer looked over a dance floor, but an array of looms weaving rolls of cloth. And where Mejia once danced, he now worked. He fashioned the cloth into forms for T-shirts. He had his creative side as well, managing a limited edition of underwear in colors a hippie could appreciate.

"The fly was a different color. The briefs were a different color. The elastic was a different color. … I gave them away to some of my friends."

In time, Mejia had other jobs as well. He was a barber for 25 years, quitting only after cancer left him unable to cut hair. He worked at nurseries. He set up a business growing and selling trees.

The years slipped by, as they always do. And now, a half-century removed from the Summer of Love, Mejia is looking back on them.

"Fifty years. It's been on my mind for years and years …"

He talked to people about those times past. He wrote down what he remembered about the Casa Grande of his youth. And about the

110

intersection of culture and his life. He titled his work: "Voila: An American Dream."

The dream had its dose of reality.

"What really affected me was 1968," Mejia said.

While '67 was about love, 1968 opened his eyes to a troubled world.

Martin Luther King and Robert Kennedy were assassinated. Mejia began thinking about the things they stood for. Equality and breaking down barriers for people of color.

"I'm a person of color, and it really hit me," he said. His father came from Mexico as a boy.

Then there was the war in Vietnam. It seemed a distant and grainy affair on the small black-and-white TVs of the time.

But the world outside was closing in, Mejia said. And even small-town Casa Grande could not escape it. Mejia viewed the town's history through that wider lens of current events. And through the ups and downs of his own life.

A life the cancer nearly ended. He was overtaken by non-Hodgkin's lymphoma. Somehow, he beat it.

"Twenty-four years tomorrow, cancer free," he said.

Still, the chemo left him with life-long neuropathy to his hands and feet. During the Summer of Love, any number of people smoked pot. Just to get high. Mejia took it up later to relieve his neuropathy.

He still has his Arizona medical marijuana card. But he no longer tokes up. It gave him anxieties and made his heart race. Not a good match for the pacemaker and defibrillator he recently had implanted.

I guess that's how it works in the span of 50 years.

At 66, you live to the beat of a pacemaker.

At 16, you're back at the Village. It's a different beat, one you can dance to.

Where Vets Can Grab
Some Joe, Feel at Home

November 10, 2018

Every Tuesday morning, veterans of all stripes and brass report to the Eagles Landing Veteran Center. Coffee is served. It comes with doughnuts and, on occasion, a full potluck breakfast.

It's known formally as the Cup O'Joe Veterans Coffee Club. It meets from 8:30 to 10:30.

Eagles Landing is on Florence Street, next to Food City. It's run by Honoring/Hiring/Helping Our Heroes of Pinal County. It goes by the acronym HOHP, pronounced hope.

Kim Vandenberg is the HOHP chairwoman.

I dropped by last Tuesday. Vandenberg was out town. So veterans at the center felt free to talk about her.

Here's what I heard. "She's a saint, I'm telling you."

More than one veteran felt that way, Paul Lenhard among them. He was a Navy Seabee, building all manner of infrastructure. Vandenberg, he said, was the driving force behind the center. Behind HOHP from Day 1.

"She's been a godsend for this place," Bill Wargo added.

"She's got one hell of a brain," Tom Helpingstine said. "She loves people."

HOHP started in 2012 as a Pinal County "stand down," something of an open-air event offering job counseling and other services for vets. It was held on the county fairgrounds at Eleven Mile Corner.

Vandenberg, then known as Kim Rodriguez, was there from the get-go. She had plenty of help. But I'm sure she carried a lot of people along as well.

The stand downs were followed by the Eagle One Mobile Unit. It began covering the county in 2015. It's the HOHP outreach component. It provides counseling and help with employment, housing and VA. It has laptops and Wi-Fi.

The center on Florence Street opened in January 2017. It offers much the same help vets get on the mobile unit. And more, including counseling for combat veterans and VA assistance. Employment help is right next door a Arizona@Work.

And, of course, there's the coffee club. Lenhard is a regular.

"I've come here a little over a year," he said. "Tuesdays is amazing. It's good to have somebody to talk to. It's like the old days where you see the guys having coffee shop in the movies. Well, it's what we have here."

I had that in mind when I stopped by. Listening in on some of the old coffee-shop chatter. Everyday gab about cars and the like. I heard some of that.

But when you walk in with a notebook and recorder and say you're with the newspaper, it changes things. The veterans next to me wanted to talk about programs helping veterans. Programs they take part in.

I was all in.

Wargo, a Vietnam veteran, is the Casa Grande outpost leader for Point Man Arizona. It's a faith-based support group for veterans. It meets Tuesday nights at Compass Christian Church.

Veterans open up to other veterans, breaking down barriers brought on by post-traumatic stress disorder.

In 1967, Wargo was part of a small Army intelligence unit. He had five days left to go when Viet Cong overran his encampment. Marines and South Vietnamese regulars were overwhelmed.

"Almost everyone was killed," he said. "I buried it for over 50 years."

Then he began attending Point Man meetings in Chandler.

"Usually, it takes more than one meeting," he said. "I didn't say anything for three weeks. About the fourth week, I opened up."

He began crying. It all came out. For Wargo, it was a healing moment.

Point Man, he added, is a ministry. The group prays and acknowledges forgiveness and salvation through Jesus Christ. The Southern Arizona Veterans Affairs center in Tucson, he added, offers its own spiritual path in dealing with PTSD. That's in addition to more traditional treatments.

Wargo learned about the spiritual angle at the Casa Grande VA clinic. He attended a group therapy session led by a VA chaplain from Tucson. It offered a broad interpretation of a higher being.

"They don't say it has to be Jesus Christ," Wargo said. "It could be Buddha. It could be Allah. It could be the stars in the sky or a rock you see on the ground."

I heard something similar from a person who went to AA meetings. You answer to a higher power. It could very well be a rock.

Jim Sylvester wanted to talk about Pinal County Veterans Treatment Court. He's an Air Force veteran as well as commander of American Legion District 4 in Pinal County. He's also a HOHP board member.

Veterans Court, it happens, is a collaboration of Superior Court, the County Attorney's Office, Public Defender's Office and Adult Probation. It's not a diversion program, according to the website. There could be jail time, followed by probation.

The court's aim is to help veterans get back on their feet.

Eligible veterans, if they take part, are placed in treatment programs for mental health and substance and alcohol abuse. They get counseling for employment issues.

Staying out of jail means staying with the program, Sylvester said.

"It's a very strict probation system, where they're monitored daily," he added.

That includes random drug screening and housing at a residential treatment center.

It's an ongoing effort. Nationwide, many veterans fall through the cracks. Lenhard's T-shirt did the math. The number "22" was printed on the front.

It's the number of U.S. veterans said to commit suicide each and every day.

"We've talked a few off the ledge," Wargo added.

Sometimes a veteran just needs a helping hand. Or something to lean on. Helpingstine, a former Marine, has that. He makes walking canes for veterans. The head is a carved eagle. He personalizes the finished cane with a vet's highest rank, medals and other service facts found on the standard military discharge form.

"I try to do stuff to help other vets," Helpingstine said.

He learned to make the canes in Montrose, Colorado, before an accident left him with a brain injury.

"I had to learn to speak again," he added.

And carve again. His newest cane was at the center, waiting for the right vet.

Across the room, Emilio rested in an armchair. He was born in Eloy. He's 68.

"I don't talk much," he said.

He served in the Army. His time there sounded brief. Perhaps he was homeless. Perhaps not. I didn't ask. I only know his social status didn't matter.

He was a vet and, here, he was welcome.

Loss of CG Greyhound Could Upset CART

October 14, 2018

Casa Grande gave Greyhound the boot in September.

It had been making five stops a day at a Chevron station at Trekell and Kortsen roads. But people complained. And Casa Grande's Planning and Zoning Commission looked into it.

It was all about the zoning, and the gas station didn't have it.

The City Council agreed. The Chevron station was no place for a bus terminal.

But this isn't just a Greyhound story. It's also about a regional bus system joined at the hip. It's called CART, for Central Arizona Regional Transit. Its daily route included stops for the Greyhound.

CART funding, it happens, is tethered to the Greyhound. Without the Greyhound stop, CART stands to lose $160,000 in federal funding. It might not kill off CART. But it could deliver some pain.

"We'd have to reexamine our service, and probably cut back," said Ernie Feliz, grants coordinator for the city of Coolidge.

Coolidge, it happens runs CART. Commuter buses run from Florence to Coolidge and Casa Grande. They make some half-dozen loops a day. A one-way ride is $2. County employees living in Casa Grande take the CART to Florence. Patients take it to Banner Casa Grande Medical Center. Students take the CART to Central Arizona College.

Until September, CART stopped at the Casa Grande Chevron station, dropping off passengers for the Greyhound. They could go onto Phoenix, Tucson and points beyond.

Here's how the money fits in. Don't yawn. This won't take long.

CART's federal dollars hinge — at least partly — on delivering riders to Greyhound. The money is tied to a grant for rural transportation. In particular to a section that deals with intercity bus service to two urban areas. In this case, Phoenix and Tucson. The buses have to carry baggage as well as passengers. And have regular stops.

Greyhound is not mentioned here. But, frankly, what else is there?

Coolidge noted its connection to Greyhound on Google Maps. The city's transit center is marked as a Greyhound stop. The Greyhound didn't actually swing by the transit center. But, of course, CART did. Routes were planned to deliver riders within an hour of scheduled Greyhound stops in Casa Grande.

CART riders could buy Greyhound tickets at the transit center. Others bought tickets online. Three or four got the news too late, said Transit Manager Michael Meyer. They showed up at the transit center with tickets for a bus that wasn't coming. They'd have to go online for refunds.

116

One hopeful rider came to the ticket window and, asking about the Greyhound, said: "I'm supposed to pick up the bus here."

He was out of luck.

Greyhound's now just a passing blur on the interstate.

For years, Greyhound buses were a regular sight in Casa Grande. In 1957, the Wiles family started running a full-service bus depot. It was on East Second Street near downtown.

Linda Wiles helped her parents run the depot. It wasn't just a gas station with a minimart.

"We had a lobby and games and pinball machines," Wiles told me in 2014. "We had a restaurant and a barbershop."

Wiles died in 2016.

Greyhound had been stopping at the Chevron station for about a year. In that time, complaints began coming into the city's code enforcement office. Planning and Zoning staff followed up. The station would need a zoning change. How neighbors felt about that played a role.

The station is next to a small commercial plaza. Plaza owner Bob Davis said Greyhound travelers "made a nuisance of themselves."

"They disturb our tenants ... and loiter under trees," Davis said in a November email to the city.

A children's association in the plaza complained. So did the owner of nearby apartments. People, they said, asked to use the bathroom. They asked for water. And, of course, loitered.

An insurance agent said people did drugs in the alley. Apparently, they toked up while waiting to catch the bus.

That's painting Greyhound riders with a pretty broad brush. Still, not a good look when you're selling insurance.

There's another side, of course.

Joe Kittelson now owns the Allstate agency at the plaza. He's been there about three months. He hadn't noticed a bus pulling up but one time, before the Greyhound stopped coming altogether. Nobody gave him or his business any trouble, he said.

It's been decades since he rode a Greyhound himself. He flies now. But others depend on the bus, he said.

"If they had it, I'd support it," Kittelson said.

The station's operator, Benny Hong, questioned the complaints.

117

He said riders could use the restroom at the station. And not that many passengers come and go, Hong added. An average of nine a day.

Hong's lawyer, Philip Whitaker, spoke on his behalf, writing to city planner James Gagliardi.

Hong hired his own private investigator. The PI spent the better part of a day watching the bus stop. The comings and goings of passengers. He saw nobody loitering or bothering the trees.

Gagliardi handled the zoning case. He staked out the Greyhound stop as well. He didn't note anybody behaving badly.

There are some perceptions at play. Greyhound riders are less well off. Some people equate that with less desirable. I've taken Greyhounds. It can be a tough crowd, sometimes. So, Greyhound stop? Not in my backyard.

Most riders, though, just want to get somewhere. On a budget. And the Greyhound out of Casa Grande did that. I imagine it took job seekers to Phoenix. Dropped off people visiting relatives in Casa Grande. Took veterans to Tucson for appointments at the VA hospital.

It carried veterans longing to see their families in places like Los Angeles, said Kim Vandenberg, director of the HOPH Veterans Center in Casa Grande.

"There are veterans who come into the area and they want to go home," Vandenberg said.

They have little money or are homeless. The HOHP center would pick up their bus fare. They could board in Casa Grande. Now that's not an option.

"If we lose the Greyhound," Vandenberg said, "it will be a hardship to get them to Phoenix."

Four years ago, Mike Smith rode the Greyhound out of Casa Grande. He went to East Texas, where he got a job selling magazine subscriptions door-to-door. Recently he rode the bus to Phoenix. He visited his father.

I spoke to Smith, 27, as he waited in the Coolidge Transit Center lobby. He was taking the CART to visit his mother in Casa Grande.

Visiting his father, of course, just got harder.

"If you're going to Phoenix," Smith said, "you'll have to catch a ride."

Greyhound could be back, perhaps soon. Casa Grande planners have some suggestions for a bus stop. Gagliardi said 24/7 Fitness might be a good fit. It's on Trekell, not far from the Chevron station. Greyhound and 24/7 would have to sign off on it.

But here's what the city likes. 24/7 has generous parking, so there's room for a 40-foot bus. It has facilities. And it's open 24 hours, something Greyhound requires. If that doesn't pan out, one of a few Circle K's might work as well.

Down the road, Coolidge officials are hopeful.

"I'm confident something will be worked out," grants coordinator Feliz said on the phone.

I wondered aloud if he had his fingers crossed. He said he hadn't. Just the same, it couldn't hurt.

Dreamport Villages
Atop CG Mountain Trails
March 10, 2018

Dick Myers stood near a poster board. He was in the Arica Road parking lot of Casa Grande Mountain Park.

Behind the board's glass was a map lined with the park's trails.

Behind Myers, saguaros bordered the slope leading up to the main ridge. If a development goes as planned, that could change. You couldn't see the saguaros for the houses.

The houses would push against the mountain, five to an acre. Two stories permitted, up to 35 feet. To the north, more houses would spring up all along the eastern edge of the park. Some just one per acre.

It's all part of a grand plan known as Dreamport Villages. It calls for more than houses. It includes a resort at the mountain's north end, just south of Interstate 8. And office parks, restaurants, a wild-animal park and maybe a zipline.

North of I-8, more amusements. Maybe a 400-mph ride in a tube, a water park and a lake. And more, much more.

If you ask Myers, 77, it's not a good fit for Casa Grande Mountain.

The Casa Grande City Council thinks it is. Last September, the council gave a final green light to Dreamport Villages, 1,500 acres in all. Block Sports Co. of Orlando, Florida, is behind it.

The project includes 304 acres owned by the city. It's zoned largely for subdivisions. Real estate developer George Chasse has an option to buy the city parcel for $1.6 million. He would sell it to Block Sports.

The city calls it the option parcel.

It abuts Casa Grande Mountain. Casual hikers might mistakenly believe it's part of the park. I'm as casual as they come. I've only hiked the park twice. Last March, I took a leisurely stroll up the 2.5-mile Spine Trail, hiking north from the Arica Road trailhead.

It was an easy hike through a rocky desert flat. The small things caught my attention, like a hedgehog cactus ringed by small purple blossoms.

With Dreamport, Spine Trail won't be the same. As zoned, it falls outside the park. Inside a proposed subdivision. But the trail won't disappear, said city planner James Gagliardi. Spine Trail would be saved and remain open. It would run the same length, though tweaked to go around buildings and such.

Much of the view would be tweaked as well. Houses, walls and fencing would replace mountain slopes. The trail would cross over streets, so hikers would have to watch for cars. And that hedgehog cactus? Developers probably wouldn't a let little thing like that get in their way.

I asked Myers about it.

"You might as well just go walking in the city on a sidewalk," he said.

Spine Trail is just part of the story. The park, as many know it, would shrink. Desert flats to the east, north from the Arica Road trailheads, would be paved over.

Well, not all of it, Gagliardi said. The city has zoned some 92 acres to be preserved as open spaces. They would be off limits to houses, ziplines or any other development.

They would border the park, for the most part. And remain open for all to enjoy.

Hikers wouldn't know where the open space ends and the park begins. They'd still be in nature, except for the red-tiled roofs just over their shoulder.

It could be a red-tiled roof tsunami. Myers himself has long been bracing for it, as the residential zoning predates Dreamport. But now change seems real. Imminent. Not just suggestions on a map.

He'd no longer enjoy the quiet life, interrupted only by quail and javelina.

He lives on Arica, a stone's throw from the trailhead. He has few neighbors. He moved there nearly 22 years ago. He's hiked and worked in the area far longer. He can tell you just about anything you want to know about the mountain's history. And a few of its characters.

There's Old Bill on the Hill. Myers can't pin down his last name. Back in the Wild West days of the 1960s and '70s, Old Bill would pack a radio and drive his Jeep up what became known as Chimney Hill.

"He built a fireplace with a chimney on it," Myers said. "He'd come up there and listen to Paul Harvey, because he couldn't get the signal, because the mountain blocked it."

Driving up Chimney Hill is frowned on now.

Old Bill is one memory of a colorful past. The future looks like a mountain under attack, at least for Myers.

"I don't see anything other than that's a detriment ... destroying the beautiful scenery that's in the heart of the valley."

Gagliardi the planner understands. He's not an indifferent bureaucrat. He runs the mountain trails himself. It keeps him in shape for the next marathon. He's competed in 16 to date, as well as two ultra-marathons across Canyon de Chelly and back.

"I love these trails," he said of Casa Grande Mountain. "It is gorgeous."

High up the ridge and to the south, the mountain trails will still be there. And Gagliardi says he'll still enjoy the view beyond the houses and the ziplines. Picacho Peak stands out.

Still, he doesn't dispute that things will change. It will, he said, be a more urbanized experience.

And Myers doesn't dispute that people have property rights. That includes developers. He just says with resignation: "That's the price of development."

And not all will be lost. Plans call for the Arica Road entry to remain. A 1-acre parking lot would accommodate cars. And hikers could follow a corridor of a few hundred feet to open space and the park.

Past the two-story houses, the walls and barking dogs.

Who wouldn't appreciate a bit of nature after that?

All Aboard in Maricopa, Except for the Luggage

Maricopa, December 9, 2019

Glen Alley began riding Amtrak in the early 1980s. He remembered his first trip. He and his wife, Pat, rode from Lake Tahoe, California, to Denver on the California Zephyr.

From there, they flew to St. Louis, their hometown at the time.

I took the Zephyr with my own wife, Cindy, many years ago. It goes through mountain passes and chugs up and down steep grades. It's a ride to write home about.

Glen worked for a St. Louis executive-search company. Pat owned a store that specialized in party supplies. They've since retired to Maricopa. One thing that hasn't changed: Their love of trains.

"We've been on at least 25 trips on the train," Glen said.

On any number of occasions, they've ridden the Sunset Limited to Los Angeles, connecting to San Luis Obispo and other points along the coast. The Sunset stops in Maricopa three days a week in each direction. Westbound pulls through every Tuesday, Thursday and Sunday night. Eastbound every Monday, Thursday and Saturday.

It was a full-service stop. You could buy tickets there. You could check baggage.

Not anymore. Amtrak stopped staffing the Maricopa station in 2017.

Alley didn't miss the ticket part. He can get tickets online. But you can't check baggage with an iPhone. Somebody has to be there to take it, tag it and load it.

He and Pat often take six- to 10-day excursions, he added.

"It's incredibly impractical to do that without checking luggage," he said.

If it's any consolation, he has company.

Amtrak has cut staffing in stations across the country, said Bruce Becker, vice president of operations for the Rail Passengers Association in Washington.

"The loss of staff is a decline in service, there's no doubt about that," Becker said. "We continue to pressure Amtrak to think about passengers first."

An Amtrak spokeswoman in Oakland had a different take. She directed me to a November news release, titled "Improved Safety and Customer Experience Drive Record Amtrak Ridership."

It pointed out a $143 million investment "to improve customer experience at several stations throughout the network."

Of course, some stations fared better than others.

And what's the big deal anyway? It's only Maricopa. But it's Phoenix, too, which hasn't had Amtrak service since 1996. Amtrak lists Maricopa as a Phoenix stop. It even began a shuttle service from Phoenix and Tempe in 2017, the same year it stopped staffing the Maricopa station.

Maricopa Mayor Christian Price would like Amtrak to do more, not less.

Last January, he wrote Richard Anderson, Amtrak president and CEO. Price signed on to the Rail Passenger Association's request for the Sunset Limited to run daily in each direction. He joined then-Tucson Mayor Jonathan Rothschild, who wrote Amtrak in September 2018.

The Sunset Limited stops in Tucson.

Both mayors argued the Sunset Limited is popular, with increasing ridership. Price pointed out Maricopa's newly constructed overpass. It carries through traffic over the tracks and allows easier access to the station. He added the Sunset Limited is a winner for tourism. Tourists take it to and from California, as well as Texas and Louisiana. (Think New Orleans.)

Ray Lang replied on Amtrak's behalf in March. Lang is Amtrak's senior director for government affairs. Not gonna happen, Lang said, though not in so many words. Amtrak doesn't have the trains or the money, he said.

Then he seemed to throw more cold water on any plans for a brighter future.

"Amtrak is taking a thorough review of the mix of services we provide including services such as the Sunset Limited that provide infrequent service over very long distances."

The management, it happens, has shown little enthusiasm for a number of long-haul routes. I'm not sure where the Sunset Limited stands. The Southwest Chief had been singled out for the chopping block.

It runs daily to and from Chicago and Los Angeles, with a stop in Flagstaff. Plans called for putting riders on a bus for 500 miles. More Greyhound than Amtrak.

Congress stepped in to keep the Southwest Chief intact, for now.

Amtrak's focus is on shorter intercity routes, say Boston to New York. That's not a good fit for much of the Southwest, where vast spaces separate cities and towns. Amtrak has floated the idea of a Tucson-to-Phoenix run, Rail Passenger's Becker says.

Glen and Pat Alley drove to Tucson for answers. There they spoke to Hazel, one of Amtrak's Tucson ticket agents. I tried but failed to get in touch with Hazel myself. So I have to go with what

Alley told me. I'll just use her first name.

"She was one of the stalwarts of the Maricopa station," Alley said.

Hazel lives in Maricopa. She worked at the station here, before the staffing cut. She would like to see it back at full strength, Alley said. She spoke to Mayor Price about it. Nothing to be done, apparently.

Amtrak, the immovable object.

So no baggage check-in from Maricopa anytime soon. Hazel offered the Alleys an alternative. They could check their luggage at Tucson's Union Station, within 24 hours of travel.

She told Alley: "I know it's not a solution, but ... if you want to bring your luggage to Tucson, we'll check it for you and then you can just get on the train in Maricopa."

Alley appreciated the tip. But he added: "Who wants to drive a three-to-four-hour-roundtrip to check luggage?"

It's not any easier after you return to Maricopa. Your luggage is still in Tucson.

The Alleys thought about boarding in Tucson. They asked about long-term parking. You need that if you're gone for a week or two. The Tucson station, they learned, doesn't offer any.

The Maricopa station does. So that's something.

Center in a Park Offers
Hope for the Homeless

September 2, 2019

Mary Ann Lucero sat on a small chair, her dog Snowball at her feet. Lucero was at CGHelps to ask about shelter. And getting the ID she needed for services like food stamps.

125

She lost her ID when her purse was stolen. It's an occupational hazard for the homeless.

She totes around a backpack now. That and Snowball are pretty much all she has. Snowball is ivory white, smallish with floppy ears. And friendly.

"She's a very good girl," Lucero said.

I met Lucero and Snowball last Tuesday at the CGHelps Resource Center. It's housed in Casa Grande's old Peart Center at Peart Park, near the library and senior center. CGHelps opened in late April, with backing from the city. The center is run by the Community Action Human Resources Agency. Everybody knows it as CAHRA.

A staffer from CAHRA is always on duty, during business hours anyway. CAHRA helps find housing for the homeless. And works with people threatened with eviction.

Shawna Storm was on hand a week ago Monday. She's a CAHRA housing relocator.

"We have a lot of families that are living in cars and vehicles that got evicted," Storm said. "They're still working. They just don't have the funds to get that deposit, first month's rent, so they end up homeless."

CAHRA helps pay move-in costs.

Lucero, 56, wasn't tossed out by a landlord. She had been staying with relatives.

"They pushed me out, but I'm not going back," she said.

She had met earlier with a representative from Social Security. Once a month, the Casa Grande office of Social Security staffs a cubicle at CGHelps.

Lucero collects Social Security disability. She suffers from severe depression.

"Me being homeless, I try not to think about it," she said.

She had stopped receiving benefits, as she had no address. But CGHelps took care of that. The homeless can use the center's mailing address. CGHelps keeps their mail in a lockbox for 30 days. The Social Security representative reinstated Lucero's benefits, on the spot, a CGHelps case worker said.

CGHelps also gave her a referral to the Casa Grande office for

126

the Arizona Department of Economic Security. They had Lucero's ID on file. Lucero got a new one.

The center put her in touch with Pets in Need, which provided dog food. Snowball wouldn't go hungry. Getting around was another issue. Casa Grande doesn't have public transit, and Lucero doesn't have a car. She walks everywhere. The resource center helped out with a new bicycle. Not brand new, but one in good condition.

It's stored behind a cubicle. Lucero hasn't ridden it yet.

"I need a lock," Lucero said.

She had more matters to settle. Housing and the like. So she waited.

It's a good place to wait. CGHelps is small, a space on a human scale. The polished wood floors add a bit of class. The receptionist, Vangie Villa, greets people with a smile as they enter. She keeps a calendar of different agencies and nonprofits that offer help. They show up on different days.

Today was for Social Security. Veterans help and behavioral health experts show up on other days. Sun Life Family Health Center offers medical screening and referrals for health care. The Lions Club offers vision screening. There's more. The center's website has a calendar of events.

And if somebody walks in a bit lost, Gloria Cardenas is there to offer guidance. She's the CGHelps resource navigator, as well as a case worker.

But Lucero couldn't wait any longer. She attends the daily 10:30 morning devotion at Fountains of Living Water Church on Second Street. It's offered by Seeds of Hope and comes with coffee.

"I'll be late," she said. It was 10:25. I gave her and Snowball a lift, then returned to CGHelps.

Eddie Reyes, 57, was seated near the reception desk, with his walker.

"I'm trying to find some kind of shelter aid," Reyes said. "I've had five surgeries in the last year and a half, and I have four more to go."

He had a shopping list of operations. Multiple hip and knee replacements, as well as foot surgeries. He's also had prostate cancer. Arizona's version of Medicaid paid for treatments.

It didn't keep a roof over his head.

"I've been working since I was 6 years old," Reyes said. "It caught up to me."

He worked 25 years at an Eloy diner, right up until June. He worked through pain until, as he put it, his hips cracked. He ended up in a hospital in Mesa. Without work, he couldn't pay the rent. He lost his mobile home in Arizona City.

From the hospital, Reyes went to a rehab center. On his release, he ended up on the street. Or right next to it.

"They told me they'd put me in a shelter, and all they did was put me on a sidewalk," he said.

They left him without a walker. Reyes called a friend who lives in Arizona City. His friend picked him up. They looked for shelter. A home would be nice. But no luck. He faces a life without a roof.

"For me, it's kind of embarrassing."

Maybe this year, he can quality for disability benefits. "I was denied last year."

At CGHelps, he waited to talk to Sabrina Valenzuala from CAHRA. Her title is homeless prevention.

Joan Harp sat nearby. She turns 82 this month. She was breathing with the help of an oxygen tank. She wasn't homeless, but her son was.

Mike Harp was at a small workbench-style table, just across the room. His girlfriend, Sylvia Stanley, was seated next to him. She was in a wheelchair. They were speaking to Valenzuela.

After their session, they joined Joan and told me their story.

Sylvia is 50. Multiple heart attacks confined her to a wheelchair.

Mike, 58, suffered a back injury in a desert motorcycle race. Vertebrae were crushed. He worked construction before that. Now he's on disability, as is Sylvia.

They rented a home in Colonia del Sol. They'd always lived on the margin. Rent, food and utilities ate up their disability benefits.

Then things began to unravel. The landlord removed utility outlets. They weren't replaced, as promised. The refrigerator no longer had power. The stove and oven didn't work. Mike and Sylvia had bought food in bulk, to save money. It spoiled.

They cooked outside. Then the landlord told them he was selling the place. They were evicted.

The couple couch-surfed for a few months. They wore out their welcome and had to leave. They had nowhere to go.

"Three weeks in the streets. ... We walk around, find shade," Mike said. "This has never happened to me before."

I asked where they slept. Park benches, Mike said. What about Sylvia? He'd help her onto a bench. Prop her legs up with something soft. Then Mike's wallet was stolen. He had no ID.

He and Sylvia had hit bottom.

But every bottom has a bounce. And things were starting to look up. Mike could use the resource center as a mailing address. He could begin collecting his disability benefits, again. And Valenzuela gave him a list of possible rentals. CAHRA works with landlords and will pay the deposit and first month's rent.

"They're going to help me get reestablished," Mike said. "They said, 'start looking.'"

I got an update Thursday from Cardenas, the navigator. Mike and Sylvia could stay with his mother, Joan, until they found a place. And Lucero moved into a unit with another woman.

Somebody who likes good dogs, no doubt.

Catching the Bus
At a Truck Stop

Eloy, July 15, 2019

I pulled up to Love's Travel Stop in Eloy shortly before noon on Monday, July 1.

The Greyhound eastbound on I-10 was scheduled to pull in at 12:20. I wasn't sure just where. Love's is a big place, with acres of asphalt. It serves truckers and everyday motorists. Loads big and little.

And now it serves Greyhound. It's a new stop. The city of Casa Grande pulled the plug on the old one, a 24-hour mini-mart at Kortsen and Trekell roads. The stop conflicted with zoning laws and the attitudes of a few nearby businesses.

Losing it created heart palpitations for Central Arizona Regional Transit, based in Coolidge. CART buses connect riders to Casa Grande, Florence and places in between. It gets federal dollars for tying into an intercity transit system. One like Greyhound, for instance.

Without Greyhound, CART faced a six-figure funding cut.

And restored Greyhound service began to look iffy. Maybe, I thought, when pigs flew. Well, I can't vouch for the pigs, but Eloy stepped forward and rolled out the welcome mat. Greyhound now pulls up to Love's four times a day, at Sunland Gin Road just south of Interstate 10. CART, in turn, adjusted its route to accommodate the new Greyhound schedule. Federal funding was restored.

PinalCentral staff writer Rofida Khairalla wrote about all this in late June.

My plan was to talk to Greyhound riders. Ask them what they think. First, I had to find where on planet Love the bus landed. I didn't spot a sign or the running-greyhound logo. I ended up at the Love's cashier for the truckers' gas pumps. She told me the bus stops in front of Arby's.

It faces the gas pumps and parking for the non-trucking public. I was told bus riders were welcome to wait inside, where it's air conditioned. So I took a seat and waited.

I watched for people with luggage or backpacks. I didn't see anyone. After a few minutes, I bought a small sandwich. They're called sliders. I figured I should pay rent for my booth. I'm not a food critic. I'll just say the slider was better than the broccoli I was forced to eat as a kid.

I finished my sandwich. Still, no bus riders. I went outside. I had a brief chat with a young man changing out the trash can liners. He lifted the full bags into a cart.

Travelers often rid their cars of debris from earlier stops, he said.

Mostly wrappers from McDonald's and cups from Starbucks.

People exercise their pets. The people have restrooms. The dogs settle for a spot of grass or the pavement. One lady walked her little dog along the walkway fronting Arby's. The dog stopped at the trash cart, sniffed and deemed it good.

It was hot outside. The puddle would dry out fast enough.

Sometimes the bus riders wait it out here, just in front of Arby's, the worker said. It's on the east side, so they get a bit of shade in the afternoon.

I didn't see the bus for Tucson. I must have looked away for a moment. It had come and gone. I thought perhaps with no passengers to pick up or drop off, it just kept on going. But a Greyhound spokeswoman later told me the bus stops in any case.

I just needed to pay more attention.

The 1:20 to Phoenix was due next. So I waited. Still, no outbound riders. The bus pulled into a spot for RV parking around 1:30. One young woman got off. She carried a backpack into Arby's.

She made a phone call for a ride. She said she was staying with her aunt and sister.

"I'm coming from Texas," she said.

She didn't want to give her name. And, beyond what she'd already told me, didn't want to talk. I thanked her and went to my car. I returned four days later.

No luck this time either. Nobody waited for the Greyhound. Nobody wanting to pull up stakes, or just get away. I thought of an old Roger Miller song: "I'm bound to catch the next Greyhound leavin' this town … hoping that dog ain't got a full load leaving this town."

The bus pulled up right about 1:20. It wasn't full and became one person lighter when Bernie stepped out. The bus driver followed him out and retrieved his bag.

Bernie wasn't happy.

"This is stupid!"

Bernie, 54, thought he'd be let off in Casa Grande proper, at the old bus stop. Not at Sunland Gin Road, halfway to Arizona City.

Bernie declined to give his last name. I think it made it easier for

131

him to vent.

"I wish they had told me this in Tucson," he said. His son was to meet him in Casa Grande, he added. "Not way the hell out here."

He called his son to let him know: Change of venue. "I'm at Love's."

Bernie planned to spend a few weeks with his family. He knows Casa Grande. He was born and raised in town. He now works construction in Tucson.

He had no plans to return by Greyhound.

I thanked Bernie for his time and headed back to my car. As I opened the door, a semi rolled by. I paused to take in the writing on the trailer. "Swifty Swine Racing Pigs."

OK, so maybe they don't fly. But they can run fast.

On the Chain Cholla Trail

November 2, 2020

I went on a hike last Tuesday. That was a week before Election Day, which — if this column lands in its usual spot — is today.

I sought refuge from the politics. The campaigning. The low blows. The guilt from watching my wife wash all those dishes.

My refuge was Casa Grande Mountain Park. There I would find solitude and peace. I was lucky. A few days sooner and I'd have been sharing the trail with 125 students, parents and teachers from a local charter school. Not much solitude in that.

I turned off Sunland Gin Road onto Arica Road around mid-afternoon. I passed a half-dozen semis from the truck stop. They were lined up on Arica to make a left onto Sunland Gin. They waited at a stop sign for a break in a steady stream of traffic.

Good luck with that, I thought. Things will get better, though.

The Eloy City Council plans to make improvements. New intersections. Stoplights. And a few other design details to be worked out.

I read about it in the Dispatch. Local coverage. I can't plug it enough.

Anyway, I headed west on Arica. Past all the trucks. Past some duplexes and houses. Past open desert. I pulled into the Arica-trailhead parking lot, landscaped with rocks not quite the size of boulders.

I put on a windbreaker. It was, after all, in the 60s. For an Arizona native, that's like a polar vortex. Still, great weather for a hike. I could always take the jacket off if I got warm.

Norm had on a T-shirt. He stepped out of his pickup. He was just out for some fresh air. I followed him south, on the East Butte Trail. He soon peeled off to poke around the desert.

I soldiered on.

On hikes past, I wrote about the desert flowers. The gaudy purple blooms of the hedgehog cactus. Little flowers that dot the trail sides. The Mexican gold poppies scattered about in no particular order.

Not this time. Not following a summer without rain. This was a stark desert. Cactus and desert trees were in survival mode. The birds and the bees would have to wait.

The unadorned landscape seemed more remote. More secluded. A world away from politics and a virus that was everywhere — but here.

So, no bursts of color. Just saguaros and cholla cactus clinging to the rocky slopes. Lots of cholla. They don't need flowers for a show, anyway. Backlit by the sun, they glow with neon brilliance.

I glanced back and saw a mountain biker. He seemed to be going slow. I was going slower. I stepped aside and he passed me, going uphill. Grinding it out.

Last March, I took part in a spinning class at the city rec center. We set our stationary bikes to high resistance and pretended to climb Casa Grande Mountain. Now I know. The real thing's a lot harder.

At some point, the East Butte Trail became the West Butte Trail.

It descended into the Chain Cholla Forest Trail. Here cholla cactus rose up to 7 feet. Their branches were needle-laden hanging stalactites. The trail weaved between them.

I thought: This would make a great haunted house ride. Or rather walk. Give the kids flashlights and dare them to enter. They'd be scared. But they'd go in, tiptoeing through the moonlit shadows of a cholla forest. Hidden speakers could play spooky sounds.

Band-Aids would be extra.

Sure, not practical. But when I'm hiking, my mind wanders. The view always brings it back. Now I could see farms to the south. And beyond them, the homes of Arizona City.

Soon, the trail turned and led up me up a ridge. This was, after all, the Ridge Trail.

Up I went. I'm not in awful shape, but the ascent — at times — left me winded. OK, I thought, no ultra-marathons across the Grand Canyon for me. Not this year.

I stopped to remove a pebble from my shoe. I took off my windbreaker. I wondered why I didn't bring water.

I know why. I didn't think I needed it, so I left it in the car. Smart, huh?

Then the sun settled below the top of the ridge. I was in shadow. The trail edged along a steep slope. My mind wandered again.

I saw myself weak with thirst, stumbling about in the dark. Tripping on a rock and rolling down the slope, through a mountainside of teddy-bear cholla and ending up in the Chain Cholla Forest.

I'd have to call 911.

"What's your emergency?"

"I'm lost in the Chain Cholla Forest. Bring Band-Aids."

That didn't happen. I dropped down to another trail. The sun appeared. I spotted a lone car in the Arica trailhead parking lot. It was mine. I reached it and headed back to the world of ugly politics and coronavirus.

And, on the plus side, clean dishes.

Memories of a Moose Lodge

Arizona City, August 31, 2020

Ron Jolly joined the Loyal Order of Moose Lodge 1038 in the fall of 1985, just a month or so after arriving in Arizona City.

He followed his wife, Becky, from Plymouth, Indiana. She'd found a job teaching in the Toltec School District. She taught seventh and eighth grades for 30 years. Ron sold insurance. A few years later, he took up real estate.

Ron and Becky brought two young daughters with them, Amanda and Deedra. Son Nick was born in Arizona.

In 1985, the Arizona City lodge was still known as the Casa Grande Valley Moose Lodge. It had been incorporated in Casa Grande in 1970. But it quickly pulled up stakes and moved to Arizona City.

"They moved part of a building out here," Ron said.

A new building went up as well. Moose officials broke ground for it in late 1971.

TV-star Rory Calhoun cut the ribbon for the grand opening in December 1972. He lent his name to the developers who donated land for it. He later had a falling out with them and sued. That's another story.

Two years after Ron joined, the lodge jettisoned the Casa Grande name. That was 1987. It became Arizona City Loyal Order of Moose.

The name changed. The welcome mat stayed. The lodge became a second home to Ron, Becky and even the kids.

Ron had his own parking spot. It wasn't marked as such, but the members knew. Reserved for Ron. Inside, he had his own space at the bar. He and Becky called it the Cheers Corner, an homage to the TV show about a neighborhood bar.

"Pretty much I was there every day of the week," Ron said. "Same old corner."

He'd be greeted by familiar faces. His lodge fellows. People he knew. People he could share a beer with. And, as Becky put it, shoot the bull.

"We'd talk about the same thing every day," Ron said. "I drank Miller Lite. I was their No. 1 Miller Lite drinker."

He rarely talked shop there. The lodge, the bar, was his refuge. His comfort zone.

I spoke to him and Becky last week. They sat next to each other at their kitchen table. I sat across from them, socially distant. Amanda, their daughter, stood nearby. Her three daughters, oldest 5, ran around and played.

Becky spoke up.

The lodge was more than a bar, she said. It was the family center. It was, after all, a place for families, she said. Not just men chatting over a beer.

"Friday nights used to be kind of a family night," Becky said. "It was a safe place to take the kids. You didn't have to hire a babysitter. You could take the kids and they would play and stuff."

Ron's Cheers Corner had a cubbyhole by the bar. It was a good fit for young Nick, when he was 4 or 5 years old.

"Nick would climb up underneath there, and just go to sleep," Becky said.

He learned to play pool, even as he could barely see over the table. It was three-ball pool. Games went fast.

The girls were older. They could stay up late. The lodge had tables and a small playroom with a TV, chairs and a sofa. And donated toys.

Every Christmas, Santa visited. Mrs. Claus helped.

"I remember we had Christmas parties," Amanda said. "Every child gets a Christmas present. Bobbing for apples was a game we used to do."

The grownups had their games, too. They played bingo in the dining room or the bar. Dinner was served every Wednesday and

Friday. Fish fry or hamburgers.

"We had a pretty full menu," Ron said.

Sunday poker was popular. Nickel, dime and quarter bets. Nobody got rich. But then nobody went away broke. Sunday was also a time to watch football, on one of a half-dozen TVs. Saturday night was reserved for darts.

"One year we had a men's leg contest," Becky said.

Contestants stood behind a curtain, raised just enough to show their legs, from the knees down. Prizes went for hairiest, most tanned and best-looking legs.

Max Moore had it all. He was decades older than the other contestants. Though he died in 2005, his legs were legendary.

"Oh, he had really nice-looking legs," Becky said. "He's a golfer and they were very tan. Athletic-looking legs."

At other times, the lodge relived the '50s.

"We had sock hops, where they wore the poodle skirts and the guys wore jeans with the cigarettes rolled up in their sleeves," Becky said.

Few members actually smoked. The lodge became smoke-free a few years back. Smokers had a place outside, on the patio.

Couples exchanged vows at the lodge. It was a place for wedding receptions and anniversary parties. Becky's own mother and father celebrated their 50th there.

Moose Lodge 1038 had its charitable side as well. Members raised money for the Arizona City Library, the Boys & Girls Clubs of the Casa Grande Valley and Toys for Tots. They contributed to Mooseheart, a school and residential campus outside Chicago. It cares for orphaned children of member families throughout the country.

The Jollys' own children grew up learning to help others.

And, as kids do, they did grow up. They didn't outgrow the lodge. Nick joined when he turned 21. He often took his own son there. Amanda joined in her 20s, as a Woman of the Moose, like Becky. She's now 38. She would take her own daughters.

"They were itty-bitty," Amanda said.

People always looked forward to seeing them.

Ron joined in his late 20s. Becky soon after. They're now both

64. The lodge was more than half their life. A lot to reflect on. Becky boiled it down.

"It was a friendly lodge," she said. "And a lot of people, because we've known them so long, are like family."

The Loyal Order of Moose 1038 also opened its doors to others. It was, as PinalCentral's Maria Vasquez wrote, Arizona City's one community gathering spot.

For Ron Jolly, it was the Cheers Corner and old friends. He settled into his spot on Aug. 13 and ordered the usual. Miller Lite.

The next day, he got a call. "The bartender said the Moose was on fire."

Thirty-five years of memories went up in flames. The Arizona City Fire District station was a block away. Casa Grande and Eloy fire departments also answered the call. But nothing could be done. The fire quickly spread in a gap between an older roof and newer one built above it.

The good news: No one was injured.

Nothing to do now but look ahead. Create new memories for its 365 members and their families. A GoFundMe page is up and running. And the fire station has opened its doors to Moose officers. They meet twice a month.

Ron Jolly is a trustee. He attends. But it's no substitute for Lodge 1038. You can't get a Miller Lite at the firehouse.

Fishing in the Desert?
Sure, If a Canal Runs Through It
March 29, 2021

The question was: What kind of fish can you catch in a canal? So asked Andy Howell, PinalCentral's assistant managing editor.

He had a point. You think of a canal as a ditch that carries water for crops. Maybe it delivers water to towns and cities, after it's been treated. Canals weren't created with fishing in mind.

Still, that didn't stop David Whitaker. He fled Pinal County Sheriff's deputies, who received a report he allegedly had sexually abused a minor. He made himself a desert hideaway, living off the grid. Surviving on javelina and rabbits he shot and fish he caught in a nearby canal.

Whitaker managed to live wild for more than three months. The law finally caught him, though. Sheriff's deputies, the Border Patrol and the Arizona Department of Public Safety closed in on him March 15.

As of Friday, he was in Pinal County jail, awaiting trial. He was booked on three counts. Indecent exposure, sexual abuse of a minor and sexual conduct with a minor.

Before the law closed in, Whitaker, 43, made his home away from home in the desert, about a half-mile north of Missile Base Road, near the Central Arizona Project canal. That's where Whitaker fished, says Lauren Reimer, public information officer for the Sheriff's Office.

He caught carp and catfish.

Case closed. Well, not quite.

I'm familiar with that stretch of CAP. In October 2019, Kent Taylor gave me a sneak preview of a trail that runs alongside the canal, from Nona Road — east of Interstate 10 — south to the area known as Missile Base. Taylor is Pinal County open space and trails director.

The county is developing a hundred miles of trail along the canal. It will tie into the CAP National Recreation Trail. When completed, the national trail will run the entire length of the CAP.

The Nona trail is the first segment in Pinal County. It's now open to the public.

Don't look for the CAP fishing docks, though. There aren't any. What's more, the canal is lined with a high chain-link fence, guarding it from the trail on one side and the desert on the other.

Somehow that didn't stop Whitaker. He apparently found a place to drop the fish a line. He already faces serious charges. But the CAP could pile on, if so inclined. Fishing in the CAP canal isn't permitted.

Nor is swimming. Here's a warning from the CAP website:

"The sides of the canal are very steep and the water moves up to 3,500 cubic feet per second. If someone were to fall in, the current would quickly sweep them away and the slope of the canal sides is too steep to climb out."

In other words, you could end up getting fished out yourself. You probably wouldn't put up much of a fight.

Whitaker didn't fall in. But he could face up to a thousand-dollar fine and 90 days in jail, if he fished in the CAP, says CAP spokeswoman DeEtte Person.

I doubt Whitaker gave the legality of it much thought. He caught the carp. He caught the catfish. But why just two kinds? The U.S. Bureau of Reclamation, in a 2015 survey, listed 17 different kinds of fish swimming up and down the CAP. Most are striped bass and bluegill.

I learned this from a 2018 article by Scott Bryan, CAP senior biologist.

The CAP fish have a tough time of it, Bryan writes. They live in a fast-flowing concrete-lined channel. No place to lay eggs really. They'd just get swept away. Most of the fish are hatched elsewhere and end up in the canal through no fault of their own.

They do get a lot of exercise, as they're constantly swimming to "avoid be sucked into the pumping plants."

They become small and lean. It's like CrossFit for fish.

CAP stocks the canal with three species. They do important work. Channel catfish control pests like caddisfly. Grass carp keep the vegetation in check. And redear sunfish go after quagga mussels, which specialize in gumming up the works.

The carp and catfish that Whitaker caught were just doing their job. If he knew that, he'd throw them back.

Not all canals ban fishing. If a canal's open to the public, you can fish it. A number of smaller unfenced canals run near Whitaker's desert hideout, CAP's Person said. He might have fished in one of them.

It wouldn't be hard. He could just walk up to an irrigation ditch and drop a line in. Nothing wrong with that, as long as you're not trespassing. And have an Arizona fishing license.

The Arizona Game and Fish Department puts it this way: A fishing license is required "for any publicly accessible water in Arizona."

So, if the city stocks the public pool with bass, you can't reel one in without a license.

I live less than a mile from a canal. It's owned by Salt River Project. I could fish there, with a license. I'd likely catch one of two kinds. White amur and the common carp.

SRP says you can keep the common carp. But you have to toss the white amur back. It eats plants that can clog a canal.

I wouldn't know the difference. So I'll just save myself the cost of a license and settle on a taco. Preferably chicken.

Recalling a Fiery Plane Crash
Francisco Grande, November 1, 2021

Frank Mejia parked his pickup along Peters Road, on the north side. Not quite a half-mile west of Burris Road, just outside Casa Grande.

Mejia once lived in the house across the street. He had 10 acres, some cows. He moved out in the '90s.

"See that tree there," he said. It was a tall tree, maybe 30 to 40 feet. It was in the backyard. "I'm going to tell you a story about that."

Mejia has lots of stories. He grew up on farms in Casa Grande. He joined the Air Force at 17. He served 1954-58, returned home and became a barber. He opened his own barber shop. He cut hair for more than 50 years, too many heads to count. Before the second

Iraq War, he had a side gig as a Saddam Hussein impersonator.

He married Angelita in 1964. They have four children, all grown up. He's 84, looks like 65.

So, sure. Lots of stories.

But a tree? "A sight like that, in all my life, I'll never forget."

The tree just begins the story. It ends with a plane crash.

It was July 8, 1979, early evening. Mejia was sitting out on the back patio, watching the sunset. Julian Bonilla sat nearby. Bonilla was a welder who lived on the property. A plane came into view, from the west.

"It was flying awfully low, on the other side of the gravel pit."

The gravel pit was south, across a field. The plane banked north and flew toward Mejia's house. Just over the tree, close enough to make the branches sway.

The house was — and still is — surrounded by farms. Crop dusters were a common sight, Mejia said. This was something else. A cargo plane. Later reports identified it as a C-119 Flying Boxcar. It had two propellers, one to a wing.

Mejia and Bonilla watched as the plane went north. It flew over farmland, then cleared State Route 84, about a mile away. It banked left again and headed west, toward the Francisco Grande Resort.

"I said, 'He's probably looking for a place to land.'"

Short of the resort, the plane hit the ground.

"There was a big ball of fire," Mejia said. "So it bounced from that fire, and I'd seen the plane, on fire, going up a second time."

It bounced again. "Then it bounced back down and then another explosion."

"I says to Julian, 'Let's go.'"

Mejia took his truck. Five minutes later he pulled up to a wreckage in flames. He got out. Julian stayed in the truck.

"There were some bodies."

Last week, Mejia took me to the crash site. It's a dirt lot covered with some desert scrub. We walked around a bit. Nothing remains of the wreckage today. Mejia remembered a plane in pieces, still burning. And the barrels. They likely carried fuel, he said. Drug smugglers could tap them without stopping.

We walked a bit farther. He pointed to the ground. He recalled a man lying there, still smoldering.

"I'll never forget his eyes … He was just looking up," Mejia said. "He was alive, and there was nothing I could do about it."

The man died shortly after. Another survived long enough to walk toward the resort, before collapsing.

First responders soon arrived. They lifted another survivor onto an ambulance. He was in shock and speaking in Spanish. The EMT asked Mejia if he spoke Spanish and could interpret.

Mejia went up to the man, badly burned. The man kept saying, "Quítate el cinturón!" "Take off my seatbelt!" Mejia said, translating.

The man also said, repeatedly, "Dios perdoname." "God, forgive me."

Mejia asked where he was from. Colombia, he said. He told Mejia he had a wife and two daughters. That's all Mejia found out.

"He didn't make it," Mejia said.

Mejia went back home and told Angelita what he saw. The horror of it. Like nothing like he had seen before. And he had seen plenty. In the Air Force, he handled dispatch for the crash and rescue team at Castle Air Force Base, near Merced, California. He also went out on calls.

The base has since been shuttered. At the time, it was a staging ground for B-52 bombers and KC-97 refueling tankers. In 1955, Mejia and a team went to a crash involving a tanker. Nobody survived.

"It was all pieces," he said. "We had to put them in bags."

Body bags.

As bad as it was, he didn't have to look into the eyes of a dying man. And know there was nothing he could do to help.

At the time, Mejia said little about the Francisco Grande crash. But reporters jumped on it. The next day's paper ran a story with a photo of flames from the wreckage shooting "high into the night sky." It was taken by Donovan Kramer Jr., then and now managing editor of the Casa Grande Dispatch.

The story quoted 14-year-old Michael Johnson of Desert Carmel, a nearby subdivision. He was in his front yard when he saw the plane come down. An engine was on fire, he said. The plane bounced twice, then exploded. He ran to get his parents.

Later stories identified the people on board, four in all. David Dwake, 29, and Sammy Middleton, 32, died at the scene. Both were from Florida.

Howard Scruggs, 37, and Luis Torrenegra were taken to Maricopa County Hospital — now Valleywise Health Medical Center. Then and now, known for its burn unit. Neither man made it. Scruggs was from Florida. Torrenegra, the man Mejia spoke to, was from Colombia.

Nobody knew where the plane was from. Or where it was going.

News reports noted the 55-gallon drums, the ones Mejia mentioned. There were 30 of them, filled with fuel. Onboard, they exploded when the plane hit.

Originally C-119s were military transport planes. Production started in 1947 and continued through the mid-'50s. With ample cargo space, they became popular with drug smugglers, an official with the U.S. Drug Enforcement Administration told the Dispatch. And this one appeared to be tricked up for drugs. It was painted black and apparently flew without lights.

But no drugs were found. No bundles of cash.

"They found some jars later with some coins in it," Mejia said.

If at First You Don't Succeed, Wait 43 Years
Tucson, December 6, 2021

I first drove up Mount Lemmon in 1978. Well, not all the way.

I was a journalism student at the University of Arizona. Tucson was somewhat new to me. I was from Phoenix. We have mountains around Phoenix. When you get to the top of them you're still in the

144

desert. Mount Lemmon was different. On arrival to Tucson, I heard stories that if you made it to the top, you'd get pine trees. And, in the winter, even snow.

And it was right outside Tucson. You could practically walk up it, if you happened to be training for Mount Everest.

I wasn't. I'd go by car.

My car at the time was a yellow Volkswagen squareback. They look like small station wagons. Like a number of my early cars, this one had a few mechanical issues. I had some work done on it after the engine caught fire.

It got around Tucson OK. Not too difficult. It's pretty much flat, like Phoenix. But one weekend I packed a light lunch and headed up the mountain. The road wound past saguaros of the lower desert. And curved up past any number of climate zones.

Or so I heard. My car never made it. It pooped out around 4,000 feet, or so I'm guessing. It must have been the rarified air. I managed to turn around and coast back to town. And say goodbye to Mount Lemmon. I should have said, "I'll be back in 43 years. Just you wait."

The mountain waited. So did I, until now. Until I had a reliable car, along with a faithful dog and a wife who was all in for an escape to the pines. As long as it didn't involve camping. We booked a Forest Service cabin at Palisades, a spot on the map. It has campgrounds and a visitors center. Palisades is at 8,000 feet, about 1,200 feet below Mount Lemmon's peak.

The Palisades ranger residence cabin was built in the 1930s. It has since been upgraded. It has central heating, a full kitchen and a bath. I had tried to book it for summer. So did everyone else. No surprise there. At 8,000 feet, it's a nice break from the desert heat.

I found three open nights in November.

The ranger no longer lives there, so we didn't have to share a bunk.

The drive up was an adventure, not counting the 8-mile crawl across town on Tucson's Grant Road. Cars lined up 30 deep at every intersection. The green light let six through at a time. Or so I recall.

Still, Tucson makes up for it with Mount Lemmon, right on its doorstep.

Here's what I know about Mount Lemmon, by way of general knowledge. It's the highest point of the Santa Catalina Mountains, north of Tucson. It's one of a number of Sky Islands that dot southern Arizona. Mount Graham near Safford is another.

There are, in all, 32 sky islands north of the U.S.-Mexico border. That's not general knowledge. I learned that from "A Natural History of the Santa Catalina Mountains, Arizona" by Richard C. Brusca and Wendy Moore.

I spent several hours flipping through a guest copy at the cabin. My wife Cindy later bought one for me through the Summit Hut in Tucson. You can't get it on Amazon. The book covers the geology, history and biology of Mount Lemmon. It's a slick spiral-bound edition with lots of pictures.

Mount Lemmon's formation begins some 600 million years ago. It took a lot geology and tectonic forces to make a mountain that big. Its name goes back 140 years.

Sara Plummer Lemmon was a well-known botanist, as was her husband John Lemmon. In 1881, they sought to trudge up the Catalinas from the north, the Oracle side. They wanted to check out the plants. They arrived at the ranch of Emerson Stratton, just below the mountain. Stratton recalled seeing John on a horse, with Sara walking behind him.

Stratton agreed to lead them to the top. They went on horseback. Once there, Brusca and Moore write, "Stratton and the Lemmons carved their names on a big tree, and Stratton named the spot 'Mt. Lemmon' in honor of Mrs. Lemmon."

She was, by all accounts, the first white woman to scale the mountain. Some native inhabitants — Hohokam and, later, Apache — likely got there earlier. If only they had carved their names on a tree.

Sara Lemmon is honored in California as well. She led the drive to name the California poppy the state flower.

Anyway, that's why it's Lemmon and not Lemon.

After Tucson, the drive up was a breath of fresh air. The road had its twists and turns. I worried a bit about traffic. I'm a cautious driver. On mountain roads, I often end up leading an impatient line

146

of eager drivers.

Good news here. The Catalina Highway has plenty of pullouts for slowpokes. I could enjoy the drive without sweating the tailgaters. And take in the change of scenery. The saguaros gave way to grasslands and oak. And so on. By Palisades, we were in a pine forest.

Cool and shady. At night, we cozied up in the cabin. We read books. In the day, we hiked through the forest. Last year's Bighorn Fire largely spared Palisades.

One afternoon we drove to the peak — or nearly to it. We hiked along Meadow Trail No. 5. It led to a lookout over Tucson, spread out along a broad valley more than a mile below. And, across the way, Mount Wrightson. Another Sky Island.

Heck of a view. After 43 years, it was worth the wait.

DOGS

Linda, a Good Name for a Dogwalker

August 2, 2013

The Valley Humane Society's summertime dog walkers are a tight-knit group. Just three in number, they're all volunteers. They show up about 5 a.m. to walk dogs, every Monday, Tuesday and Wednesday.

And, "We're all Lindas."

That was Linda Dodge, I think. It could have been Linda Lenderman. It could have been Linda Jensen. But I'm pretty sure it was Dodge. She was the first Linda I talked to Tuesday morning.

"There is a fourth Linda, believe or not," Jensen said.

The fourth Linda is a dog walker in winter, when dog walkers are at full strength. The three Lindas, however, are year-rounders. Without them, the dogs of summer would have no walks the three days the shelter's not open. They'd have to settle for hanging out in kennels. Getting bored and maybe plotting a raid on the kitty compound.

I paid the three Lindas a visit on Tuesday morning, driving out to the VHS shelter off Trekell Road.

It was a little after 8:30, and most of the 40 or so dogs had already been walked. The three Lindas start early — and finish early — to beat the heat. Erin was still on the patio, having completed her rounds with the great outdoors.

Erin is a pit bull with a head like a concrete block and a tongue you could mop a floor with. She is mild-mannered, easy-going and friendly. Not pit bull-like at all. And she's good on a leash.

"She's a delight," Lenderman said.

As a dog everybody likes to walk, Erin ranks right up there with

155

Ghost. Ghost is part Dalmatian, part cattle dog, part this and part that. She's all white.

"That's why we call her Ghost," said Lenderman, a member of the VHS board.

Good-on-a-leash is a high bar for some dogs.

"Some of them are more challenging than others," Lenderman said. "Angel, she only wants to go at one speed."

Maybe someday Angel will learn. She can't go any faster than the arm straining to hold her back.

The standard dog walk here is about three-quarters of a mile.

Not all dogs complete the course, or are expected to. Twinkles the boxer gets to hang out in a large pen and play with other dogs, as best she can. Twinkles is 10 years old. Her age is reflected in a graying muzzle and eyes that tell you they've seen it all. In her former life, before the shelter, she was probably a breeder — made to pump out puppies, then disposed of. Twinkles doesn't hold a grudge, though. She's a gentle soul.

Douglas is the brown dog of the bunch. Medium build, he's a new arrival. He's learned more about nature than most dogs ever will. He was found in the desert covered in so much cactus it had to be surgically removed. One of the Lindas suggested he should have been named Cactus Jack. At the shelter, Douglas is still learning the way of the leash.

He sees the leash is something to be fought and cast off. He'll come around, in time. The leash will be his friend, his third favorite thing, after dog food and Milk Bones.

When my little dogs — a pair of roguish Shih Tzus — see a leash, they often dance in circles and yap. They know there's a magical land beyond the front door. And they can only get there by leash.

The VHS dog walkers give all dogs their due, their morning walk, whether they're leash savvy or leash averse. Here, there are no bad dogs. Just a few that call for the patience of Job — though God never asked him to walk to Montgomery the Chihuahua. Little dog, big energy. At the end of the leash, he's like a 5-pound bucking bronco.

As the thermometer rose with the sun, walk time was over. Erin

156

had to return to the kennel. Lenderman tugged on her leash, but she sat firm. A tree stump. This was one walk she didn't want to take.

Brain-Dead Puppy Revived!
April 19, 2013

The scene doesn't change much in the lobby of a veterinary clinic. People wait with their dogs. They're called in. A few minutes later, they leave with their dog in tow and perhaps a bottle of pills.

But every so often, somebody comes in with a dog and leaves with only a collar, crying.

So it went for my wife and me last Monday. The dog we had for 14 years, Sammy, could no longer stand on her own. She had a neurological disease, progressive and debilitating. We got the diagnosis about two months ago and put off the decision to take her in, one last time, as long as we could.

It's a tough call, especially with a pet that's been in the family for more than a decade.

We have a picture of Sammy as a 12-week-old puppy playing with our daughter in a nearby park. The back of the photograph reads "Spring 1999." Sarah was 10. In the 14 years since, Sarah has finished elementary school, high school and college. She's now in graduate school. Sammy was her lap dog, even though she wasn't really a lap dog. More of a stunted golden retriever.

So when I called Sarah about Sammy, the tears flowed. But we had the memories, I said.

We got Sammy from a newspaper ad. She was born in a rough neighborhood. The car on the driveway had bullet holes. The teenage girl who showed us Sammy said the dog was born brain dead and had to be resuscitated. Maybe a stretch, but that would explain a lot. Sammy didn't like to socialize or play with other dogs. I took her to a dog park once. She spent all her time chasing butterflies — or would if she could. Other dogs would approach and offer to play. She'd snap. They'd snap back, and a fight would break out.

We never went back to the dog park.

Sammy was a runner. I used to take her to South Mountain Park in Phoenix. And, in violation of city code and perhaps some international agreement on dogs I'm not aware of, I'd let her off the leash. She'd bolt into the desert. The first time this happened, I spent an hour looking for her. Then I gave up, figuring she was never to be found.

I walked back to the parking lot, some two miles away. And there was the dog, waiting by the car.

But I soon cut back on Sammy's wild desert runs. It wasn't the threat of getting cited, though that was always in the back of my mind. It was the rattlesnake bite. Sammy ran up a desert wash one warm September morning. Something caught her attention. She stopped to smell it, then leaped about 3 feet straight up. I ran to her. I saw two rattlesnakes coiled together. I saw her nose. Not good, I thought.

I took her to the vet, who showed us why they earn the big money. The dog pulled through.

After that, I kept Sammy on the leash, mostly, though she would pretty much just run in place. It was like walking a sled dog. I told passers-by she was training for the Iditarod.

Sad as the loss was, she had it pretty good for a dog. She wasn't one of the strays or lost dogs I see almost every day, dodging traffic — sometimes not making it. She didn't end up unwanted at a shelter.

I'm not sure dogs have an afterlife, but I can imagine one. Dog heaven, as I see it, is one big off-leash park. The Milk-Bone River runs through it. Stealing food off the dinner plate is not a crime.

And there are plenty of cats to chase. Dog heaven, I imagine, is where the bad cats go.

Big Welcome for a Small Dog

September 27, 2013

I got my first little dog late in life. Of course, I've been late in life for a while now.

It was about 15 years ago that Twinkie walked into my life. Well, rolled into it would be more accurate.

I first saw her in my rearview mirror, rolling out from under a station wagon. I had been on my way to work. The wagon just kept on going. I turned around and drove back.

The small white dog lay in the middle of the road. Dead, as far as I could tell. But she hadn't yet been flattened, so I figured the least I could do was move her off to the side.

I picked her up and felt a heartbeat.

I was conflicted. The dog was alive. That was great news. But I couldn't just toss her to the side now. I would have to take her to the vet, and that would mean vet bills. And patching up a car-damaged dog could run into big money — and I'm not a big-money guy.

Twinkie, it turned out, was not too messed up. The diagnosis: a big bonk on the head. It was her lucky day. The car went right over the top of her and knocked her out. She would have been unscathed but for some low-hanging piece of the undercarriage.

The vet sized her up. She was about 10 to 12 years old and had a bad heart. We kept her, of course. Twinkie was just a mellow little dog of unknown origin.

She moved in with the big dogs and — for the most part — got along.

The biggest was Homer, a 100-pound Old English sheepdog.

159

He was deaf. We got him from a breeder in Williams — I should add a legitimate breeder, not a puppy mill. She wanted to find the dog a good home and — through my mother — found us.

Homer was free. Of course, that doesn't mean he was cheap. He broke half the dishes in our kitchen. He couldn't help himself. He liked food and perfected smash-and-grabs off the kitchen counter.

But he was friendly, in a big dog kind of way. He'd greet me at the door with a bounding body block. Like all big dogs, he needed big pets. You could almost thump him with affection. And he was a good companion on long walks through the desert — all in winter.

Homer's gone now, as are the other big dogs we had in the family. So's Twinkie. But she's been replaced by other little dogs. A bichon frisé rescue dog and two Shih Tzus. The Shih Tzus were strays we picked up.

They had no IDs. We got them vaccinated, fixed and tagged. The male, Benji, is a true lap dog. My first. He's a natural at it. If you give him a pet, he looks up at you with big puppy-dog eyes. They seem to be saying: "Don't stop."

The little dogs are friendly. They like walks, too, though I don't go five miles through the desert with them. Just like big dogs, they're always glad to see you — however bad your day. And they don't eat much, when they eat at all. They can be picky. Cleanup doesn't require a real big shovel.

Before Twinkie, I'd have to say, I wasn't a little-dog person. Now I see the good in most dogs, big and small.

And, as you read this, there are big and small dogs, at this very moment, just waiting for a good home. You'll find them at Casa Grande's Animal Care and Adoption Center.

I got a look at some of the shelter's big and small dog offerings on Thursday, thanks to shelter Supervisor Linda Garcia. The shelter doesn't discriminate, she said.

"We have every shape and size," Garcia said.

They have Chihuahuas small enough to fit in a big pocket, though putting one there is probably not a good idea.

On the other hand, Garcia said, "The biggest dog we had in the shelter ... was a 198-pound English mastiff."

Coco is currently the resident big dog. OK, not huge, maybe

some 60 pounds, but big enough. She has medium-longish white hair and a golden muzzle, along with a greyhound-like build. And, a quality I like in a dog, floppy ears.

She's adorable and adoptable.

Well, so are Flutter and Echi. They're in the super flyweight division.

Kennel assistant Julie Tiemann brought them into the lobby. Both Chihuahuas, they showed a lot of versatility. They're more than lap dogs. They're good shoulder dogs. If you're torn between adopting a dog or a parrot, Echi would be a good choice.

The shelter would love to find homes for all their dogs — big, medium and small.

So if you're looking, they'll find your size.

Search Party for Alice

July 11, 2014

The runaway dog had everybody out looking for her. An artist, a letter carrier, Dispatch front office workers and downtown Food City employees. Maybe some others I didn't know about. They drove around looking for the dog. They put the dog's picture on Facebook.

Somebody even offered a reward.

"Everybody knows Alice," Nancy Davids said. She's the letter carrier.

Alice, in turn, knows everybody. She knows all the stops good for a handout. She'll park herself outside the door until she gets her treat.

She's a regular at the Dispatch, where Davids delivers the mail. Workers at a chemical plant greet Alice with snacks. Bob Foughty, a retiree, keeps a bag of treats at the ready. He's a friend of the artist, Campbell Auer.

Everybody knows Alice. But nobody knew Alice like Dan Elliott.

Alice was his best friend. They went everywhere together.

They were easy to spot. Alice was medium-sized with a strength to match her friendliness. Elliott used a thick rope for a leash. Elliott is 60 and doesn't get around like he used to. His knees bother him. He had arthroscopic surgery at the Southern Arizona VA Health Care System hospital in Tucson. He had no complaints about the service.

I wrote about Alice and Elliott in February. Elliott had Alice since she was a puppy. Where he went, she went. Alice seemed to be his connection to the world.

He lost that connection on the Fourth of July, last Friday. Elliott was getting ready to take Alice for an evening walk. They shared a mobile home south of downtown. Except for Alice, Elliott lived alone.

"She just went out the door," Elliott said. "I was about to put the leash on. And one of those sparklers went off. And she ran. I thought I'd never see her again."

The sparkler actually was a small rocket fired a few blocks away. It burst in the air with a bang. Alice freaked and ran into the night.

It's no secret. Lots of dogs go missing on the Fourth, said Mary Dill, a Casa Grande animal control officer.

"We had a bunch of calls throughout the weekend," Dill said. "I believe we had at least 15."

Dogs went missing. And dogs were found, some far from home.

"They can run so far away because they're scared," Dill said.

When Alice ran, Elliott hopped on his bicycle, bad knees and all. He called out for Alice. He stopped and asked people if they had seen her.

"I talked to the trash collectors," Elliott said. And four or five policemen, he added.

Alice was nowhere to be found.

Elliott ended up at Auer's house on the west side, near the railroad tracks. Elliott and Alice were frequent guests. This time

Elliott was alone.

"Where's Alice?" Auer asked. Elliott replied, "She's gone."

On Saturday, Elliott and Auer set out to look for Alice. They took Auer's pickup.

Auer was part of a network best described as Friends of Alice. It wasn't just about the dog. The Friends of Alice knew what Alice meant to Elliott.

Auer and Elliott stopped by the Dispatch office.

Beth Woodward was Alice's go-to source for Second Street treats. She put Alice's picture on her Facebook page and helped prepare a lost-dog classified ad. After work, Woodward and receptionist Bonnie Green drove around in search of Alice.

Facebook became a social-network milk carton. Woodward, Davids the letter carrier and even somebody from Food City — all posted pictures of Alice. Food City was where Alice got her dog food.

Auer and Elliott continued the hunt. They hit the dog shelters. They stopped a number of times at Casa Grande Animal Control. Nobody had seen Alice, Dill said, though everybody knows her.

She visited the shelter often.

"If she sees our front door open, she'll run in," Dill said. "We'll give her treats."

Alice was welcome anytime. She had her city tag. She was up on her shots. And Elliott would be right there with her. He lives across the street.

Dill and the other animal control officers belonged to the network, Friends of Alice. They'd watch for her.

On Sunday, Auer and Elliott drove out to the Valley Humane Society shelter off South Trekell Road. Early Monday, they stopped by the Pinal County Animal Care and Control shelter at Eleven Mile Corner. No Alice here. No Alice there.

Each time, Elliott left with less hope than he had going in. And he didn't have much to begin with. He was in tears.

Then late Monday morning, Rex rolled into the parking lot behind the city shelter. Rex is a person, but Dill didn't get his last name.

He wanted to drop off a dog, Dill said.

"I happen to look in his van. I said, 'That's Alice.'"

Maybe she said it with an exclamation mark.

"I put a leash on him," she added, "and walked through the back door and out the front door, and ran her back to Dan's."

It turns out Rex had Alice all along. He spotted her in a lot next to Powell Feed & Supply, about a half mile from Elliott's home. She had been loose less than an hour. Rex gave Alice shelter through the weekend.

Rex probably doesn't know it. But he's now a member of the Friends of Alice.

She'll be around for her treat anytime now.

Patience for a Dog
That Had It Rough

January 16, 2015

Parents are diplomatic when asked to name their favorite child. They're all favorites.

We have one child, and she's definitely our favorite.

Dogs are different. They come and go out of our lives. We fondly remember our favorites. For me, it was a deaf Old English sheepdog. His name was Homer. We got him free from a reputable breeder. She wanted a good home for a puppy whose world didn't include sounds.

He learned sign language. Waving your hands up and down, palms down, meant sit or lie down. Wagging your finger. Bad dog. Clapping your hands. Good dog.

He took those to heart. Clap your hands and Homer wagged the little stump he was left with. Sheepdog tails are docked. It's customary, though I don't see the need for it.

What he lacked in hearing, he made up for in appetite. He loved to eat. As I set down his bowl, he'd spin around. He'd drool. It would fly out in a centrifugal spiral. A pinwheel of slobber. But whatever we fed him, it was never enough. He'd go for dinner plates left on the kitchen counter. He'd wait for his moment, when no one was around. Then you'd hear the sound of three plates breaking.

He got a severe finger wagging for that.

My wife, Cindy, would shout: "He's a beast!"

Her favorite, just the same.

We lost him a few years ago. He had cancer.

I bring up Homer to talk about Mindy. She is — to put it tactfully — the dog equivalent of least favored nation. We love her. It's just that we've really had to work at it.

She came with issues. They weren't her fault. Mindy was likely a breeder in a puppy mill, churning out more copies of herself, bichon frises. She probably got no more affection than a chicken in an egg factory. And when her puppy-making days were over, she was turned out on the street.

She ended up in the shelter at Maricopa County Animal Control. A poodle rescue group claimed her and found her a foster home in Tucson.

At that time, Cindy and I had said a final goodbye to Twinkie. She was a little dog, light as a feather. She had strayed into the road and was hit by a car. Not mine, I should add. I picked her up off the pavement. I felt a heartbeat. She had no ID. No one in the neighborhood claimed her. We got her patched up and took her home.

She was already old, but she hung in there for another five years or so.

When we lost her, we looked for a replacement. That was probably a mistake. Dogs can't be replaced like goldfish. They're all different.

I'm not sure how Cindy, my wife, found out about Mindy. Maybe online. Maybe newspaper classifieds.

We spoke to somebody in the poodle rescue group. They gave us the number of the Tucson foster home. But we were cautioned. The dog was uncomfortable around people.

Cindy and I live in south Phoenix. We agreed to pick up Mindy about halfway. We met the foster mom at the outlet mall, now CityGate. She handed over Mindy. The dog wasn't as light as a feather like Twinkie. She was a bit dumpy. She had a large sagging mid-section. It was all those puppies she had to make.

The foster mom said Mindy was shy. She never came out of the bedroom closet.

When we got her home, she ran and hid. She was never aggressive but always scared. It took her at least a year before she let us show some affection. She still doesn't wag her tail.

If guests showed up, she'd stand in the corner and bark, incessantly.

She was sort of housebroken, sort of not. She probably spent most of her life in a cage or pen. I don't think she understood that indoors was different than outdoors.

And she wasn't an easy dog to walk. More like dragging a stone. She'd take five minutes to reach the end of the driveway.

We've had Mindy now for about eight years. She's part of the family. She sleeps on the bed, maybe half the time. It's up to her. She greets me at the door with the two Shih Tzus. They bounce around with excitement. She stands there like a statue, but at least she shows up.

Her reflexes, though, are geared to past abuse. If you brush her from behind, she freaks and bolts. In her puppy-mill days, people probably just kicked her out of the way.

Mindy was middle-aged when we got her. She's a senior citizen now. She's pretty much blind and deaf. Never fast to begin with, she now shuffles about like a slow-crawling crustacean.

Poor Mindy. We gave her what she needed, though. Love, patience — sometimes strained — and understanding.

And she still outranks the cat.

Road Trip Becomes
Detour for Lost Dog

March 28, 2016

Benji went in for his booster shots recently. Rabies and some other vaccines. I asked the desk clerk at the veterinary clinic about his first visit.

She thumbed through his file. It was February 2010, she said.

So we've had Benji for six years. It seems like just yesterday we picked him up as a stray. My wife and I were headed down a busy Phoenix street. We were out for a Sunday drive, en route to Tucson.

We spotted a small furry dog, his coat a panda pattern of black and white. Shih Tzu in type. This was Benji, a name he'd come by later.

Over the years, I've passed up countless strays. They trot along the sidewalk. They dart in and out of traffic. I put on my blinders and keep driving. If I picked up every stray on the road, I'd need my own island to house them.

The few times I did stop, dogs would panic and run. Benji, on the other hand, simply stood in the crosswalk. He wasn't scared or shaking. It seems his plan was just to wait there until somebody offered him a ride.

That turned out to be Benji's way. Take life as it comes, even on trips to the veterinarian.

Our other dogs seemed to regard the veterinary clinic as a house of horrors. They shivered in the lobby. They quivered in the exam room. They dreaded whatever was in store for them. They weren't keen on the specifics. But they knew it was bad.

Benji? Our latest trip to the vet told a different story. After I put him on the exam table, he stood there like he expected nothing more than a scratch behind the ear. The vet, in fact, gave him a pat — and a shot. He took Benji's temperature, the old-fashioned way.

The dog took it all in stride.

"Is he always this calm?" the vet asked.

"Yeah," I said.

"I wish they were all like this," he replied.

I didn't tell the vet that Benji has his moments. At home, he can be touchy, at least when it comes to food. He patrols his bowl. It's like a sovereign state. If the cat crosses the border, Benji snarls and gives chase. Then he returns to the bowl. He usually pushes around a few leftover crunchies with his nose. Maybe he counts them, makes sure they're all there.

When we first saw Benji, we had just pulled up to a red light. He was in the far crosswalk. He stood there a moment, then trotted to the other side, if only to follow a man walking a dog. Benji kept pace with them, like he was part of the walk, too.

He had a plan, it seems. He'd just follow the guy all the way home and through the front door.

We turned up the street. We followed the dog following the guy walking his own dog.

The guy turned around and shooed away Benji, who turned and sauntered off. We drove alongside. He went back across the busy street. Unscathed somehow.

He was one lucky dog.

We caught up to him in a parking lot. Cindy opened her door. Benji jumped on her lap and began licking her.

He was, it turned out, our first lap dog. It was something I had to get used to. Until Benji, our dogs were the type to lie at your feet. Too big for laps. For Benji, though, a lap is like oxygen. Something he has to have, especially if it's parked in front of the TV.

He's gained a bit of weight since we first took him in. So now he's a lap dog with the body of a seal pup.

The name Benji was far from original. But it seemed to fit a little dog lost.

So he settled in with our other two dogs, since passed on. A golden retriever, of sorts. And a bichon frise. Three wasn't a crowd

168

but it was a good place to stop. Four dogs? In Casa Grande, it's the limit. Five's a citation. For me, in south Phoenix, four was one dog too many.

So I was content.

Perhaps a year later, Cindy came home from shopping. She had a dog with her. A small black dog of the Shih Tzu variety. She picked the dog up at Safeway. The dog had spent two or three days there, begging for scraps.

"Big mistake," I told Cindy. "You should have driven it straight to the pound. But, no, you had to bring it inside. Now, we have to keep it."

So Maggie became lap dog No. 2.

She's what you call a people dog, like Benji. They greet all with affection — tail wags and the like. Other dogs are another matter, especially on walks. They don't bother Benji. Maggie, on the other hand, strains to get to them.

She goes all mental, as the Brits might say.

There's only one dog she's ever really taken to. That's Benji. From Day 1, they became best of friends.

Benji's cool with that, as long as Maggie doesn't forget: He's still lap dog No. 1.

Dogs Earn Their Wings
Flying Sardine Class

October 24, 2016

We did the drill a half dozen times, perhaps more. I'd set down the soft-bodied pet carriers. They were bigger than a breadbox, but not by much.

The two dogs watched. They knew the drill.

"Airplane ride!" I'd shout. Then: "What fun!"

The dogs remained unconvinced. Still, I placed each one through an opening in the carriers. And zipped them up. I placed the carriers under a chair and pretended to be the captain.

"We'll be cruising at altitude of 28,000 feet, which is a good altitude, unless we encounter Mount Everest. So buckle up and enjoy the flight. And remember, only one peanut per passenger."

Then I'd make noises like the airplane taking off and flying. And landing. Five minutes later we were on the ground and headed for the gate.

That fell a bit short of the five-plus hours they actually spent on the airplane. But I wanted them to get a feel for air travel, so they could join my wife and me on a New England vacation.

The cat would stay behind and guard the litter box. My sister would check in on her. We would be in western Massachusetts visiting our daughter.

It was our first time flying with pets. Most airlines welcome dogs. Big dogs have to go in the cargo hold. Little dogs can go as carry-on luggage, as long they fit under the seat.

Some 2 million animals fly every year, the U.S. Department of Transportation says. The figure includes pets and maybe a few goats. I can't say for sure.

The federal government has some rules. Things like how many hours an animal can be cooped up. And how many fleas each pet is allowed. (I made that one up.) Airlines have their own rules as well. Things like how big a dog is allowed in the cabin. Usually it's 16 pounds or less. They have to fit in a carrier that fits under the seat.

I checked the blogs. People had stories about dogs escaping. Dogs running loose on the airplane. Well, I had my doubts about that. Airplanes are engineered to suppress the free movement of anything larger than a microbe.

Perhaps things were different in some golden age of air travel. Perhaps the flight crew even invited dogs to join them in the cockpit. I could see Benji, my Shih Tzu, seated on the captain's lap. The captain would let him fly the plane.

"All right, Benji, take us to Philadelphia." And with that, Benji would bite the captain on the arm. Benji would not want to go to

Philadelphia.

In truth, Benji rode coach, as did Maggie. First they had to clear security at Sky Harbor, just like everybody else. We carried the dogs through the metal detector. I took Benji. Cindy, my wife, had Maggie.

They went through with nary a beep. And they didn't escape and run amok. I could only imagine the PA announcement: "Whoever lost their dog please report to security for shaming and ridicule."

Cleared for takeoff, we placed the pups back in the carrier. "Airplane ride!" I said. "What fun!" It was seven hours of fun. That included a short hop to Las Vegas, a transfer and a long haul to Hartford, Connecticut. Bradley International is the closest airport to western Massachusetts.

The dogs stayed at our feet, under the seat in front. They were unable to get up, stretch and move about for the entire flight. They had it almost as bad as the people.

Personally, I only had to endure hours of severe pain in my left knee. I couldn't extend my leg, blocked – in part – by Benji's carrier. It was a small price to pay for a buffet of salty snacks.

Our daughter, Sarah, picked us up at the airport. We were all relieved to walk the planet like normal people.

I shouldn't complain too much. We made better time than Lewis and Clark. And it became one of our favorite vacations. Sarah and her friend Kinsey were our guides. Here are a few highlights. We spent a night at a dog friendly bed and breakfast in Danby, Vermont. The house was built by a lumber baron in the 19th century. I think it still had the original paint.

The next day we hiked part of the Appalachian Trail, a short drive from the bed and breakfast. It was like a picture out of a travel log. Tall trees in every shade of fall.

Two days later, we picked apples from a New England apple orchard. Acres of trees lined grassy fields. The dogs weren't too interested in the apples, but they enjoyed the walk.

The apples, I should add, were excellent—something to write home about. Of course, I didn't bother. The cat can't read.

The week went by in a blur. It was time to go back. We settled into the sardine can and headed home.

The dogs returned a bit wiser. Now they know "Airplane ride!" does not mean "What fun!"

Chillin' with Dogs
In the Arizona Heat

August 4, 2018

I take the two Shih Tzus for walks around 7:30 or 8 a.m. It's no walk in the park. OK, it is a walk in the park. But it's a very warm walk.

By 8, it's already 90 degrees. I happen to live in what must be North America's largest heat island. Phoenix. On July 6, the low was 94 degrees. It was a record high for a low on that date.

If I had a time machine, I'd go back and tell Dante about it. He'd invent a new circle. One where hell is right outside your front door.

OK, not that bad. Casa Grande certainly isn't. The lows here have been in the low 80s of late. Better than the sauna I enter every morning.

And it probably pays to go out early.

Ed Van Blaricum and Saydey, his 10-year-old Shetland sheepdog, head to Dave White Regional Park at 6. They get in a mile every morning, Van Blaricum wrote in an email.

Up with the sun. That's the coolest part of the day.

But even in Casa Grande, the nights used to be more pleasant. Sometimes you'd even feel a chill. Let's take July. It is the hottest month. The last record low for any given date in July was in 2004. It was 57 degrees. Sounds chilly. You'd need a light sweater. Saydey would feel right at home in her Shetland fur.

Here are a few more numbers. I got them from the website Intellicast. In 1912, Casa Grande had 12 days with record lows for

July. They ranged from 63 on July 20 to 52 on July 24. That really was Christmas in July.

In Phoenix, the last record low for any July date was in 1955. Let's face it. The planet's getting warmer, and Phoenix is leading the way. Casa Grande's not far behind.

And it's not exactly a dry heat. The monsoons add a dose of tropical humidity.

We prep the Shih Tzus with summer cuts. And they go out early enough to avoid burning their paws. Asphalt can reach 140 degrees by afternoon. Ouch.

Still, a minute into a walk and they're panting. It's especially true for the senior dog, Benji. Our best guess on Benji is 13, 14 years old. Maggie is, oh, 6 or 7. She certainly has more spring in her step. But even Maggie starts to slow after 10 minutes or so.

Shade offers some relief. Dave White has shade trees around the lake. I suppose there could always be more. In Phoenix, shade is the talk of the town. There's a shade master plan. And a tree and shade subcommittee.

Rio Salado Park is a few miles from my house. It's shady. Overhanging branches from cottonwood trees cover part of a trail. The leaves are big and unruly. They make excellent shade. One trail below them runs a few hundred feet, if that. It leads to a little babbling brook, fed by a pump atop a small rise.

A fallen cottonwood trunk rests by the bank. I'll sometimes take a seat. And I'll sometimes drop the leashes. Maggie stays with me. Benji, the old-timer, just kind of wanders off. There's a perimeter of stones about 20 feet away. When Benji reaches them, I grab his leash and we're on our way.

It's a nice little nook. It's like being in the woods. It's quiet. The water is calming. Some people find it a nice place to sleep. I don't know them. They sometimes leave their laundry out to dry. Washed in the creek, no doubt. And they leave their trash. The city does a pretty good job of cleaning it up every few days.

If I see somebody's gear, I just turn the dogs around. We don't socialize.

City park rangers patrol the area. But it's probably a cat-and-mouse game. Rio Salado Park takes in miles of the Salt River (such as it is). And urban rivers have long been a haven for the homeless.

I have a lot of sympathy for them. And they're welcome to enjoy a public park as much as the next guy. But maybe they could pick up after themselves.

A traditional city park is within a mile of our house. I drive there. I call it the grassy park. A walkway winds around the park's perimeter. There are trees. Some provide shade. There are some palm trees. Very stately but poor shade. Some eucalyptus trees here and there. Very tall but not much canopy.

The walkway passes beneath a few shady mesquite trees. Otherwise, it's largely shade-free. The dogs love it just the same. The lamp posts are especially worth checking out.

It's about a 20-minute walk at most. By the time we get back to the car, the pups are panting like they just finished a marathon in sweats.

I load them into the back of the Prius. It's in dog mode, with the backseats down.

"Time for AC," I tell them.

Maggie knows. She plants herself in front of the vent. It's better than a walk in the park. It's the ride home.

My Dogs Will Eat Garbage, But Settle For Dog Food
March 3, 2018

The two Shih Tzus have different tastes in dog food. The girl, Maggie, approaches it like a hung jury. She's never sure if this day's offering is up to her standards.

Her standards are high. Did I top the crunchies with freshly roasted chicken? Or did I just toss in some old burger?

The boy, Benji, likes dog food. Every day in almost every way. As I approach with his bowl, he dances in circles. And barks. It's a little dog bark, with a hint of tenor. Kind of a low-frequency yap.

By the time I set down his bowl, he's nearly out of breath. But he can't bother with oxygen. He inhales his food instead.

But of all the dogs I've had, Benji still takes second in feeding frenzy. The gold medal would go to Homer, the deaf Old English sheepdog. He did circles. He barked, a true tenor. Almost a bass. He also let loose a stream of drool that spiraled out from his pivot point.

We had two or three other dogs during Homer's time on earth. He wasn't big on boundaries. He'd finish his meal well before the others. Then, if he could, he'd push them aside and start on theirs.

We began to feed Homer in a separate room. We made one exception. Sammy ate with Homer. Sammy was an undersized golden retriever. But she fought above her weight. She was a street brawler. Homer left her — and her food — alone.

Over the years, dog food has evolved. Before my time, I imagine dogs got the kitchen scraps. The first dog I remember is a reddish English-Irish setter named Rusty.

We had Rusty when I was still in grade school. We fed him dog food from a can. You'd open up a can and plop the contents into a bowl. Rusty liked it.

Years and numerous dogs later, I began to shop around for higher-end brands. The first specialty dog foods were sold by veterinarians. Then along came PetSmart and other stores that offered selections that took up aisle after aisle.

I began shopping there. I browsed among packages that had pictures of wolves. I don't remember the main ingredient. I think it was something a wolf might hunt down, like a slow buffalo.

If your dog wasn't into big game, not a problem. The shelves were stacked with lamb dog food. The packages pictured dogs big and little, all apparently happy to be eating lamb.

Humanely harvested from cuddly little lambs.

Chicken was big, too. Beef seemed to come in a distant third. Some dog foods were even vegetarian. Some set themselves apart by what they didn't have. No corn! No byproducts! (Like chicken

175

beaks, I'm guessing.) No gluten!

But not one said, "Made with real garbage!" It would be a sure bestseller. I've never known a dog that, if given a chance, wouldn't dive into a bucket of garbage.

At the pet store, the large variety made for some intense browsing. I liked browsing. But more often than not I was stopped by a wise old dog food expert. He or she would help me choose. What am I looking for? They'd recommend brands. They'd offer tips.

One kindly woman said if my dog's a picky eater, top his food with broccoli — or something like it. Broccoli? I couldn't force-feed my dog broccoli.

I suppose the dog food whisperers meant well. But I tried to avoid them, usually without success. I found them annoying. I stopped going to the pet food palace.

I turned to Amazon and bought dog food online. Apparently, I wasn't alone. Millions of others were too bothered to drive 3 miles for doggy lamb. By 2017, Amazon had cornered more than half the online market. So said Petfood Industry.com.

No surprise there.

But ordering from Amazon had its downside. The Shih Tzus don't eat much. So I ordered the small 2.7-pound bag. Each bag came in a cardboard box. And each box had to be broken down and set out for recycling.

It seemed a waste. Maybe Amazon or its retail partners will figure out a way to deliver dog food in a container you can send back. It could be cleaned out and reused. It worked that way for the milkman.

Yes, I'm old enough to remember the milkman. I don't think I actually saw him, though. You just put out the empties. And the next morning, you took in bottles of fresh milk.

For now, I'm back to buying dry food off the rack at the supermarket. I get the small package with a little white dog on the front. It says: "The first ingredient is beef!" It doesn't brag about the rest of the ingredients.

I also get what's advertised as gourmet food. It comes in little plastic containers. It's kind of gloppy looking. The dogs seem to like it.

Still, it's not garbage.

Two Dogs from the Street, Now at Rest
February 2, 2020

We buried Benji Thursday before last. He's near Twinkie, beneath the cover of an old palo verde.

The two dogs never met. They led separate lives under one roof. They share something of an origin story, though.

We claimed them both from the streets of Phoenix. Strays. Twinkie shuffling across the road until a car knocked her down. Benji standing in a crosswalk, waiting for somebody to pull over and take him home.

I happened on Twinkie in the mid-1990s. It was morning. I was driving to work on a two-lane blacktop. The road, at the time, had little traffic. A little white dog sauntered out in front of me. I slowed, let her pass.

She was hit by a large station wagon headed the other direction. In my rearview mirror, I saw her come tumbling out from under the car. I pictured the next passing car making a mess of her.

I turned around and pulled off on a gravel shoulder. My plan: Move the dog off the road. Sure, dead was dead. But I'd spare her the indignity of looking like bad road kill.

I picked her up and felt a heartbeat. She had no tags. I took her to the vet. He patched her up. She became family. She was small, so we named her Twinkie. She was already 8 to 10 years old. She lived another five.

Twinkie was a gentle dog, shuffling around the house. Just as she shuffled onto a two-lane blacktop.

She wouldn't stand a chance nowadays. Housing developments now line that same road. Traffic is steady. Heavy at rush hour, sometimes bumper to bumper.

Benji apparently didn't get the memo. Stay off the busy streets. At least, he had the good sense not to wander onto Southern Avenue in Phoenix at rush hour. He chose a Sunday morning instead, 10 years ago this month.

My wife, Cindy, and I were stopped at a light. We saw him standing in the crosswalk, across the intersection. I think he was auditioning for a new home. "Hey, check me out. I'm a good boy."

No takers, so he wandered off.

We followed him to a parking lot. Cindy opened the car door. He jumped in and began licking her. Just like that, he had a new home. His breeding was something on the order of a Shih Tzu. He came with hair mats, ticks and a full set of puppy-makers. A vet removed the puppy-makers. The groomer removed the mats. We dealt with the ticks.

We named him Benji. Not all that original, but it seemed to fit.

Benji had a heart condition. It didn't appear to bother him much, until later last year. He began to slow down. He'd have trouble keeping up on walks. I wrote about it, and a couple of readers suggested I get a stroller. A baby buggy for dogs.

I wrote back, thanking them for the suggestion. I told Cindy what the readers advised. She said: "Order the stroller."

I ordered the stroller. Benji took to it like a fish in water. It was just his size. He'd sit up and gaze over the edge as Maggie walked alongside. Maggie's also something on the order of a Shih Tzu.

Hoisting Benji in and out of his stroller was always a bit tricky. What he lacked in size, he made up for in density. Sort of the neutron star of dogs. And his center of gravity was off center. You had to hold up his back end, to keep from losing him.

But I managed, until I broke my left wrist, two days before Christmas. Spiral fracture of the ulna. I didn't know my ulna from my funny bone before I read the ER report.

Anyway, getting Benji in the baby buggy was a real pain, until our daughter came to the rescue. Sarah flew in from Massachusetts on Christmas Eve. She had a break from her graduate coursework.

We teamed up for dog walks. Sarah helped with the heavy lifting. That would be Benji. She pushed the buggy as he sat up and took in the scenery. I walked Maggie.

Sarah also gave Stitch, our aging cat, much needed attention.

She returned to her studies the second week in January. I handled Benji on my own. Once again, I managed, though Cindy helped. Benji got his buggy walks.

But he was in decline. He no longer sat up in the buggy. He lay on his stomach, staring out through a mesh window.

We had him on heart medicines. They helped for a while. They weren't a cure, however. He stopped eating, then drinking. Then he couldn't get off the floor. Maybe it sounds corny, but the shine had left his eyes.

It was time. Afterward, Cindy and I reminisced about Benji. And what a good boy he was.

Four Paws on Four Wheels
October 19, 2020

I usually take Maggie for a late-afternoon stroll. In a stroller. She can walk on her own, but she's taken to the stroller.

I'll be reading. Shortly before 6 o'clock, she parks herself in front of me. I feel something's up. I lower the book and see a dog staring at me. It's not a sad puppy look. It's not a plea. It's an assertion.

"Time for my scooter walk."

I've taken to calling the stroller a scooter. Don't know why. Scooter sounds more fun, I guess.

I admire her assertiveness. I'm somewhat passive-aggressive myself. I mumble something and get mad when my wife tells me to speak up. I mumble louder. Like Maggie, Cindy's assertive. So's my daughter. I'm surrounded by assertive women. It keeps me from having to overthink things.

Back to the dog. Maggie is mostly Shih Tzu. Cindy picked up her at the local Safeway, some years back. The dog had been running in and out of the store, days on end. The manager handed her over to Cindy.

The year before, we picked up Benji, another dog of Shih Tzu bearing. He was wandering the streets of Phoenix.

Later in life, he developed a heart condition. He had trouble keeping up on walks. I wrote about it. A couple of readers suggested a dog stroller. I thought about it, then ordered one.

It worked great. Benji would sit quietly as the world slowly rolled by. Maggie would walk alongside. She learned to stay wide of the scooter, after a few close calls.

Benji died in January. I folded up the scooter and put it in a nook next to the piano. Why we have a piano is another story. Nobody in our house has a clue how it works.

I continued to take Maggie on walks. We went to the park in the morning. And around the block in late afternoon. As the days warmed to toaster-oven levels, we cut back on the afternoon walks. The asphalt was too hot for little Shih Tzu paws.

The dog, however, expected walks. She let me know it. She has that look down pat.

So I pulled out the scooter. And set her inside and off we went. She took to it like Benji.

They did differ a bit in style points. Benji took on the air of dictator of a small country. He'd look straight ahead with the bearing of somebody important. He'd welcome the greetings of his adoring subjects. "What a nice dog!"

Maggie, on the other hand, is always on the lookout. This way. That way. She watches for people. She likes people. She watches for dogs. Dogs upset her. She watches for Richard. Sometimes he'll be in his garage. He'll come out to say: "How ya doin', doggie?"

She'll wag her tail and bark. And bark. And bark. She likes attention.

Two houses down is a man with daughters. One of them always seems to be washing a car. One day he saw me pushing the stroller.

He shouted, "Congratulations!" He thought I was a new grandfather. When I got close, he looked in.

I'm not sure he liked what he saw. A dog or an extremely hairy baby.

Deandre is a whole different story. He likes Maggie. He lives around the next corner. Sometimes he's out playing on the driveway. He's maybe 9 or 10. He first met Maggie when I took her for walks with Benji, a year or two ago. Before Benji became scooter-bound.

Benji and Maggie made a good team. Benji would nonchalantly approach Deandre, as if to say, "Pet me." Maggie took this as her cue. She'd put her little paws on Deandre as if to say, "Me too!"

Benji gave her courage. Now, without him, she seems a bit more shy. More cautious. At least with people outside the home. She holds back a little. Benji's not there to assure her it's all OK.

I've read that dogs can mourn loss. I think there's something to that. I know Maggie misses Benji. There is a silver lining. Maggie now gets all our attention. And she has a laser-like focus on the here and now.

And so, late afternoon, she lets me know. It's time. I make it official. I announce: "Scooter walk!"

I unfold the scooter. Maggie runs right past it, for the door. I call her back. She runs up to me. She stops. And rotates like a train car on a turntable, so I can pick her up.

I put her in the scooter, open the front door and we're on our way.

Three turns later, we're back on our street. C.M. lives on it. One time, as we strolled by, he pulled into his garage. I paused to tell him I was walking the dog, in her scooter.

"She's spoiled," he said.

I smiled. If only I had thought to say: "We're doing our best."

Dictionary for Well-Heeled Dogs
November 15, 2021

My nephew Ryan and his wife Aga are getting a new puppy. A golden retriever. They live in Chicago. They found a good breeder in Utah. They recommended the breeder to Cathy and Joe, my sister and her husband in Maricopa.

Cathy and Joe had golden retrievers before. Ginger, then Portia. In time, the dogs died, as dogs do. It's always a painful loss. Cathy and Joe didn't have plans to replace them.

That is, until Ryan and Aga told them about the special breeder, with the special golden retrievers.

So Joe and Cathy reached out. The breeder asked Joe what he and Cathy would like in a dog. A girl, he said. And a dog with a big vocabulary.

Their previous dogs were friendly and well-behaved. They also had big vocabularies. They knew sit, stay and many other words. Many more words than your average dog. Graduate-level canine lexicon.

Their new puppy doesn't have to know all the words. Somewhere between a junkyard dog and Chaser the border collie.

Chaser was a girl. She had a 1,000-word vocabulary. She was tutored by John Pilley, a retired psychology professor in South Carolina. He had taught at Wofford College, a good name for anything involving dogs.

Chaser learned to fetch any one of 1,000-plus toys, balls and Frisbees. Each by its own name. (Yes, each Frisbee had a different name.)

Pilley published his findings in 2013. The New York Times later wrote: "…Chaser was taught to understand sentences containing a prepositional object, verb and direct object."

That's more than I know.

The quote came from Chaser's obituary. She died in July 2019. She lived to 15, a good run for any dog.

Pilley died the year before. His wife Sally and daughter Robin cared for Chaser in her final year.

I'm sure Chaser missed Pilley. I'm sure she was sad. Maybe she even understood the word "sad."

I believe Maggie does. She's my dog, a Shih Tzu mix. It so happens she's a very good girl. She definitely understands that, if you say it right. Something like this: "Maggie is a good girl!" — with the emphasis on good.

She wasn't formally trained. She's like the dog who dropped out of high school and went on to become a self-taught genius. OK, a bit of hype on the genius angle, but to my wife Cindy and me, Maggie's a "smart little cookie."

Her vocabulary is not standard doggerel. Sit is a suggestion, not a command. Stay works if there's something not worth chasing. And "no bark" doesn't work if she spots another dog within 20 feet. Then we just pick her up and point her in another direction. Easy enough. Maggie weighs 9 pounds.

Homer, our Old English sheepdog, had a different issue. He was deaf from birth. We got him as a special needs case. You could yell "sit" all you want. Homer would stand there and drool. But he knew a sign language. Simple gestures. Some we made up. Some we got from a magazine.

A wave toward us, palms up, meant come. A one-hand wave downward meant sit. Two hands waving emphatically downward meant lie down. A finger wag meant bad dog. Homer could be a handful.

A handclap meant good boy. He got a lot of applause.

One thing you couldn't do, if he took off, was call him back. He did that once. He gave chase to a coyote. We found him around the block, staring down the coyote. He got a good finger wagging for that.

Homer died some years back. He had cancer.

Maggie used to take off down the street when she was a puppy. She stays put now, except for walks. And her buggy trips around the block. It's a baby buggy just for dogs. We usually go by Richard's house. If he's out and about, he'll drop whatever he's doing and give her a treat.

Maggie loves that. She lets out a happy bark. But if Richard's not around. I'll say: "Richard's not home. It's sad. Very sad."

So now she knows sad.

Here are a few other entries in Maggie's dictionary.

Walkies: Any outdoor venture involving a leash. She hears that word and she runs around. It's a dog's way of saying: "Let's do this!"

Jiggly tags: Connoting the noise dog tags make when I put her collar on, as in "jiggly tags!" This is often a substitute for "walkies!"

Food: As in, "Does Maggie want food?" She wags her tail at that. She likes the attention shown by the service — even if she sometimes snubs the actual food.

Scooter walk: A walkie in her dog buggy.

Lifties: Whereupon she gets lifted up to a bed or a couch. She'll rotate in place to get into position.

Down-de-down: Lifting her off the bed or couch. She wags her tail for this one. Another signal for "Let's do this!"

A tail wag is one way to make a point. The imploring look is another. Say Maggie has to powder her nose, she approaches with an expectant gaze. You reply: "Does Maggie want to go out?" She runs for the door, signaling "yes, yes, yes!"

If she wants a lap sit, she'll park herself at your feet. And stare. It's not talking. It's mental telepathy.

I get the message. After all, she is a good girl.

LOOSE
ENDS

'It Might Be Like This'

Lincoln Star (1955)

A House Divided
On TV and Dinner

July 26, 2013

I share a common bond with many cable TV subscribers. We open our cable bills. Our first thought is, "That's it. I'm cutting cable."

Actually, that's the second thought. I can't print the first.

When people want to trim expenses, they usually start with cable. They talk about cutting cable TV as if they're going to take to the streets with large industrial cable cutters.

The reality is not so dramatic. Cutting cable comes down to returning a box and a channel changer, and perhaps engaging in a bit of tug-of-war with the clerk before finally letting go.

Anyway, I am weak-willed. Many times I've told my wife, Cindy: "We have to cut cable."

She calls my bluff. "If you want. Sure."

And it could be she's bluffing, too. The old double bluff. She works hard, and when she's home, she likes to relax in front of the TV. She knits and watches Hallmark-channel movies. The plots are all the same. After a big misunderstanding and many tissues later, the guy and girl finally get together for a happy Hallmark ending. You don't get that kind of entertainment on Fox.

Surely, my spouse wouldn't want to give that up.

But she can afford to bluff because she can read me like a book. She knows I have a jones for Jeopardy. And that without cable and DVR, Jeopardy in real time would be one commercial after another, most aimed at old people in need of pain relief. And then there's baseball. If there's no cable, there's no nightly baseball.

189

So for me, TV and cable have become necessary evils. My wife, on the other hand, likes TV. She watches without shame. She's smart and she reads a lot, but she likes TV.

Our differences go to our upbringing. My wife's father, when she was little, unplugged their television and tossed it. She grew up without a TV.

She became popular in school. She made good grades. She took pity on those less fortunate and ended up with me. When she became an adult, she got a television. And watched and watched and watched. She would never again suffer the deprivation she experienced as a child.

In my case, we were a TV family — all through the '50s and '60s. TV trays and Swanson's TV dinners. That was us.

I was not popular. My grades were adequate. I couldn't dribble a basketball. I had pimples. All because of television.

Then we found ourselves with a child of our own. I didn't want our daughter growing up like me, unable to dribble a basketball. I wanted to her to be as free of TV as possible. I had a vision of our family all gathered around the dining room table for dinner. We would pass the butter and bond with small talk. Just like the Cleavers and the other families I watched from behind the TV tray.

When our daughter turned 5, however, I got resistance. Sarah liked to eat in front of the TV and, frankly, so did my wife. It was time for compromise. I drew up a schedule. Sunday would be TV. Monday through Wednesday, we eat at the table. Thursday through Saturday, TV. I taped it to the wall for all to see.

That was many years ago. The schedule is still there, a constant reminder that I didn't get my way. It was TV at dinner time every night.

Our daughter became popular. She had starring roles in high school plays. She graduated magna cum laude from a small Ivy League college. She reads a lot. And now she's halfway through graduate school.

OK, so TV didn't lead her astray. But one day she will be filled with remorse. The day she gets her first cable bill.

Money Goes Down the Drain
When Nothing Else Will

December 20, 1013

When plumbing goes bad at the North Pole, Santa probably hands an elf a wrench.

I looked all around for an elf with a wrench a few Sundays back. I had a plumbing issue. The bathtub had been draining a bit slowly. No elf in sight, I found a wrench, shook it at the drain and made threats. That didn't work.

So I got my handy drain cleaner. The amateur's Roto-Rooter. I bought this many years ago at a major hardware store. Frankly, it never worked. But hope springs eternal when you're trying to get your money's worth.

So I pushed the end of a snake into the drain. And turned a crank. And hit something of a dead-end. Well, that was it. Mission accomplished. I pulled the snake out, and I no longer had a slow-drain problem. Water came oozing up from the bowels of the house.

And it smelled like it.

I told my wife this was no big deal. We could shower in the other bathtub. First, I had to remove the cat litter. Everybody calls it Kitty Litter, but that's a brand name protected by lawyers who send letters to reporters who misuse it.

The cat litter, by the way, is not in the shower for the convenience of the cat. To the cat, everything is an inconvenience. We put it there to keep it away from the dogs.

They have a keen sense of smell. And it always leads them right to the cat poop. I won't lie. They eat it.

But we needed a shower, so I set the cat litter box in the bathroom corner. I unplugged the drain. And up came the water, filled with rich organic nutrients. Good for growing bacillus cultures.

It rose several inches. And there it stayed. It didn't drain slowly. It didn't drain at all. I now had two tubs filled with bad water. Sponge baths were out.

I thought about the inter-connectedness of plumbing. The two plugged drains lead to a bigger pipe. And they lead to even bigger pipes.

Years ago, I worked briefly for an engineering firm that designed sewer systems. It wasn't a good fit. But I stayed long enough to learn about the mother ship of sewer pipes. It's called the Salt River Outfall and takes in everything from just about every drain and flushed toilet in greater Phoenix. It ends up at the 91st Avenue wastewater treatment plant.

Our house isn't connected to the mother ship. We're on a septic system. And when drains don't drain, I worry. A bad septic system can be a life-altering experience. Shortly after we moved in, nearly 20 years ago, we were awoken one night. We heard our dogs, part-Old English sheepdogs named George and Martha, sloshing around.

We turned on the light and saw them standing ankle deep in water. It was flowing out of the toilet like a mountain spring. That's when I bought my first shop vacuum.

And when I learned about the workings of our septic system.

Pipes deep under the ground had to be replaced. Half our landscaping was removed to make way for a backhoe. A large transfer of money occurred.

So when the tubs didn't drain, I checked the toilets. They flushed without giving back. All the other drains checked out, too. I felt relieved. But still we couldn't shower.

I had done all I could do, so I threw in the towel. I wouldn't be needing it anyway.

I called the 24-hour Roto-Rooter hotline and made an appointment for Monday morning. I could wait. They charge extra for Sundays. I'd only pay extra if we needed life jackets.

The technician showed up the next day. He put his snake through one of the pipes on the roof that somehow have something to do with plumbing.

He finished up and all the water drained away. The bill was $197. "It was a big ball of hair," he said.

I paid the man, then told my wife about the $200 hairball. We came up with a plan. We'd blame the cat.

Tough Tortoise Not Down in the Dumps
September 19, 2014

Ruthie Armendariz spent last Friday morning at the Casa Grande landfill. She watched from her car as workers searched for her tortoise.

"I call her Turtle," she said.

Turtle had been thrown in the garbage. And so Armendariz came here in hopes of finding her.

The night before, Sept. 11, Turtle had been stolen. Neighborhood kids told her they saw four other kids take Turtle.

Armendariz, 78, spoke about Turtle's theft on Monday. She was seated at the dining room table in her neatly appointed house on Cameron Avenue, a few blocks east of downtown. She'd had Turtle for about five years. Her daughter Dorina gave her Turtle for Mother's Day.

She has turtle bric-a-brac throughout her house. Gifts mostly.

"People found out that I like turtles," she said.

Turtle wasn't her first tortoise. She had another before Turtle. She called it Turtle, too. About six years ago, somebody stole Turtle No. 1. A young man came up to Armendariz's back fence.

She recalled his words. "Are you guys missing your turtle?" For a reward, he'd tell them where it was.

Armendariz and her husband, Eduardo, refused to pay ransom. They never saw Turtle No. 1 again.

I asked about her husband. Eduardo was a meat cutter at Bashas' and Food City for 34 years. Everybody knew him as Lalo. They were married for 58 years. He died a year ago this coming Saturday. For Armendariz, it will be a sad anniversary. Not one she can easily talk about.

Turtle, in the meantime, has kept her company. Turtle No. 2, that is.

Apparently turtles — in this case, African tortoises — bond more easily than people think.

"When I'm outside working on the yard, I have to be careful I don't trip on her, because she's always following me around," Armendariz said.

All tortoises are "she" to Armendariz. Spanish for turtle, tortuga, is a feminine noun.

Early that Friday morning, Armendariz noticed Turtle was gone. She searched all around. A man on his way to work, Mark, helped her out. Kids at a nearby school-bus stop spotted Armendariz and yelled to her.

"Lady, we saw them take off with your turtle," they told her. "And they dumped her in the garbage and they dropped her on the road three times to see if it would break."

Turtle is tough. She didn't break. But she must have had a hard landing. Turtle weighs 30 to 40 pounds.

They dropped her first, then dumped her. Turtle ended up in a big round rubber bin in an alley across the street.

The kids from the bus stop pointed it out. They get around, as kids do, and see things. They're sort of the neighborhood's Baker Street Irregulars, Sherlock Holmes' young band of informants.

Armendariz knew this much. Turtle was in trouble. The garbage truck had just rolled through earlier that morning. Everything in the can had gone right into the truck.

"I called the landfill," Armendariz said.

She drove there with Gabby Rodriguez, a good friend. She wasn't allowed to get out and look for the tortoise herself. But the workers did. They sifted through freshly dumped garbage.

They used a front-end loader, Rodriguez said. A small one, Armendariz added. "So they wouldn't crush her."

At the Dispatch, we first heard about Turtle from one of the reporters. She lives around the block from Armendariz. We speculated about Turtle's chances for survival. Some thought she'd turn out OK. The trash from the truck was still loose. It hadn't yet been tamped down by the 60-ton compactor. And there'd be food. Turtle could live on scraps. Turtle liked lettuce. What better place for old lettuce than the landfill?

Armendariz, however, wasn't hopeful. She went home after an hour. She didn't find Turtle. She began to cry.

The school bus came by later that afternoon. The kids got off. They had some news for Armendariz. She had come to meet them, along with a Casa Grande police officer. They told her: Turtle didn't go to the dump. The kids who stole Turtle took her out of the garbage can before the truck came. She had been atop a pizza box. Two of them took Turtle home. They were all of 7 and 9, police said. I'm pretty sure the 7-year-old didn't haul Turtle around without a little help.

They live with their mother in a small apartment. She's a single mother. She works at Wal-Mart. Maybe she can't afford after-school care, leaving the boys free to make mischief. And bring home a tortoise.

The apartment's about a block from Armendariz's home.

The officer went there. He returned with Turtle. Armendariz said she almost cried herself silly.

Turtle wasted no time. She went right back to her routine. She likes to settle under the car in the driveway and watch other cars go by. A chain-link fence keeps her from running into traffic.

The bus-stop kids — the Cameron Avenue Irregulars — told Armendariz the boys' mother was mad.

Mad because her kids stole the tortoise? Armendariz asked.

No, they said. "She's mad because the turtle pooped in her house."

A Small Contribution
To the General Welfare

March 28, 2014

I rarely carry money. I'm a debit card type. I might swipe my card to buy three bananas.

The swipe machine will ask if I want money back. I usually tell it no. I'm cheap. If I don't have money, I don't have to spend it. Sometimes, though, I'll treat myself. Gimme five, I'll tell the machine.

And so, a month or so back, I walked into the parking lot flush with a five. Maybe it was my body language. Maybe I looked like a soft touch. Maybe my money just longed to be free.

In any case, there he was. An old grizzled guy on a bicycle.

"I wonder if you could spare some change for dinner," he said, as I recall.

I asked about his situation.

He said he had a mental illness and lived on about $700 of Social Security a month. His rent was $500. He begged every night for the $3.50 or so needed to eat at McDonald's.

I opened my wallet and handed over all my liquidity.

He thanked me and pedaled off. I loaded a 12-pack of beer in the trunk, hoping he wouldn't spend my money on liquor.

I believed the guy, though. I felt like a philanthropist donating to a worthy cause.

Some panhandlers, of course, aren't as bad off as they make out to be. I used to get cornered by people who told me their car had run out of gas. The whole family was stuck inside it — grandma, the kids and the family dog. It sounded like the Joads. They just needed a little help and, by gosh, they'd make it to California.

The car always was on other side of the parking lot. I never actually saw it. I don't think it existed.

I've heard of people offering jobs to panhandlers. They could work for a living. In at least one case, I was told, the offer was turned down. Why work, if you can beg?

In a way, begging is work. It's not glamorous. It's repetitive. Hot and sweaty in summer. And it's the ultimate sales pitch. You're asking people to give you money, because you could really use it. And like any good salesman, you have to be primed for constant rejection.

Panhandlers, in any case, leave me alone most of the time. They seem to know when I've got some walking money and when I don't. And I usually don't.

Admittedly, my ship came in recently. I opened up a piece of mail and found a two-dollar bill. It was free money from the government, which chose me for a study. I slipped it into my wallet. And a day later, I handed it over to a young woman in the same supermarket parking lot.

She had a stroller. It was a double decker. An infant on top and a kid no older than 3 or 4 on the bottom.

She asked for money to eat, and I asked about her situation. She was trying to get food stamps, she said.

It was probably about 8 o'clock at night. I felt sorry for the kids. Who wouldn't? And maybe that was her game. Of course, it wasn't a game for the kids. I wished I had the five I had given the guy on the bike.

She took the two and, for a moment, looked at it like I had given her Monopoly money. Then she thanked me and strolled off with her kids. I muttered something about hoping it helps them, if just a little, but I don't think she heard me. I had already dropped off her radar.

But good fortune soon smiled on me again. My wife left a dollar on the dresser. This time I just shoved it into my pocket. The dollar went to work with me. It went with me to downtown Florence, where I looked for an office I didn't know had moved.

I stood too long in one spot. My dollar sent out an all-points bulletin. A young woman seemed to appear out of nowhere. She greeted me with a smile, then said she was kind of homeless.

And I kind of handed her my dollar.

Seeing the World
From a Car with Big Fins
June 26, 2015

Nothing says America like the family road trip. Everybody piles in the car to see the USA. It could be in your Chevrolet. Or your Ford.

Our family car was a Plymouth station wagon. It was a 1960 model, but that's a guess. It had fins. It was pea green. And the size of a diner.

In the summer of 1967, it went from Phoenix to Montreal. The whole family went with it. My dad and mom. My two sisters, Christine and Cathy. My brother Jim and, of course, me.

I don't know who first pitched the idea. I suspect my mother. I can't imagine my father thinking: Hey, wouldn't it be neat if we spent 10 hours a day in a metal box with four teenagers?

We went to Montreal to see Expo 67.

We took turns riding in the back seat, which faced the rear. We all wanted the back seat. It had the best view. A panorama of a receding highway — leaving it all behind.

We didn't have seat belts. Nobody did. We were on a highway full of crash-test dummies. That was OK. We hadn't yet been told seat belts save lives. I don't know if our ignorance reached the level of bliss. But we had no worries.

The news wasn't all good. The radio got AM stations. We heard about Jayne Mansfield. Her car met with a big rig. It wasn't a pretty picture.

This was my first trip to the East. A lot of details escape me, though Detroit comes to mind. We drove through it. I remember freeways and skyscrapers. In Phoenix, everything over 10 stories was a skyscraper. Phoenix had one freeway, Interstate 17.

Montreal? I don't recall a thing.

Expo 67 was part of a dying breed — the big world's fairs, where nations and businesses had over-the-top pavilions. Displays featured all the neat stuff we'd have way in the future, say 1985.

Here's what I remember about Expo 67. The U.S. exhibit was a big Buckyball, a geodesic dome designed by Buckminster Fuller. The Soviet exhibit showed the good side of oppression, probably with tractors.

We went on to New York City. We didn't see the Yankees. And we didn't go to the top of the Empire State Building, tallest building around then. Instead, we took a Circle Line cruise.

We went around Manhattan. The water was choppy. The air was heavy, warm and muggy. So I can't blame my sister for getting sick.

Later, we piled back into our barge on wheels. We took a bridge out of Manhattan. In those days, workers painted bridges with a thick coat of oil-based battleship gray. At least that was the color of the paint dumped all over our car. It came from a workers' scaffolding on high. If we were true New Yorkers, I think we would have yelled obscenities. Even if no one could hear us.

But we just figured that's life in the big city.

On the way back, we took a southerly route. We visited a great aunt in Atlanta. In Mississippi, I took the helm. I was 16 and a licensed driver. What could go wrong?

A lot of course, but nothing happened. I did make my mother nervous. It began to get dark. We were on a ribbon of back road.

My mother snapped. "The speed limit's 25!"

I was doing 26 or 27. That didn't put her at ease. In her mind, I was a maniac at the wheel.

Texas, as always, took forever. But we made it back.

Five years ago, I took a solo road trip to Massachusetts. I had a mission. Return our daughter's car to her. She was in college then.

I never thought of myself given to panic. But that was before I found myself on a bridge crossing the Mississippi River. I was on

199

U.S. 62, a leg of U.S. 60. The bridge was narrow with just two lanes. What it lacked in width, it made up for in length. And height. It was a sunny day. I remember the shadows of the framework flitting past as I drove. Like a strobe light without end. The panic set in. I gave myself pep talks: "You can do this! You can do this!" I didn't believe me.

I thought I'd never make it. I did, eventually. I pulled off at a small park.

Now all I had to do was cross the Ohio.

When Kindergarten Was All Snacks and Naps

March 27, 2015

Miss Wells was my kindergarten teacher.

She's not in the picture my mother saved, an August 1955 clipping from the Lincoln Star. It's now the Lincoln, Nebraska, Journal Star.

Four tots are seated on a carpet. The photo caption says: "It might be like this."

They're imagining what real school is like. In front of them is a book, apparently thrown in as a prop. In 1955, kindergartners didn't read. Other people read to them.

I'm one of the kids in the clipping. (Why else would my mother save it?)

Here's what I remember about kindergarten. We had graham crackers and milk for a snack, then we napped.

Joe Ayres remembered a bit more. He's in the picture, too. I found him through an Internet search. Ayres still lives in Lincoln, where he sells real estate.

He was born 12 days before me.

"I've been in Lincoln 54 of my 64 years," he said.

Out of college, he spent 10 years in Washington, D.C. He was an aide to Nebraska Congressman Charles Thone and, later, a lobbyist. He moved back to Lincoln, the state capital. He worked for the government and, once again, as a lobbyist. He took up real estate in the early 1990s.

"It's still the people business, like lobbying," Ayres said.

Throughout his life, Ayres lived history in the boomer bubble. He remembered just where he was on hearing Kennedy was shot. He recalled the Beatles on Ed Sullivan. "They kind of changed the world." The music was good, too. Later, he was in the first lottery for the military draft. Ayres remembered his number: 247. High enough to keep him out of Vietnam.

"My brother was a Marine in Vietnam," he said. "I really didn't want to do that."

Neither did I. My number was 324.

Of course, in 1955, I knew nothing of Vietnam, only that communists were bad.

Our kindergarten class met in the basement of Sheridan Elementary School, Ayres said. I didn't remember that. We went from 9 to 11 in the morning. There was an afternoon class, too. Maybe we had coloring books, did building blocks. I don't remember. Neither did Ayres.

But our teacher, Miss Wells, was as nice as they come, he said.

Our family didn't stay long in Lincoln. By second grade, I was going to school in Guam. We shipped out with my father, an Air Force officer.

Ayres went to Sheridan through all six grades.

He'd see Miss Wells about the hall as the years went by.

In the clipping, the caption hewed to the old style of identifying parents. Mine were ID'd as Mr. and Mrs. Harvey Coates. For the record, my mother's name was Virginia.

Ayres' parents were listed as Mr. and Mrs. Joyce Ayres. I asked him why his mother got the credit. Joyce happened to be his father's middle name, he said. His full name was Warren Joyce Ayres.

He used his middle name for an advertising business he started in 1946. The name stood out.

"He used to get letters, 'Mrs. Joyce Ayres.'"

Mr. Joyce Ayres, it happened, wrote the Sheridan school song. It's still the official song. And Sheridan remains a top-notch school, Ayres said.

"It's still one of the best schools in Lincoln. It's kind of in the country club area."

Yet they let me in. The picture proves it. I'm on the left. Ayres is third from left. The little girl identified as Polly Rohrs sits between us. Ayres remembered her as Patty.

They were both born on the same day at the same Lincoln hospital. Patty married an FBI agent, Ayres thinks.

I wasn't able to reach her.

The other little girl, Sandy Rosewell, sits on the right. She sports eyeglasses in the kind of frames "Far Side" cartoonist Gary Larson took as his inspiration. She looks quite studious.

I spoke to Rosewell on Wednesday. The glasses weren't hers.

"I didn't wear glasses," she said. She put them on for fun. "I was a ham."

Rosewell now lives in Boulder. She's a career counselor at the University of Colorado. She goes by Sandi now.

Like my father, her father was in the Air Force. Irvin Rosewell retired as a colonel and opened a floral shop in Lincoln.

"He loved that," she said. "We had flowers all the time, and we had a big parrot that lived in the flower shop that always talked to us."

I forgot to ask what the parrot talked about.

Ayres and Rosewell were friends in grade school. They used to play in his backyard, she said.

She, too, became a Beatles fan. What's more, she had advance warning of the British invasion.

"I had pen pals in England," Rosewell said. "I thought that was really cool. I could get all the inside scoop about what was really happening."

She remembered Miss Wells the way Ayres did. She was very nice.

I picture Miss Wells as young and pretty. No doubt, she's

changed in 60 years, if she's still alive. Kindergarten has changed, too.

Amber Gutierrez can tell you that. She teaches kindergarten at Cottonwood Elementary School in Casa Grande.

"There're no naps," Gutierrez said.

No time for that. Children in her class are too busy reading, writing, adding and subtracting. They keep journals. They write opinion pieces — what they like, don't like.

And their progress is measured.

In short, "they're pretty much tested on everything," Gutierrez said.

And, at that age, it's all good.

"They're just ready for all this, and they love it."

They don't have to imagine what real school is like. They're already there.

Knitters, a Force to Be Reckoned With
February 6, 2015

My wife, Cindy, knits. She sits in front of the TV. She likes the English murder mysteries. They're often set in a beautiful green countryside. There's a manor house about the size of a Hilton.

The landscaping is immaculate. But inside, somebody's been bludgeoned. It's not pretty. Then the murderer has to cover his, or her, tracks by killing more people. And Cindy just knits away as the bodies pile up. Knitting apparently has a calming effect. She gets knitting endorphins.

I think of the knitters in "A Tale of Two Cities," Dickens' take on the French Revolution. They have a front row at the guillotine. They're calm.

Cindy has her moments of frustration, though. She has to keep count. It takes concentration. She doesn't want me to interrupt. It's not a good time to ask: "What did you do with the butter, because I have no idea where I put it."

This counting thing is apparently key to knitting success. If Cindy loses track, she has to unravel the whole sweater, then start over.

That's speculation on my part. Knitting is a great mystery to me. Somehow, by pushing yarn around on needles, you can make all kinds of stuff. Sweaters, mittens, lacy things.

Cindy is not alone in her pursuit. There's a worldwide alliance of knitters. They belong to a social media site called Ravelry. Some 5 million knitters in all. They wield power. I think they were behind the defeat of Mitt Romney in 2012. He looked bad in a sweater.

Ravelry knitters, as I understand it, are in every town in every state. In every country. A while back, I asked Cindy if she could find Ravelry knitters in Casa Grande for me. She could, but she refused.

It's a tight-knit community.

They post their work so others can see it. Some knit sweaters with political messages. I recall Dickens' notorious knitter, Madame Defarge. She'd knit in the names of spies and French aristocrats. They'd get theirs. I think she knitted a hoodie that said: "Meet me at the Bastille. Bring your pitchfork."

Cindy knitted me a nice winter sweater. I sometimes hold it up to the light. I can just make out: "Pick up some milk on the way home."

Ravelry is as much about yarn as knitting. It's a marketplace for yarn. Some knitters build up large stores of yarn. They call it their stash. Cindy's stash takes up a corner of a spare room, piled high in plastic bins. She's preparing for the end times. Yarnageddon.

Sometimes Ravelry knitters look to sell off their entire stash. It's called destashing. They need the money. You can tell a lot about the economy when knitters destash. They unloaded yarn by the boatload during the Great Recession. When banks failed in Iceland, Icelandic yarn flooded the market. It came packed in ice, or so I'm told.

204

Even now, in the United States, knitters destash to pay medical bills. You have to be careful around knitting needles.

We have a knitter in the newsroom. Melissa sometimes sells her knitting online. That's a great idea.

I'm thinking of our own home-based sweatshop. It'd work like this: Whenever Cindy finished a sweater, I'd bring her some water and a bagel. But she won't sell her knitting. She likes to give it away.

She's knitted free stuff for me, for our daughter and members of our extended family. That includes my niece's three daughters. Cindy knitted a lacy blanket for each of them. The oldest is 3 or 4. I'm not sure. I lost track. Megan, the niece, sent us a photo of them with their lacy blankets. Word is they love their blankets. And they regard their Aunt Cindy as super. Somebody with a special talent.

Probably the best they can say about me is I'm a moderate drinker.

MVD Up to Challenge
Of Making Old Man Look Awful
August 14, 2015

The man pictured in the driver's license:

A. Flunked out of meth rehab.

B. Survived rabies, by some miracle.

C. Was run over by the 9:10 Greyhound.

D. Was exposed to MVD technology that — after many years of research — finally perfected the truly bad photo.

Correct answers in multiple choice tests are usually the longest. So you probably guessed right. The answer was D.

The poor man in the photo is me. I feel sad for him. He looks like he could use a social worker.

I went in for my new driver's license two or three weeks ago. I was about to turn 65. Arizona pegs 65 as the first of your declining years. Your hair falls out. Your reaction time slows. Your eyesight dims.

Arizona's Motor Vehicle Division really only cares about the third thing. You take an eye test. Here, you read letters and try to spot some flashing lights on the side, for side vision.

Then you get your picture taken. My old picture wasn't so old. I had to update it less than two years ago. It was a suitable photo. Way above MVD's usual standards.

I imagine officials worked on a fix. Extra pixels were assigned to sags and wrinkles. Color was set to funeral-parlor pallor. New

206

training materials included "The Picture of Dorian Gray."

But maybe bad photos and bad service just come naturally. It is, after all, MVD.

Don't take my word for it. An April state audit of MVD reported: "MVD field offices do not consistently provide a good customer service experience."

OK, hardly news.

I went to the MVD office in south Phoenix, near where I live. As I walked in, I saw people lined up along a rope. On the other side of the rope a sign read "Line forms here." Nobody was there.

What to do? Go where the sign says? Or follow the crowd? I joined the crowd. I think most people would. Then somebody in charge of crowd control told me to get in the other line. I became a line of one.

I was called for the eye test. It was set up at the information booth, which was short on information. And long on confusion.

Through it all, the clerks were reasonably cordial. I couldn't blame them for the way things worked. They were stuck in a system they had no control over.

After passing the eye exam, I was in line again. Now two people were in charge of crowd control. They had a running dispute. The line goes here, one said. No, the line goes there, the other said. I had no idea what the line was for. No matter. I joined it.

It was, of course, the wrong line. By some fluke, I ended up in the line for photos. They, too, were being taken at the information booth.

People were herded through, lickety-split. Flash! Next! Flash! Next!

My turn. I was told to remove my glasses. All the better to show off my ghostly eye sockets.

Flash! Deer in the high beams. Next!

I took a seat and waited. The last time I went in, the license took just minutes to prepare. It was ready on the spot. Now they have a new system. The wait is inversely proportional to the time spent snapping your picture. Picture in a flash. Then a wait in purgatory.

In time, my name was called. The clerk handed me a sheet of paper. It was my temporary license. The real one would be in the mail.

Two or three days later, I had a flight to catch. I remember standing at the TSA checkpoint. I took the license out of my wallet. I unfolded it like a note from home. The TSA agent wasn't impressed by an ID printed on copy paper.

It didn't fly. Neither would I, had I not brought my passport.

It had a decent photo. Not great but not the picture of Dorian Gray.

Colonoscopy? The Fun's in the Prep
February 8, 2016

The instructions could have come from the torture memo the CIA overlooked. They involved subjecting people to compounds with names ending in -lax. Dulcolax. MiraLax. Purge-alax. Maxilax. And Please-Please-No-More-alax.

The last three weren't actually on the list. They're still undergoing testing, I think. You don't want to be in on those trials.

The MiraLax is torture enough. But don't blame it on the CIA. It's part of a ritual I undergo every five years in preparation for a colonoscopy. I had one last week. It went well. The doctor found a polyp and nipped it in the bud.

I have no idea what a polyp looks like. I imagine it's something like a sea anemone, swaying in a gentle tide. Then came the MiraLax. I'm surprised the polyp survived that.

As it happens, I outdid myself.

In the doctor's own words: "The quality of the preparation was excellent."

That means he had unobstructed view. Here's the key to preparation. Everybody eats but you. The wife eats. The dogs eat.

Even the cat eats.

You get to suck on a Popsicle. Then comes the main course: a 64-ounce Double Big Gulp of Gatorade. But it only works if you stir in the MiraLax. Open up the MiraLax. Pour some in. Stir. Pour in some more. Don't stop. Keep pouring. Just keep pouring. Pour and pour, until the whole bottle is empty.

Then drink a glassful every 15 minutes. Until it's all gone.

I'll spare you the details, except for step one of the helpful guide labeled "Colon Cleansing Tips."

"Stay near a toilet! You will have diarrhea, which can be quite sudden." Not to worry. It adds: "This is normal."

That's a relief. Really.

I started regular colon screenings after 50. They're a good way to prevent colon cancer, which often starts with the little polyps. Sixty-four ounces of spiked Gatorade is worth a pound of cure. You just keep telling yourself that.

Besides, my father had colonoscopies. Now it was my turn.

I went in for my first exam about 2000. The doctor had recommended a half measure, known as a sigmoidoscopy. It's like a colonoscopy, but the doctor doesn't go all the way up the ladder. I focused on a bigger difference, as I understood it.

With a colonoscopy, I'd get mind-numbing drugs. With a sigmoidoscopy, I'd get a bullet to bite on, at best. But no drugs. Nothing to distract me from — well, you know. So I came up with my own prep. I drank two, possibly three beers the morning of the procedure. My wife drove.

Maybe the doctor was onto me. Maybe he saw me stumbling into the exam room. But he didn't let on. He simply went down a checklist. He asked if anybody in my family had polyps. My father, I said. And there it was. My ticket to a full colonoscopy. Drugs and all.

I rescheduled. And I learned colonoscopy prep was so much more than a couple of Budweisers. On exam day, I must admit, I looked forward to the buzz. What a guy has to do for a fix.

At it happened, I wasn't out of it enough. I was in a haze but still felt some discomfort.

This last time around I felt nothing. I was hooked up to an IV with a knockout drug. I was told it would take in about five seconds. I didn't buy that. Nothing works that fast. The anesthesia specialist hit the plunger. And faster than you can read this, I was out. The doctor went to work.

He noted in his report: "Patient tolerance to procedure was excellent."

I finally found something I was good at. Lying inertly on a table while heavily drugged.

I woke up maybe a half hour later, thanks to my wife's constant prodding. She's had a lot of practice. I got dressed, once I figured what foot went in what shoe. Cindy drove me home.

My discharge papers said I could resume my normal diet. Too bad. I was starting to like the Popsicles.

How Was Your Colonoscopy, On a Scale of 1 to 10?

April 5, 2021

I recently shopped for paint at one of the mega-hardware stores. Enough to cover a plank for a gate falling off the hinges. A pint would do it.

While the clerk mixed the paint, I noticed a sign taped to the plexiglass. You know, the plexiglass barriers now standard in most retail stores. They help protect the workers from COVID.

The sign asked you to take a survey about your experience. On your phone, I think. You could win $500.

The sign added: If your shopping experience wasn't a 10, see the management.

Nothing less than a 10? That's a pretty high bar.

What if my experience was a mere eight or nine? Would I get a refund? Would the paint-mixing clerk lose her employee-of-the-month parking? Would they put the work gloves out where I could find them?

I passed on the survey.

But there'll be others. There's no escaping them. They're known as feedback surveys and they're everywhere. Wherever you shop. Whenever you visit a doctor or a veterinarian. Interact with government, all the way up to Amtrak.

I know about interacting with Amtrak. I interacted with Amtrak reservation agents a half-dozen times last year.

Every call began with a recording. Would I stay on the line, at the end of the call, for a survey about my experience?

OK, let's see. The coronavirus kept pushing back my travel plans. I would book a trip, then cancel, rebook, then cancel again. The calls would often run a half-hour, poring over timetables and connections. I began to get the sense I couldn't get there from here, especially after cuts to train service.

I never waited on the line for a survey. Why torture myself? I'm sure some people took it. Amtrak probably got an earful.

Last February, I had a colonoscopy. A day or two afterward, the doctor's practice sent me a text. Would I take a survey of my experience? I didn't really have anything to offer. I don't recall my experience. That's the beauty of anesthesia.

It wasn't just the doctor's practice. The surgery center also wanted me to rate my experience.

What would they ask? "On a scale of 1 to 10, how would you rate the pillows?"

Answer: "A nine. Could be fluffier. No chocolate."

A week or so later, I visited the dermatologist. It was an annual screening. Afterward, the practice messaged me. Would I take a survey?

Not much to say. The doctor gave me the once over and said I was good to go. I asked him about the rough spot above my forehead. He said it was just age.

"So I have barnacles," I said. He kind of laughed. Feigning amusement at a lame joke. I'd give him a 10 for that. I didn't take the survey, though. Enough is enough.

211

Professor Anne Karpf wrote about feedback surveys for The Guardian newspaper. Karpf is a British sociologist. Feedback surveys follow you everywhere you shop, she said.

It wasn't a recent discovery on her part. The article ran in 2016.

She recalled standing at a supermarket checkout line. The cashier handed her a card. It read: "How did we do today?"

Now the question shows up on cash-register receipts.

Karpf wrote about emails piling up. Every time she shopped, she was asked: "How was your visit?"

She didn't answer. Who has time?

A single survey can run 15 minutes. Responding to all of them would add up to a full-time job, without pay, she said.

Karpf did answer one question. Why all the surveys? Because, companies say, they're used to improve customer service.

Like Amtrak is going to take my advice.

Feedback surveys, Karpf said, go back to the Second World War, when the German military asked how they were doing. Maybe they recorded your responses for quality purposes.

Anything less than a 10, you were probably shot.

Anyway, the feedback survey seeds were planted. University of Michigan researchers, Karpf writes, designed surveys in the 1940s and '50s "to help create less authoritarian styles of leadership." Sounds ironic.

But it got me thinking. I could use a bit of feedback myself. I tend to think everything I do rates somewhere between a five and a seven. Maybe I'm better than that. I turned to Maggie, my dog.

"How am I doing with — WALKIES, WALKIES, Maggie!" Her feedback was amazing. Running around the house. Vigorous tail wagging. Excited barking. A definite 10.

Survey question No. 2. "Maggie, treats, Maggie! How am I doing with TREATS!" Another 10.

This after I arrived home from an errand: "Maggie, on a scale of one to 10, are you really glad to see me? You are? What a GOOD GIRL!" Another 10.

Thank goodness, perfect 10s. Maggie won't report me to the management, AKA the wife. She offers a lot of feedback. I don't even have to ask for it.

Getting from Point A
To Point B Never Felt So Hot

June 13, 2016

The woman had just finished her shopping at Wal-Mart. She settled into her 1989 van. She soaked a handkerchief in cold water, then wrapped it around her neck.

"When I know I'm going out, I try to get my water bottles frozen," she said.

By now, the ice had all melted. It didn't take long on such a day. It was Monday afternoon, and my car's dash said 112 degrees. The official Casa Grande high was 111.

It could be worse, though perhaps not for this woman.

She's a member of a small but miserable club. People in cars without air conditioning. I drove to Wal-Mart, my own air conditioning at full blast. I had set out to gauge the misery index of drivers without such cold comfort.

For that, I had to leave my icy bubble. I trekked across the plain of baking asphalt. What's it like without air conditioning? I asked. After a few interviews, I got a sense some drivers would rather be waterboarded — if it involved cold water.

The woman in the van was my first stop. She was 51. She declined to give her name.

She and her husband bought the van five months ago. A few months later the compressor went out. They plan to get it fixed. For now, she sweats it out with a wet handkerchief and fewer trips. She avoids stop lights.

"I take the back roads," she said.

For cars without AC, the imperative is to keep moving. The only

213

thing worse than hot air blowing through an open window is no air at all. Red lights mean a half-minute pit stop in hell.

I say this from experience. In high school and college, I drove cars that barely had working pistons. Air conditioning wasn't part of the option package. Seat belts were a luxury add-on.

In a way, I didn't miss what I never had. Still, red lights were a killer. And yellow meant step on it.

I got married, settled down and joined the middle class. Our cars had air conditioning. But compressors did go out a time or two. I dreaded the cross-town drive in a convection oven. It was hard on the wife and daughter as well.

Now I cherish my air conditioning. It's a must-have feature. I no longer take pride in arriving somewhere drenched in sweat. I had that attitude once: "I'm a native and I'm all about toughing out the heat."

Now I'm not so tough. And the summers are getting hotter. Record highs are nearly as frequent as sunrise and sunset.

At Wal-Mart, I followed a Chrysler PT Cruiser into a parking space. The windows were open, a sure sign of suffering.

Aaron Weatherford of Stanfield said he was in a wreck. He lost all his refrigerant. But the hoses were back in place now. All he had to do was replenish the coolant.

Weatherford, 26, said he had had the Cruiser less than a year. His last car had no AC to begin with.

"I'm way used to driving without AC," he said.

Even after he gets it working, he'll use it sparingly. He has a 35-mile drive to his job, and air conditioning eats up the gas.

I spotted Adrian Tapia, 31, loading a box into the back of his 2006 Scion. He lives in Picacho and is a department manager at Wal-Mart. The Scion didn't have AC. His first car, he said, did.

"But it really didn't work," he added.

Tapia was young and heat resistant in any case. He didn't mind the scorching drive, too much.

William Beyer gave me a different story.

"It's absolutely miserable," said Beyer, 26.

He was loading up his 1986 Ford F-150 pickup with bag after bag of groceries. His wife, Alex, was with him — along with their

214

7-month-old daughter, Sarah. Helping out were John Higgs and his two daughters, 5 and 6.

Beyer and his family were new to Arizona. They're from Michigan, where they bought the truck. It was a good deal. But many old Michigan trucks don't come equipped with air conditioning.

The Zen of Dish Washing

March 4, 2017

Like most well-run organizations, our household has a division of labor.

My wife, Cindy, is the generalist. I count on her to do most generally everything.

When I worked full time, she cooked. She did dishes. She did the wash. She sometimes even got down on her hands and knees and scrubbed the floor, just like Cinderella.

I would come home after a hard day of assembling words and there would be dinner. And she'd only just gotten home herself a half-hour earlier. I was impressed. All that after a hard day of practicing law.

How did she did do it? I didn't ask. Why spoil a good thing.

I'm the specialist. I specialize in waste management. I take out the garbage, as often as twice a week. And I handle maintenance issues, like plumbing. I spend six hours fixing a leak, then call a plumber.

The division of labor changed somewhat after I retired. Well, semi-retired, if you count this column.

Now I do dishes, without the assist of an automatic dishwasher. And I do some cooking, which usually means roasting a chicken.

The chicken takes time. And so do the dishes, at least the way I go about it. Cindy can clear a sink-load in 10 minutes. I have to line up all the plates on the counter. Dishes here. Silverware there. I stare at the pots and pans: "You, end of the line."

I run the water. I test the water. As I wash each plate and fork, my mind wanders. I think about things. Have I planned well for retirement? Too late for that. Is it planting season? I'd hate for the gophers to go hungry. Is that guy with the hair still president?

Well, I've never been known to rush things, especially household chores.

In my youth, I often approached them like the protesters who go limp as cops try to haul them off. I opted for passive resistance.

That was especially true in my teen years.

When I was 9 or 10, I was more accommodating. I enjoyed mowing the yard, for one thing. We were on Guam. We lived in base housing, courtesy of the U.S. Air Force, which employed my father. All the lawns had to be shipshape, though I guess that's a Navy expression.

The Air Force supplied the mower. It was like a rental, except there was no charge. You picked it up. And returned it.

The mowers were big gasoline-powered jobs. I could barely reach the handles. It didn't matter. I didn't have to push. The mowers had a special feature. They drove themselves. All I had to do was walk behind it and steer.

Sure, there was always the risk I might fall down and get run over. Or at the least, lose a foot. But those were the days. Kids could do grownup stuff and nobody worried about them. And, when you're 9 or 10, you don't know any better.

At 13, of course, I would have been old enough to handle self-driving mowers. But by then, I had already scratched mowing off my to-do list. It got in the way of sleeping in or hanging out.

My father, however, made sure to pencil it back in.

It was the year of mowing reluctantly. Saturday mornings, I trudged to the shed like a wrongly convicted inmate in a chain gang. It was so unfair. I could have been watching an old Tarzan movie on TV.

We had resettled in Phoenix. Now I had to push the mower

216

using my own muscles. Where was the justice in that? And once I got it started — after 20 minutes of yanking on a rope — I would slog through a quarter acre of freshly irrigated Bermuda grass. It was like mowing a swamp, without the snakes.

Not that I'm complaining. My experience paid off. On graduating from college, I landed a job as a groundskeeper for a grade-school district.

I lasted about three months. Apparently the shovels weren't just for leaning on.

Today, in our household, I still take care of the landscaping. I don't mind. It's pretty much desert. We don't have grass. We had a small patch at one time, but I let it die out to spite the gophers.

I liked mowing it, in any case. I still have the simple reel mower. No gas required. I just pushed it and went at my own pace.

Maybe, this spring, I'll replant the grass. That sounds about right. Throw some sod down. Get out the old mower. And the shovel, in case I need something to lean on.

Pre-COVID, Pre-K
Germ Factory

February 24, 2018

I had a nice time week before last. I got to see a dental hygienist teach preschoolers all about dental care.

The tots were enthusiastic, but not rowdy. They smiled and listened intently to good advice. Then they filled the air with viruses that could bring down Dumbo.

Well, I'm no elephant. But I was brought down.

I sat in on the class Feb. 12, two Mondays ago. By the following Wednesday, my throat felt funny. Like it was trying to tell me to forget the green bananas. By Thursday, I was a walking cesspool of viral infection.

Sure, you can call it the common cold. But I don't take any suffering lightly. I sniffle. I sneeze. I cough. I shuffle and moan. I diet on gooey elixirs. Gooey cough syrup. Sticky cough drops.

I'm choosy about my cough drops. I first just scavenged for whatever I could find about the house. Kitchen drawer. Sock drawer. Under couch cushions.

But all I found were drops with trite messages stamped on the wrapper.

Here's one: "Dust off and get up."

I'm lying in bed. I'm a mess of mucus. And I read a message that sounds like my father telling me to shake a leg. That was a favorite of his. "Shake a leg."

It was his way to remind me about Saturday chores. Through sickness and in health. Yes, even sickness — lying in my bed moaning and groaning. Maybe not as loud as I'd like, on account of my weakened condition.

And there's my father at the door with a new saying: "Dust off and get up."

I'm sure the cough drop maker meant the message to sound upbeat, like Andy Hardy trying to cheer up a mopey Judy Garland: "Hey, let's put on a show!" But that's not how I took it.

So, after I dictated my do-not-resuscitate order, I asked my wife for new cough drops, the kind that didn't nag you. She got me a whole new bag. She was my Florence Nightingale. Maybe she didn't hold my hand and say softly say, "You poor boy," like the real Florence Nightingale. But at least she didn't tell me to dust off and get up.

I'm 67. I'm rethinking whether to enter another preschool class, even for a good story. Tot viruses are just too virulent. I'll try to explain it with a thought experiment.

A team of physicists find Schrodinger's cats and place one in a preschool class. It comes out dead. Fortunately Schrodinger had lots of cats. Scientists go through them all. One-by-one, they're placed in the classroom. One-by-one they're carried out feet up — do-not-resuscitate orders attached to their little collars. Kids cry.

They want their kitty back.

Scientist are scratching their heads. These cats are not alive and dead. They're just dead. All from exposure to Ms. Holly's germ lab. Quantum mechanics is turned on its head. But not all scientists are convinced.

"Let's try Einstein's puppies!" one cries.

She's voted down. No puppies. The optics are bad.

My thought experiment does have some flaws. I don't think cats can catch kid germs, for one. For another, I'm not sure Schrodinger had any cats left. Maybe he did. Maybe he didn't.

But there is evidence kids in preschool are Petri dishes on legs. I combed the internet. OK, maybe I just clicked the first thing that popped up. I found Dear Julia, who answers health questions on Vox, a media website.

Here's her take, August of 2016: "Kids' immune systems are developing, they pick up everything." They also spread germs parents don't have an immunity to themselves. And, of course, there's the germ-factory theory. Kids are thrown together in a single room, where they put their germy fingers in each other's milk, creating a production line of sickness.

In the classroom I visited, there were sinks. Kids could wash up. Clean hands can stop a lot of germs.

I recall my days as a substitute teacher. I taught kindergarten for a day. I didn't see a sink. And the boy with the runny nose still haunts me. I was helping a little one with some letters. I turned. And there he was, his nose a waterfall of mucus. He wiped it away. Then he reached out with the hands. The hideous hands.

Naturally, I got sick.

But kids are kids. You can't blame them for passing germs. They just do. And we've all been there. My own pre-K and — later — school-age daughter introduced me to sties and pinkeye. And norovirus. I still get queasy thinking about that one. And, yes, colds.

I was a germ-carrying tot in the 1950s. We dealt out more than colds and pinkeye. Our viruses really were threats to life and limb. We carried measles, whooping cough, chicken pox and — before 1955 — even polio. Vaccines have since been developed for all those diseases. And more.

So, on reflection, the common cold isn't so bad. Not that I'm ready to dust off and get up. I'll just lie around and do a little moaning. And wait for Florence Nightingale to hold my hand.

Guess Which CG Story Is Fake
March 31, 2018

A few years back I asked my boss about doing an April Fools' Day story. He nixed the idea, for good reason. People might not get the joke. They often don't.

My favorite April Fools' bit was on the old Jack Paar show. I don't think it ran as an April Fools' joke. But it had people fooled, including me. I was only 12 or 13 at the time, so I was an easy mark.

I think I wrote about this before. But if your memory's as good as mine, you've already forgotten what I said. I have.

The show's segment was presented as a mini-documentary on the spaghetti harvest in Italy. Strands of spaghetti had ripened on the trees. Field workers carefully picked the spaghetti strands and placed them in baskets. A narrator described the care and effort that went into a harvest destined to be smothered in Ragu sauce.

It wasn't until later, much later, I thought: Hey, spaghetti doesn't grow on trees. They dig it out of the ground, like potatoes.

My point is, I don't have an April Fools' column. But if I did, I'd write something like the following news items. Two are made up, just like harvesting spaghetti from trees. One is a true story. You can probably figure out which is which. But I'll fill you in at the end. No fooling.

I-10 to Phoenix to get additional lanes

State highway officials announced that Interstate 10 north from Casa Grande will get additional lanes and make driving to Phoenix pure joy.

"All the stars are aligned to make I-10 bigger and better," said an ADOT spokesman. "See, the Big Dipper's now in the third house. So, by the looks of it, we'll have a 10-lane freeway by August, and Bob's your uncle."

My uncle's name was actually Harold. But highway officials cited the extraordinary cooperation of federal, tribal, state and county governments. It couldn't have happened without Ronnie Baker of Casa Grande Troop 1193, who locked all the agency heads in a room until they came to an agreement, as part of his Eagle Scout project.

The freeway will be equipped with giant fans to blow any dust storms toward California, where they belong. It will also include rubber bumpers for drivers who have trouble staying in their lane while texting.

"I got the idea from my last trip to the bowling alley," the chief engineer said. "They have a special bumper lane for subpar bowlers and kids. No gutter balls. And no one should end up in a gutter just because they're texting at 80 miles an hour."

Kitty Splash-Down to make debut at city pool

Casa Grande officials announced a pool day for all cats at the aquatic center. The event is being dubbed "Kitty Splash-Down."

"It's like our annual Doggie Dive-In, but with cats," a city spokeswoman said.

Cat owner Roberta Brown first approached recreation officials with the idea.

"People have a misconception that cats don't like swimming," Brown said in an interview. "That's just not true. I take my cat swimming all the time. She loves it, once I get her floaties on."

Event organizers said cats should really take to the new water slide.

City buys nice photo of desert 90 miles away

Casa Grande city officials bought a photo of a scene near Lake Pleasant, north of Phoenix, because it looked like a nice desert.

The city used the photo to promote Casa Grande as a good place to live and work.

The city's public information officer told the Dispatch the

picture was "a stock photo of the Sonoran Desert."

Close enough for government work.

OK, now to separate the truth from the totally made-up.

The I-10 item is clearly bogus. The Arizona Department of Transportation claims poverty whenever it hears complaints about the need to widen I-10 to Phoenix. And the Gila River Indian Community apparently isn't keen on granting the additional right of way.

Cats hate water. My cat barely likes me.

The last item is true. Thanks to the Dispatch, we weren't fooled.

No Birdies, but Maybe a Hawk
February 3, 2018

I played my final round of golf last Monday.

I owe it all to my wife's newfound freedom. She recently retired and commenced to clear out years of household clutter.

Everything must go!

The golf clubs sat in a corner, long neglected and collecting dust. I couldn't quite bring myself to toss them. But I tried not to think about them. They reminded me of a lifelong quest to get better at something I would never get better at.

I first golfed when I was 9 or 10. My brother, Jim, and I accompanied my father at the Navy golf course on Guam. I think it was called Nimitz, like the aircraft carrier. I remember hunting for errant balls in the boondocks.

Jim and I golfed with our dad any number of times. He was a font of advice. Before every swing, he'd offer tips. "Slow your backswing." "Close up your stance." Or maybe it was "Open up your stance." He'd dispense advice on your grip. On keeping your head down. On follow-through. He proffered any of a dozen tips to improve your stroke. Right there on the spot.

And then this final bit of advice: "Relax your swing."

Of course, I was all tensed up and primed for a duff.

Later on, he lightened up a bit. He even invited me to team up with him for a father-son tournament in Ahwatukee. We finished dead last. I think I brought his game down to my level.

He meant well. But when he died, I thought it might improve my game. It didn't. So it wasn't all his fault.

Over the years, I played with friends and colleagues. One golf shot stands out. I was probably in high school. At Encanto Golf Course in Phoenix, I hit a 7-iron, as I recall. The ball didn't go toward the green. Instead it bounced off a palm tree, came straight back and hit me in the chest. I forgot to duck.

I hit a lot of trees Monday, too. This was at Dave White Municipal Golf Course, where I'd golf one last time. All things must pass.

On my arrival, Dave White was thick with golfers. Golfers at the driving range. On the putting green. And foursomes following each other around the course — in carts and on foot.

The woman checking in golfers said she had a full plate. Tee times were booked from 7 in the morning to 3:30 in the afternoon.

I had to admit, I fit right in. Few golfers fell outside the retiree demographic. And all were white, as far as I could tell. Many, if not most, were winter visitors.

"I'd probably say about 90 percent of our business is 50 and up," said Ryan Porter, assistant golf pro.

No surprises there. Casa Grande is a mecca for retirees and winter visitors. And the golf course is a mecca within a mecca. But you have to wonder: Where are the younger golfers? Nationwide, the trend isn't promising. They're not teeing up. They apparently have better things to do than duff shots and toss 5-irons into a lake.

Dave White is reaching out to the youth, just the same. It offers classes and leagues for all ages, according to its website. And it's the home course for two high school golf teams — Vista Grande and, recently, Coolidge. Central Arizona College offers golf classes at Dave White, Porter added.

Porter himself is a young golfer. He took up golf shortly before high school. He picked it up quickly.

I did not. But hope springs eternal in golf. Every duffer has his or her moment. A par there, a bogie there — and things start looking up.

My hopes faded at the driving range.

Still, they already had my $28 for 18 holes on foot. It was the cheaper afternoon rate. Why pay more to embarrass yourself?

Part of golf is the camaraderie with the golfers in your foursome. My foursome included Dan, Hal and Cletus. Dan and Hal are retired. Like me, Dan walked. He usually followed a straight path from tee to fairway. Hal and Cletus shared a golf cart. They drove up ahead and helped locate my tee shots. They tracked them down in the desert rough. And on fairways for other holes. I hit three in the lake.

Hal and Cletus couldn't help me there. Their golf cart wasn't submersible.

As walks went, it was pleasant. A stiff breeze kept the sun from getting the best of us. I joked the wind was playing havoc with my 30 handicap.

Well, my game wasn't a total loss. For one thing, I made everybody around me look better. For another, I did have two pars. Both par 3s. The yardage marker on one of them, the 14th hole, is dedicated to the memory of Phillip Glenn. "Ugliest hole-in-one ever."

I'd take that any day. But no holes-in-one for me. No birdies. No eagles, though I did catch a glimpse of a red-tailed hawk as I walked off the 18th green. It floated like a kite in the wind. Free and wild.

That sounded about right. So I freed myself of my own burden. I left my clubs at the clubhouse. Dave White takes donations of golf clubs for youth leagues.

I might donate the scorecard to a grade school. Students can learn to add big numbers.

Reporter's Car:
Dumpster On Deadline
April 20, 2019

In years past, my car was stocked like a survivalist's pantry. Maybe a few open cans of soda, some not yet moldy. Half-eaten Snickers bars, still in the original wrapper. And health food, like granola bars. All conveniently stored about the floorboards and folds in the seats.

If I ever ended up in a ravine, trapped in my car, I'd be all set. People would drive by, unaware I was already on my second Snickers.

Sure, at some point, I'd want to be rescued. And I might need to use the bathroom.

For years, I had what might be called a reporter's car, a rolling trash can. I heard the name somewhere. I guess it means a reporter's too busy getting scoops to bother with hygiene. Or a clean car.

It fit me in the sense I kept a messy car. But I was not the reporter rushing to get the scoop on a widely reported story, like guys you'd see in an old movie. Guys in rumpled suits, dashing from the courtroom, grabbing a phone and screaming: "Get me rewrite! The judge threw the book at Lucky the Lip Lupino today but missed, so he got a bigger book!"

I gravitated toward writing feature stories instead. I wouldn't join the rush to announce the verdict. I'd rather try to get an interview with the judge, check out her law library. See if she had any favorite books she liked to throw.

I suppose it'd be Title 13, the Arizona criminal code. But the judge might want to throw the book for a parking violation on state property. That's Title 41.

I did cover a few trials, from time to time. I never yelled, "Get me rewrite! It's curtains for O'Casey!"

In one 1990s trial, or retrial, the defendant was charged with murdering his cellmate. He had etched the word "Banzai" on the victim's back, with the sharpened end of a toothbrush. The defense attorney pointed out a handwriting expert had not been brought in to match the wound with the defendant's own handwriting.

The defendant, Robert Vickers, was convicted anyway. He was sentenced to death, a second time. He also faced a separate trial and retrial for murdering another inmate. Guilty as charged. So Vickers had four convictions total. Two of them stuck. One was enough. He was executed.

I drove from Phoenix to Florence for the trial. I probably stopped off for a burger. I probably tossed wrappings and a paper cup on the floor. I'd get to it later. But the refuse just piled up.

A sort of reverse psychology took place. The more the trash accumulated, the easier it was to ignore. It was a matter of critical mass. It reached the point where I simply couldn't face the cleanup. It added up to too many man-hours. I looked the other way, as best I could.

The car clutter wasn't always refuse. There were used notebooks. Some with blank pages. They could be used in a pinch. And, like a trash picker, I could sort through stuff and usually find a pen.

Sometimes I hauled around things I'd have use for later. I once had a half-full gallon can of paint resting on the floor. This was in my 1996 Saturn. I planned to take the paint to the hardware supercenter. It was house paint, and I wanted to make sure I got the right color. I think it was an amber of sorts.

Every day, I told myself: Next weekend, it's off to the paint center.

Then July came. And, before I went, the can blew. Basic physics, I guess. The heat created a pressure cooker and I got a car interior to match the color of my house trim.

I've since turned a new leaf. I trace it to the day we came home with a new car. The Prius we have now. I know. I'll be forever marked as a Prius-loving liberal. If you're a fossil-fuel-friendly

226

conservative, feel free to slap an anti-Prius bumper sticker on your Ford F-150. I looked up a few online. My favorite said: "Prius Repellent."

For whatever reason, I've kept the car reasonably clean. I even pick up the register receipts my wife leaves on the floor, after I've scanned them to monitor her purchases. They usually say something like: "Handbag from Savers, $2.99."

Sometimes I ask: "What's this? What could possibly cost $18?"

"Your beer."

She has an answer for everything.

We've folded the back seats down, leaving room for my liberal-loving Shih-Tzus. I put a sheet over the carpeting. The sheet becomes a reflection of my dogs' daily walks. It harbors mud, dirt, dust, pebbles and twigs. But it's easily cleaned. A shake or a run through the wash usually does it.

I can't catch everything, of course. Dogs get sick. They throw up, especially in cars. My two often manage to miss the sheet, and hit the carpeting.

I don't get mad at them. They can't help it. And just maybe it'll match the trim.

Should Have Been Listening To 'Running on Empty'

January 12, 2019

Cindy, the two dogs and I were headed down a Kansas freeway, not a care in the world. We'd left it all behind.

The road would lead to Holyoke, Massachusetts, an old mill town along the Connecticut River. And home to Sarah, our daughter and creative writing graduate student at the nearby

University of Massachusetts at Amherst.

We planned to spend Christmas with Sarah, her cat and roommate Kinsey.

A road trip seemed like the way to go. No hassles with overworked TSA agents. No airplanes stuffed like sausages. Just the open road in a Prius, The Beatles' "Abbey Road" blasting away on the CD player.

A sign came up for a rest stop. It said something like 96 miles to the next one. OK, this stop wasn't critical. But better than having to wait three hours. So I pulled in, parked and saw a little square blinking on the gas gauge. The Prius gas gauge has little squares. The more squares you had, the more gas in the tank.

I was down to my last square and it was blinking. I checked another gauge. This one told me how many miles I had left in the tank.

My exact words, according to Cindy, were: "Oh, ----." Except I didn't say dash-dash-dash.

I was down to my last 10 miles. I was almost out of gas. How was that possible? I was in a Prius. It's a hybrid. It uses battery power. You can't run out of gas in a Prius. It violates some kind of Newtonian law of perpetual mileage.

OK, not a big deal. Ten miles would get me to the nearest gas station, easy. I asked a fellow traveler, somebody familiar with the Kansas roads. He told me 10 miles would get me halfway to the nearest gas station, in WaKeeney. I could walk from there.

A bit of panic set in. I didn't show it, though. Not to the dogs. I assured them we'd get to Holyoke, no sweat. Only 1,600 miles to go, once I figured out how to make the next 20.

Cindy did not panic. She's good in a crisis. On the road, she was my chief navigator. She let me know which lanes to take at freeway junctions. Things like "Stay right for I-81." I called her Siri Cindy.

We did have one disagreement. We decided on coffee at a Dunkin' Donuts in a small New York town.

"Turn left here," Siri Cindy said. She spoke with authority, just like the real Siri. And so I turned in, going right of the car coming out. I didn't see the orange barrel. The kind of big orange barrel highway crews use to block off lanes.

I stopped inches short of ramming it. I had to back up in traffic to get around it.

I was upset with Siri Cindy. "Why didn't you tell me about the orange barrel?"

"I thought you saw it. How could you not? It's big and orange."

Siri Cindy and I fumed over that one for a while. But, it was a small hiccup in an otherwise fine road trip.

In Santa Fe, Cindy was able to visit an internationally known folk-art museum while I walked dogs around a tundra of a city park. It was cold. In New York, we took a detour through Cooperstown. I took in the Baseball Hall of Fame and Museum.

It was almost a religious experience. Plaques honoring the saints of baseball adorned walls along a vast marble-floored hall. Columns rose up to a high ceiling. It only needed Michelangelo's touch: God with an outstretched hand, giving life to Babe Ruth.

Cooperstown came after St. Louis, where we spent a few nights with Bill and Mary McClellan. I met Bill years ago in Tempe. It was 1970-71, or so. I was a student at Arizona State University. He was back from Vietnam, having mustered out of the Marines. He lived in a nearby apartment with his newly acquired pug, Primo.

Bill was an astute observer of people and life's ironies. He also happened to be a writer with few peers. And a great storyteller. He went on to become the lead columnist for the St. Louis Post-Dispatch. He's semi-retired now, sticking to one column a week. He used to crank out four.

Back in the day, Mary lived in that same Tempe apartment building, next door to Bill. Somewhere along the way, they got married. They moved to St. Louis, where Mary went to dental school. She recently sold her dental practice and retired herself.

Our dogs, a pair of mixed Shih Tzus, didn't know all that. They just knew the McClellans were good hosts. Benji made himself at home under the Christmas tree. He liked the comfort of a felt cloth meant to hold gifts. And the warmth of a nearby fire.

We made it to St. Louis later than planned. While we were still in Kansas, Mary left a voice mail. She wondered where the hell we were. I called. We were taking our time, I said. And I added I had 10 miles of gas and the nearest station was 20 miles away. I was

229

waiting for AAA.

That apparently was the coward's way out.

"I would have gone for it," Mary said.

Cindy and I agreed. Better safe than screwed.

Two hours later a guy showed up in a tow truck, lights flashing away. He retrieved a 5-gallon can and tipped the nozzle into the tank. A family in a gas-guzzling SUV laughed as they drove past. I knew what they were thinking: "Not so smug now, are you, Mr. Liberal?"

Humbled, with gas in the tank and Siri Cindy at my side, we finally made it to Holyoke. We had a great Christmas. Sarah gave me a pair of socks. And not just any old-man socks. But socks with artwork of an ancient warrior in a chariot yelling, "Hark! To the microbrewery at once!"

Sarah and Kinsey also spent four hours preparing a Christmas dinner. It was vegetarian. Much in the way Supreme Court Justice Brett Kavanaugh likes beer, I like meat. But the meatless dinner was delicious and filling, though I avoided the avocado paste. I had my limits.

On the drive back, we just wanted to get home. We stuck to the interstates. And I came up with a new rule. I didn't let the fuel gauge drop below three dots.

Even smug liberals need gas once in a while.

Great-Uncle Found
Adventure in Gold Rush

July 6, 2020

Last Christmas, our daughter Sarah visited from Massachusetts. I brought out a box of old family photos. Some family documents and old news clippings. A bit of family history.

She wasn't too keen on the Coates side of things. Follow it back to my great-great-grandfather, Nathan Coates, and you get a Georgia slaveholder. Nothing to see here.

Sarah found more to like on my mother's side. It's a side that speaks to immigrants who came to our shores by the boatload, for real, in the 19th century.

In our case, it was Norwegians.

Severt Olsen and Christina Johnson were among 800,000 Norwegians to enter America between 1825 and 1925. Or so I read. Name spellings often changed from old world to new. "Johnson" is likely an anglicized version of Johansen. Severt was listed as "Sivert Oleson" on his naturalization papers.

They came to America for a better life. A cliché, but probably true. Sarah told me that Norway in the 1800s had a program to unburden itself of its poor, huddled masses. The government paid them to leave.

So here came the Norwegians.

Severt and Christina likely spoke no English. They settled in Wisconsin, where they first met. Much of what I know comes from a magazine submission by Bill Olsen, my great-uncle. We knew him as Uncle Bill.

Sarah spotted the piece among the papers spread out on the dining room table. It was the original 1955 typewritten manuscript, three pages. It was passed down from my mother. Maybe my older sister gave it to me. I didn't read it. Not right away. Instead, I scanned it into the computer, slipped it into in a manila folder and filed it away. Somewhere.

Sarah pulled it from the pile. She took a seat and began reading. It was a tale of adventure. Men in the wilderness, searching for Alaska gold.

I read it myself, eventually. I know. I shouldn't have waited so long.

The submission is addressed to "Editor of B.L.E. Magazine." B.L.E., it happens, stands for Brotherhood of Locomotive Engineers.

Uncle Bill was a longstanding member. He hired on as a fireman with Southern Pacific Railroad in 1897. Southern Pacific was later taken in by Union Pacific.

He shoveled coal to power-steam locomotives. Five years later, he was promoted to engineer. For the next 40 years, he hauled freight and passenger trains across southern Arizona.

I don't know if the magazine published his story. It touches on his life before the railroads. He starts from the beginning. He was born in 1874 in Merridian, Wisconsin. That's his spelling. Perhaps he meant Meridian.

Soon after, the family moved west to Union City, Washington. Severt went into the logging business. Christina gave birth to Clara, my grandmother. I never knew her. She died well before I was born.

The logging business was hard on Severt.

"Father lost his health," Uncle Bill wrote.

The family moved again, to the Wilmington area of Los Angeles. Severt worked as a shipbuilder. Christina gave birth to a daughter, named, well, Christina.

I don't think they called her junior. We knew her as Auntie. She would later move to Phoenix. She adopted my mother, Virginia. She was just 7 years old when Clara died.

Uncle Bill learned shipbuilding from his father. He later moved to Tucson and worked for the Tucson Bridge and Building Department, as he puts it. He was 17. Still plenty of time for adventure.

Three years later, he booked passage on a steamer with a friend. His name was Morgan Wilson. It was 1895, early days of the Klondike gold rush. The ship set a course for an inlet near the Kenai Peninsula, Alaska. Forty men were on board

"We were in a couple of bad storms and nearly shipwrecked," Uncle Bill wrote. "Just escaped being blown into an active volcano island."

And perhaps being blown out again, only with lava.

They landed across the inlet from Kenai Peninsula. He spelled it Kenia, but I'm sure he meant Kenai. It was a 20-mile crossing. It was part of the plan. The ship came with materials to build a boat for the crossing.

Uncle Bill knew how to build boats. He pitched in. A few days later they crossed the inlet. They made their way to Fort Kenai, a village comprised of Eskimos, American Indians and Russian exiles. Not far from Anchorage.

"Nice people," Uncle Bill wrote.

They ended up on the Kenai River and traveled by barge. At one point, the river iced up. They dragged the barge onto an ice floe and rode it part way. When the ice cleared, they camped and prospected. They didn't get rich. They did nearly get buried in an avalanche. They got riddled by mosquitoes.

Otherwise, Uncle Bill wrote, "all we got was a wealth of experience."

They ate well, he said. Fresh salmon and all manner of game. Porcupine, he added, "was better than any chicken."

They headed back down the river by boat. They went through rapids, whirlpools and waterfalls.

"It was dangerous fun," Uncle Bill wrote. "Several men lost their lives because of no experience in boat handling.

"I was an expert with a boat because I was practically raised at boating."

He made his way to Seattle. He was broke and took a job at the docks. The boss bawled him out. Not worth it, he decided. He quit after three hours. He made 15 cents, 10 of which bought him lunch.

He borrowed some money and made his way back to Tucson.

He married. Years later, he became widowed and moved in with Auntie. I remember him as a big, rounded man. His shirt had holes where his cigar ashes fell. Still glowing. He was an easygoing sort.

I didn't know it at the time. He was heir to the American dream. All those Norwegians ago.

I'm Not Unfriendly,
Just Social Distancing

April 6, 2020

Maybe I should call Bennie, my barber. Let him know I'm thinking of him. It's been months since I last visited.

It's starting to show. My do is something of an unruly hedge surrounding a barren field. I don't mind too much. I had longer hair in my college days. So I guess I'm reliving my youth, with less overall coverage.

I hope Bennie understands, in any case. These are the days and weeks — and perhaps months — of social distancing. Better that than getting sick. Or getting somebody else sick.

For Cindy and me, sheltering in place is an inconvenience but not a hardship. We're retired. We don't face the hardship that comes with being put out of work. Or shuttering a business. As rent, mortgage and other expenses pile up.

Our daughter is still working. We're thankful for that. She lives in Holyoke, Massachusetts. It's in the western half of the state. She's a graduate student and teaches a class at the University of Massachusetts, Amherst, about a half hour up the road.

Until March, she taught in the classroom. Same time a few days a week. The students have since been sent home. Sarah now teaches remotely. It takes more time. Students can't all attend at a set hour. They live in different times zones. Some halfway around the world.

She and her roommates are playing it safe. They have groceries delivered. They hike in woods and parks that allow a good social distance.

I planned to visit her in mid-April. I had booked Amtrak for a

234

cross-country excursion. Sarah thinks I should cancel my train trip. I think so, too. It's just not a good time to travel.

I had reserved a flight back. American Airlines sent an email about doing its part in the age of coronavirus. Like only serving beer in first class. The schlubs in economy get soda pop. I'll cancel that reservation, too. I can't see paying an extra $1,000 for a beer.

I'm social distancing for this column. I had planned to meet with Rose Gipson and ask her about growing up in Pinal County. I met Rose after a memorial for George Mack, my neighbor. He was an art and antiques dealer. He had cancer and died on Feb. 29.

George and I practically shared mailboxes. We'd chat about politics. We were of the same mind. We liked Obama. We'd chat about music. George was African American, about my age. He liked jazz and The Beatles. Sometime I'd hear him play the piano, soft soothing melodies coming out of his garage-turned-studio.

George's memorial was early last month. Cindy and I attended. It seemed safe at the time. We're still healthy anyway. One of the speakers was the Rev. Grady Whatley, now retired. He used to preach in Casa Grande. I said hi afterwards. He's a cousin of George's wife, Valorye.

Valorye's brother, Darryl Farthing, attended as well. He lives in Casa Grande, as does Rose. She's also a cousin of Valorye.

Rose told me she planned to write a book about her life. An interesting life it was. I told her I'd like to interview her for a column, in person. I'd call after I got back from the train trip.

Well, the train trip's off. And so is the interview, for a while anyway.

We're all sheltering in place now. Some things we all share, like social distancing, and where'd all the toilet paper go?

How far we have fallen.

During the Cold War, toilet paper was America's Exhibit A in our case for the free enterprise system. Commie Russia was always short of toilet paper. So I was told in the '50s and '60s. I pictured the average Russian trudging gloomily to his unheated bathroom. The average Russian, in my mind, was always gloomy. He'd cart in the latest issue of Pravda, but not for reading.

Our American shelves, on the other hand, had stacks and stacks of toilet paper. The hardest part was choosing. Mr. Whipple told us not to squeeze the Charmin. Of course, we were going to squeeze it anyway. And think, it's so soft. Much softer than Pravda. We could fill our carts with Charmin. It was always there.

Under capitalism, there was no toilet paper rationing. Except in gas stations. I recall this on family trips in our very large 1959 Plymouth station wagon. We'd stop at a gas station and everybody had a turn in the bathroom. The gas station did not stock Charmin. Maybe recycled Pravdas. Still, it was toilet paper, if you could get at it. The roll was usually secured inside a very stingy dispenser. Ten minutes of wrestling with it yielded one lousy square.

Now you can't even get that. Toilet paper aisles at the market look like a scene out of Venezuela. Empty. In our case, it's not a failure of socialism, Venezuela style. It's a shortage borne of good old American panic-buying. It's every man and woman for themselves, so grab all you can.

Here at retirement central, anyway, we're good for now. And if we do run short of toilet paper, I have an old issue of Pravda handy. It'll be my moment of truth.

Gardening Column
Lives On in the Internet

May 3, 2021

CASA GRANDE -- Last December, we bought an Arizona yellow bell. We made it our Christmas tree, though it's more of a bush.

We put it in a pot and put the pot in the living room. We put presents under it.

After New Year's, we moved the pot outside. True to its name, the yellow bell produced bright yellow flowers. Bell-shaped. I can see them now, through the living room window.

The rest of the bush isn't faring too well. Whole branches are bare. What leaves there are look shriveled. Some have large circles cut out of them. Salad for pests.

Just what the pests were I had no idea. So I Googled a long description of the problem.

The first item on my search was a 2018 column by Rick Gibson. For years, once a week, his column appeared in PinalCentral's Tri-Valley Dispatch.

Until recently, Gibson was director of Pinal County Cooperative Extension, as well as an agricultural extension agent. He retired last year. He's stepped back from the column as well.

But the columns are still out there, in cyberspace. Just Google his name, PinalCentral and your garden issue. You'll probably get an answer.

Here's what I learned. My yellow bell, Gibson tells me, likely has a bad case of Tecoma leaf tier, a moth larva. Tier is pronounced "tire," as the little bugs have a way of wrapping themselves in leaf tissue. They then tie it down with silken thread. Inside their little bubble, they have at it with the leaf.

Yum, yum.

Like a lot of problems, this one's best caught early. And I could be too late. My yellow bell looks ready for last rites.

But in reading Gibson's columns, you know better than to give up. He's not one to throw in the towel on plant problems. He's a master gardener. Master gardeners come prepared with remedies. And for treating leaf tier, Gibson recommends a pesticide packed with larvae-killing bacteria. It's what you might call nature's way. A far cry from the DDT that nearly wiped out the bald eagle.

I remember DDT. Well, I remember the mosquito foggers making their weekly passes through the neighborhoods on Guam. They spewed a mist of DDT from the back of a truck. It was the late '50s. I was a kid of 8 or 9. We'd all run behind the fogger, into the mist. What fun!

No mosquitoes on me. And no brain damage. At least not so much I couldn't work for newspapers.

Thankfully, DDT was banned and the eagles have rebounded. They're no longer considered endangered.

Gibson, it happens, is a fan of organic gardening. I paid him a visit a few years ago. He uses scorpions for pest control. They eat the bad bugs. If the scorpions get out of control, he hunts them down with a blacklight and whacks them with a hammer.

He stocks a small lily pond with mosquito fish. True to their name, they eat mosquito larvae. Much more kid-friendly than DDT, as is the bacteria-based pesticide Gibson recommends. It's safe for plants and animals, he writes. The main ingredient is Bacillus thuringiensis. Bt for short. You spray it on the leaves. The larvae eat the leaves and get a terrific stomach ache. Then they die.

I suppose that's kind of sad. But it's either them or your yellow bells.

For Gibson, gardening isn't about achieving perfection, not if it calls for overuse of chemicals. That goes for organic pesticides, Gibson says. However much you spray, you can't kill them all. And the few remaining bugs will pass on their genes.

It can escalate. The more you spray, the more bugs develop a resistance. So you spray more. Resistance grows. The bugs move into the house. Raid the refrigerator. Steal your beer. Take over the television.

Sure, they likely won't go that far. They'll just kill the plant.

Best to listen to Gibson, in any case.

"We avoid resistance by using existing tools, including Bt, wisely and according to label directions," he writes.

Just the same, I look at my poor larvae-ravaged yellow bell and think: I sure would like to nuke them.

I can't at the moment. I don't have any Bt spray handy. I couldn't find it in the garden department of my local mega-hardware store. It was probably there, right on the shelf, and I just didn't see it. I could have asked for help, but I have my pride.

Instead, I ordered Bt from the internet shop. It's not same-day delivery, so it's something of a race against time. I worry that when the Bt arrives, it might be too late. The leaf tier larvae will have chewed through every last leaf, only to starve.

I guess that's some consolation.

Maybe I'll get the Bt in time. Maybe I'll go nuts and attack the larvae like a madman with a super soaker. "Take that leaf tier! Ha! Ha! Ha!"

Maybe not. Maybe I'll follow Gibson's advice and read the label. Do the right thing. I'll think about it.

Going Against the Grain
In Kitchen-Cabinet Redo

July 18, 2021

My laptop rests on a desk my father made. It might be made of oak. It's very sturdy in any case.

He made the desk next to it as well. Cindy's computer sits atop that one. It might be oak, too. I wish I knew. It's the larger of the two. Plenty of space on which to pile papers, books and the odd scrap.

It took me a while to recognize the quality of craftsmanship and the patient labor that went into them. I think I told my father: Nice job. Now I'd tell him: I don't know how you did it. It's a really nice desk. Sorry about the coffee stain.

I can't tell him now. He died in 2004.

He got into woodwork when he retired. His garage had a showroom's worth of power tools.

The centerpiece was the table saw. A jagged-edged disk you could run big pieces of lumber through. He also made use of the wood shop across the golf course. It was popular among the retirees who lived in the area.

Sometime after he died, I did a freelance piece on the wood shop for another newspaper. Everybody I spoke to remembered Harvey. Fondly. I could see that. He was definitely a Golden Rule guy when it came to other people. He treated everybody with — what's the word — respect? And he was cordial. A gentleman.

He was always ready to offer advice. I wasn't always ready to hear it.

Maybe I should have spent more time with him in the garage. I could have become a craftsman, like my father. OK, probably not. Not at his level.

I learned a little about woodworking in eighth grade shop, a requirement for the boys. The girls took home economics, which was a fancy term for learning how to cook.

It was old school, in the truest sense.

I made a chess table. I was very proud of it. Not everybody felt the same. My mom put it outside, on the back patio. It eventually succumbed to the weather. The little squares fell out. Then the whole thing fell apart and ended up in the landfill, around the time The Beatles broke up.

It was a painful reminder. Nothing lasts forever, especially if it's poorly glued. Or when the hinges start falling off. My chess table didn't have hinges, but my kitchen cabinets do.

We've been in the same house, using the same kitchen, for 26 years. The cabinets were showing their age even back then.

Hinges broke. The doors sagged. And the finish had that abandoned-farm look.

Something had to be done. And, by gosh, I would do it. I would put the past behind me and fix the cabinets. All on my own. I'd channel my inner Harvey. No more thinking I'm not up to the job, all because of a lousy chess table. And all because my wife once made me toss the bookshelf I'd sweated over in college. It was a tasteful arrangement of yellow concrete blocks and planks of wood, painted blue.

Cindy pointed to the curb. I carted the bookshelf there, piece-by-piece. The garbage man cometh. The bookshelf is now in the landfill, probably some 100 feet above the chess table.

So here I was, facing my fears. I would engage wood, once again. A kitchen redo. OK, not the whole kitchen. I would refinish the cabinet doors. If some were too far gone, I'd replace them.

And I wouldn't even have to roll up my sleeves. I'd wear T-shirts.

I went to the hardware store. And I went online. I bought sandpaper, a power sander, a jigsaw, stains, brushes, new hinges, door pulls, magnetic catches and paint thinner.

I started with the cabinet doors under the sink. There are two of them. The edges met when they closed. The doors couldn't be salvaged. A number of places sell custom-fitted doors online. I measured the openings, as instructed, and submitted my order.

The new doors arrived. I stained them, attached the hinges and fitted the doors to the cabinet. A job well done, almost. The doors overlapped by an eighth of an inch. I went to YouTube, which has more handyman videos than the ocean has fish. I came across one just for my predicament.

The guy demonstrated. You take a towel, put it between the two doors and push hard as you can. I'm sure my father would have said: "Don't do it." But he wasn't around, so I did it. What a waste of a good towel. It didn't work, except perhaps to screw up the hinges slightly. So I just started sanding, by hand. Two days later, it was a tight fit, but the doors closed.

The doors on nearby cabinets were still usable. I sanded and stained them outside on a patio table. I put on new hinges. And new pull handles. I attached the magnetic catches to the openings.

So far I've done six cabinet doors. They're OK. Not great. Far short of my father's craftsmanship. But Cindy approves. So, safe from the landfill, for now.

Bumpy Career Path
January 18, 2021

I was lucky to land in a job I could handle with some

competency. And one I like. Writing for newspapers.

It was a job I largely backed into. I didn't write for the student newspaper in high school. I didn't write for the student newspaper in college. Not as an undergraduate.

I studied political science. In 1972, I got my degree and thought: Time to apply for political science work. The want ads, however, were not encouraging. I never saw: Political scientist wanted. Degree in political science required. B-average preferred. Sociology majors need not apply.

My degree, I figured, would open the door to a comfy desk job. I would move papers around. I didn't have a preference. Any papers would do. The job would come with some risks, of course. Carpal tunnel syndrome. Paper cuts.

I never found that job. Instead, I answered a want ad for groundskeeper at Madison School District in Phoenix. I don't recall if I wore a tie to the job interview. Probably not.

I think I told them, growing up, I mowed the lawn most Saturdays. I was hired on the spot. Mowing the playground? I could do that. Back and forth, back and forth on a John Deere riding mower. Not a desk, but sitting down just the same.

I was handed a rake instead.

The city was redoing a street next to one of the schools. After digging up the old road, the city was left with a big pile of dirt. The school grounds-crew chief got a good deal on it. He wasn't one to pass up free dirt.

He had it dumped on the infield of the school's softball field. Our job was to rake out the chunks of asphalt that came with it. The dirt was very asphalt-rich. We might have missed a few pieces.

I lasted three months. I was fired before I could quit.

Years later, my daughter went to that same school. I should have advised her: Life's full of bad hops, especially at shortstop.

I then got a job as a grip. My then brother-in-law, Alex, was a film director. Mostly commercials. A friend of his directed short subjects for the U.S. Information Agency. These were snippets of American life, to be shown in foreign lands.

My brother-in-law must have told him: Get a grip! That was me.

Anyway, I moved some stuff around. Boxes of equipment, that

242

sort of thing. I wasn't fired. But the shooting lasted little longer than a week, if that. One segment lasted two days. It featured the late heart surgeon Ted Diethrich. Each day, Diethrich performed a heart bypass surgery. It was a new thing at the time, in the early '70s.

Now it's pretty routine. I think I'll settle for a colonoscopy.

With few job prospects, I doubled down on political science. I entered a master's program at ASU. I was surrounded by smart, conscientious grad students. Many of them went on to get their doctorates.

Stephen Mumme was one of them. He told me his father was a minister. And that he had lived in Eloy. I didn't know anything about Eloy, at the time. Now I know it has a history rich in agriculture. And is home to Pinal County's first pot dispensary.

I learned Stephen's late father, Jim Mumme, was a well-respected and well-liked pastor. Everybody knew him.

Steve went on to get his doctorate at the University of Arizona. He's a professor at Colorado State. He was always professorial. He'd sit back, draw on his pipe and discuss politics at a level I could almost grasp.

I was not one of the smart, conscientious students. A professorship was not in my future.

Mumme, it happened, was a Vietnam veteran. The closest I got to military service was a semester of ROTC my freshman year at ASU. We marched around a field one hour a week. I wasn't very good at it. I got two demerits.

Bill McClellan was another Vietnam veteran. I met him my junior or senior year at ASU. He had written for Stars and Stripes. He could tell a great story. By the time I entered graduate school, Bill was editor of the State Press, the ASU student paper.

He made journalism seem like fun. And he wasn't afraid to ruffle a few feathers. If something needed calling out, he'd call it out. He wrote with a wry sense of humor. His irony was usually spot on.

In the 1980s, Bill became a columnist for the St. Louis Post-Dispatch.

He's since retired, but still writes a weekly column.

The Riverfront Times, a St. Louis weekly, once described Bill this way: "He was frequently mischievous, but never malicious."

Anyway, hanging around Bill, I thought: Maybe I could do that.

So I embarked on a second graduate degree. This one in journalism at UA.

It was a good move. As a reporter, I've talked to people from all walks. From governors to an orchard worker running for president. I spoke to the orchard worker in the 1980s. He ran on a platform of somehow doing away with political parties. George Washington, he said, warned about the dangers of "faction."

Just like Washington, the orchard worker was ahead of his time.

And so I found a career that had all the right elements. Job satisfaction. A desk. And no rakes.

Wildlife at the Watering Hole
July 5, 2021

Critters often gather at the small pond out front.

By pond, I don't mean a small lake. It's more of a concrete-lined bird bath, sunk into the ground and shaped like a small missile hit it. It's about 2 feet wide, if that. About a half-foot deep.

Cindy and I watch the comings and goings from our study. A window overlooks the pond.

Just now, a curved-bill thrasher is getting a drink. A Gila woodpecker waits its turn on the limb of a long-dead ironwood tree. A white-winged dove cuts in line. The woodpecker squawks and flits off.

Coyotes often stop by for refreshment. I've seen rabbits. Lots of rabbits. Rabbits and more rabbits. They reproduce faster than the coyotes can eat them. Or maybe the coyotes are just choosy eaters.

I've set up a trail cam in times past. An owl visited one night. It sat on the edge of the pond. It must have stopped by to wash down its dinner, perhaps a mouse or a squirrel.

Roadrunners have bellied up to the pond. Other birds and rabbits know to give roadrunners, owls and coyotes a wide berth. They hide and wait their turn. Why serve themselves up on a platter?

Nobody, it seems, wants to hang around the javelina. Sometimes one or two show up. Sometimes a whole herd. Or, as it's formally known, a squad. Sometimes mom and dad stand watch while the wee ones quench their thirst.

I'm told javelina are very protective of their young. I don't make a point of finding out. They certainly don't trust coyotes. They've been known to pick off a baby javelina or two.

I've never seen a javelina share the pond with a coyote.

Frankly, nobody wants to share with javelina. They don't just drink the water. They cool off in it.

Occupancy is limited. One javelina per dip. The biggest one gets dibs. It eases a hairy body into the pond, almost all the way in, kind of like a nesting bird. A very large bird. You could sell tickets: "Seeing is believing! A whole javelina in 6 inches of water!"

A minute or so later, the javelina stands up and, dripping wet, trundles off — leaving the pond with 3 inches of sludge.

Just like the javelina to ruin it for everybody else.

I'll flush the pond out with a hose. I often refill the pond in any case, at least in summer. Evaporation runs high. And I have to get everything ready for Gambel's baby quail. They generally show up in May or June.

Newly hatched, they're little bigger than cotton balls. I fill the pond to the rim for them, whenever I can. They can't bend way down for a drink, like mom and dad.

I've watched them try. They dart along the edge, searching for a perch to drink from. Sometimes they fall in. They flap the downy stubs that pass for wings. Somehow that works. They pop out of the water and join their cotton-ball siblings, already trailing after their parents.

Often, a baby chick looks up and realizes everybody's left. It spots the family and makes a mad dash to get in line.

Cindy and I look forward to baby quail sightings. If I spot them,

I yell: "Baby quail! Baby quail!" Cindy alerts me, if she sees them first.

But this year has us scratching our heads. What happened to all the baby quail? In summers past, they'd show up several times a week, sometimes by the dozen. This summer? We saw one baby trailing a pair of adults. That was a month ago. We've since spotted a small brood, maybe a half dozen.

Not a good showing.

For answers, I called Tom Cadden, a spokesman for the Arizona Game and Fish Department. He's done his own quail survey. A very informal one. Cadden lives near a Phoenix mountain park.

"Normally we get a lot of quail around our yard this time of year," he said. "I've seen some, not many."

As for why, he added: "I gotta believe it's the lack of rain that's affected those numbers."

Monsoon rains were a no-show last year, he said. And the winter was pretty much one long dry spell. It meant little in the way for quail to eat. A brutally hot week in June didn't help.

Game and Fish tracks quail populations statewide, for hunters. Game managers recently completed a survey in spring. It's based on listening for quail mating calls. You know, the courtship that leads to baby quail.

"The numbers seemed lower this spring," Cadden said.

A quail-hunting website concurred. It reported few, if any, baby quail were spotted in May.

Cindy and I aren't hunters. We just enjoy watching baby quail stumble around like little Keystone Kops. Well, not so much this year.

Thanks to a lack of rain. And javelina behaving badly.

Burn after Reading

October 18, 2021

Google apparently thinks I'm interested in being cremated. I am of an age where I might soon be eligible for it.

Google knows that. And so does the cremation company.

They follow me all around the internet with ads suggesting I can pay now, burn later. The ads are framed in purple. Why purple? I don't know. Maybe it's the color for mourning.

In the ad, though, nobody's mourning. A smiling couple are shown. They're a lot younger than me. They're planning way ahead. The woman is looking at the cremation salesman. She's wearing a purple sweater. The husband is looking at her. Maybe he's thinking: "You go first."

They're getting the inside dope on getting cremated. I'm thinking: What's there to discuss? Your body goes into the fire. It comes out a pile of ashes.

Maybe the color of the urn.

The wife might say: "I'm thinking of something in green, to match my eyes."

"Hum," the husband might say. "Could clash with the moose head over the mantle."

To be honest, I'm not interested in talking to my wife about cremation's finer points. Cindy will figure it out after I go. Of course, if I had a say, I'd say opt for cheap. Just go down the list by price. Then say to the funeral director: "That one there. The tire-fire special."

I have not seen cremation ads on the PinalCentral site. The car-dealer ad at the top is fine with me. I subscribe to other newspapers as well. And that's where "plan your cremation" usually shows up.

I don't like it. If it pops up, as it invariably does, I click on a small "x" in the corner. I get a message. It says something like: "What about this ad don't you like?"

I click "not interested." Google says: "We'll try not to show this again."

Maybe they could try harder. The ad will not go away. I keep clicking not interested. Google keeps insisting I am. It'll drive me into an early grave. Or urn.

Let's face it. I'm no match for Google. I won't give up the internet. I like reading the newspapers online. And the web can otherwise be useful. I shop online. Who doesn't? For tools and the like, I'll check out websites for the big-box hardware stores.

Just the other day I inquired about screen doors. Our bedroom has a sliding door to the patio. The nights are getting cooler. With a screen door, we could let the cool air in — without the bugs.

A website for a nearby big-box store said it had just the size I needed. Only three left! Or, if I wanted a more expensive model, only five. Only five's better than none. I drove to the store. I wandered around until I found the screen door section. I got hold of a worker for more assistance.

I showed him the pictures on my phone. The three screen doors that were just what I needed.

"We don't have those."

I showed him the five pricier ones.

"We don't have those."

"Your website says you have three of these, and five of those."

"We don't have them."

Who was I going to believe? The internet, or the guy who knows what's actually available? I was leaning toward the internet, but I didn't argue. I just pointed to a screen door. It looked the same.

"How much?"

"Ninety-four dollars."

"I'll take it."

I walked it through self-checkout. I loaded it into the back of the Prius. I slid it over the passenger seat, all the way to the dashboard.

I got it home and followed the directions.

"Take out the weather stripping. You can put it back in later." Easy enough. "Loosen a few screws. The bottom and top will pop up. Put the door in the frame. Let go and watch it fall down because it's too short."

I made up that last part. It wasn't in the instructions.

I should have paid more attention to the labeling. It said the door was for 80-inch-tall frames. It also said the actual door was only 79½ inches tall. Short by a half-inch. I decided to return it.

I shed my ratty casuals and jumped into my best cargo shorts.

I drove back and carried the door to the return desk, along with the weatherstripping. I couldn't get it back on at home. I'd let the store handle it.

Apparently that's not how it works. The clerk at the return window told me I had to reattach the weatherstripping. I set the door on its side and pushed down on the weatherstripping this way and that. I wasn't having much luck. The weatherstripping kept popping out. Minutes went by. Long, slow minutes. People waited in line behind me. Impatient people. The door slipped. I nearly shoved it into the guy at the next window. I chuckled. He didn't laugh with me.

I was getting flop sweat. What could be worse? I looked down. My fly was open.

A good time to plan my cremation.

Watering Pinal County
With a 1,000-mile straw

August 2, 2021

Dick Powell knows Pinal County farmers. His father, Dewey, opened Powell Feed & Supply in 1951. Dick took over later. He ran the store until it closed for good in 2019.

The store sold just about everything to run a farm.

Except water. And right about now, the farmers could sure use some. Lake Mead is at about 35% capacity. That's not even glass half-full. It's fed by the Colorado River, which has been running a bit low lately.

Pinal farmers know what's coming. They're last in line for water. To put it another way — they're first in line for likely cuts to Arizona's share of the Colorado, delivered by the Central Arizona Project. They can turn to groundwater, Powell says. But not forever.

He quotes the former director of the Arizona Department of Water Resources, Herb Guenther.

"If we pump the aquifers dry," Guenther said, "we have the Gobi Desert."

We'd be living out of yurts. And there'd be nothing to hold down the dirt. No crops. The abandoned farmland would become the next dustbowl. The dust storms would only get worse.

There's little hope for improvement, if you're counting on Mother Nature.

"Most of it's climate change," Powell says. "It really is. A lot of crusty old farmers … don't believe in it."

Recognizing climate change isn't exactly a Republican talking point. That makes Powell, a Republican, a bit of an outlier. But he wants what the farmers want. And need. Water.

He's on the side of the crusty old farmers. Farming is big business in Pinal County, he says. He doesn't want to see it vanish.

I met up with Powell last week at the CookEJar. He treated me to my usual coffee and cookie. He told me a little about himself. He was born during the Second World War in San Diego. His father was stationed there. Dewey was a chief petty officer in the Navy, training sailors for the Pacific Theater.

When Dick was 7, the family moved to Casa Grande. He helped out around the feed store. After high school, he left to attend what became Northern Arizona University.

"I can remember leaving Casa Grande in the rearview mirror and thinking I was gone forever."

On graduating, he worked for Ralston Purina, now defunct. He did an eight-year stint with the Army National Guard. He returned to Casa Grande in 1970 and took up running the family business. He was elected to the Casa Grande City Council in 1997. He's still there, though at 77 he doubts he'll run again.

He represents the city on a regional water panel. It goes by the name of Pinal County Water Augmentation Authority.

Last Tuesday, he showed up at the CookEJar in his signature cowboy hat.

As things stand, he said, we just can't rely on the trickle coming off the Colorado River. We'll have to shop around. And Powell knows just the place. The big box store of rivers. The mighty Mississippi.

His plan? Tap into the Mississippi and build a pipeline to carry the water. Boston had the Big Dig. We'll have the Big Straw.

This is not a new idea. Powell, for one, has talked of tapping into the Mississippi for some five years. The Dispatch's Aaron Dorman recently reported on Powell's Mississippi dreams. Without new water, Powell said, farmers won't be the only ones left out to dry.

So will developers. They dream of a master-planned community known as Superstition Vistas. Houses everywhere east of Gold Canyon.

But not without water, Powell says. And what better source than the mighty Mississippi. We'll take the water nobody there wants anyway. Floodwater.

Powell's wife Nancy came up with that idea.

She and Dick had watched coverage of flooding along the Mississippi. Damage ran to the billions. Davenport, Iowa, alone sustained $30 million in losses.

Nancy said: "It's a shame we can't get that flood water. We have an issue with not enough water. And they have an issue with too much water."

So Powell went to work on his win-win. With help, he drew up plans. They call for a diversion dam and reservoir along the Mississippi, right in Davenport's backyard. Maybe its front yard.

This would be upstream water, Powell said. Clean mountain-fresh snowmelt. Not the Big Muddy you get downstream.

Next, you lay a pipeline in the Interstate 80 corridor. It's known as the Federal Corridor. There would be few, if any, right-of-way issues, Powell says. No need to shell out money for digging through somebody's property. You just follow the interstate for a thousand miles, all the way to Rock Springs, Wyoming. There, the water spills into the Green River, which feeds into the Colorado. And flows into the farms of Pinal County. And into the taps of all the new houses in the shadow of the Superstitions.

I pointed out you'd have to build lots of pumps. The water has to clear the Continental Divide, something I read about in high school. In this case, it's the Rocky Mountains.

Powell wasn't too worried about that.

"It's flat till you get there," he said. An acquaintance driving through Nebraska told him: "It's so boring I drove into a corn field."

I read of a $14 billion-plus price tag for a Mississippi pipeline. It was based on a 2012 report by the Bureau of Reclamation, "Colorado River Basin Water Supply and Demand Study." The pipeline would take 30 years to complete. The report considered other ways to import water. Towing icebergs to California from Alaska was one.

Powell doesn't have a figure for his plan. The Arizona Legislature approved a resolution asking Congress to fund a feasibility study, one that would ballpark the cost of a pipeline. The resolution passed by large majorities in both chambers. Powell played a big role in making that happen.

The bottom line will run billions in any case. The feds could front a few billion. Arizona could split the remainder with the other six states in the Colorado River Basin. Maybe California will raise its hand: "Waiter, check please."

But what about the people of Davenport? What do they think? Powell says they'll be glad to rid themselves of all that extra water lapping up against their front doors. And maybe, I'm thinking, pay us to take it.

I called Davenport just to make sure. I spoke to Corri Spiegel, Davenport city manager. She knows all about Arizona and water. She once worked for the city of Goodyear. She saved on water herself. She had rocks for a front yard.

But now she's looking out for Davenport. As it happens, she said, Davenport doesn't have a position on the Big Straw.

She did dampen the idea of Arizona tapping into their floodwater. For one, the Mississippi doesn't always flood. And, two, the river has no water to spare just now.

"It's about 5 feet lower than normal," she said.

It's all of 4 feet deep. You could stand on the bottom, or try. The current would probably sweep you away. Flood stage is 18 feet. The 2019 flood crested at 22 feet.

Iowa farmers rely on Mississippi water, Spiegel says. So do communities up and down the river.

Pinal farmers would still be last in line.